A GUIDE TO GENEALOGICAL RESEARCH IN MARYLAND

A GUIDE TO GENEALOGICAL RESEARCH IN MARYLAND

FIFTH EDITION
REVISED AND ENLARGED

Henry C. Peden, Jr., F.M.G.S.

Maryland Historical Society

BALTIMORE

Published with the support of the
Joseph Meyerhoff Family Charitable Funds

Copyright ©2001
Maryland Historical Society
201 W. Monument Street
Baltimore, Maryland 21201

First Edition, 1972
Second Edition, 1976
Third Edition, 1983
Fourth Edition, 1992
Fifth Edition, 2001

Library of Congress Cataloging-in-Publication Data
Peden, Henry C., 1946–
    A Guide to genealogical research in Maryland / Henry C. Peden,
    Jr.--5th ed., rev. and enl. p. cm.
    Rev. ed. of: Genealogical research in Maryland / Mary Keysor
    Meyer. 4th ed. 1992.
    Includes bibliographical references and index.
    ISBN 0-938420-72-0 (pbk.)
    1. Maryland--Genealogy--Bibliography. I. Meyer, Mary Keysor.
Genealogical research in Maryland. II. Title.

Z1293. P43 2000
[F180]
929'.1'o720752--dc21   00-045209

CONTENTS

FOREWORD

Mrs. Mary K. Meyer, who was responsible for the first four editions of the *Guide to Genealogical Research in Maryland,* once remarked to me that family history researchers always had to contend with more turmoil than one would expect of an avocation which concerns itself with something as constant as the unchangeable past. Archives switch locations or hours, libraries acquire—or, much more rarely, part with—collections, and the staff member who was so helpful on your last visit has retired and been replaced by somebody who's not even too clear on the location of the rest rooms. Since Mrs. Meyer made this observation, the "Information Revolution" has stirred things up still more: genealogists now lie awake wondering if the information they've needed is adrift somewhere in cyberspace and, if so, how they'll ever be able to find it.

While the present work can't actually surmount any of these obstacles—nothing in it, for instance, can open the doors of the Maryland Historical Society's library to you as a researcher on a Monday afternoon—it does alert you to common problems, suggests ways around them, and gives you insights into useful but often neglected tools for Maryland research. I think of it as being divided into three sections: the "where and when," the "what," and the "how." Most researchers have no trouble supplying their own "who" and "why" in respect to their work.

WHERE AND WHEN

The opening pages list not only the "Big Six" institutions for genealogical research in Maryland, their locations, hours, and unique resources, but also the "Smaller Six Hundred," which name is only a slight exaggeration in characterizing the denominational archives, local historical and genealogical society collections, public libraries, and web sites that concern themselves with the past and present of the Old Line State. Thanks to Mr. Peden's up-to-date telephone numbers for all of these, as well as the e-mail and web site locations he supplies for those institutions that have them, an attentive reader need never fear being the only car in a library's parking lot, and he may very possibly find it conceivable to dispense with traveling to the library at all.

WHAT

Most of this fifth edition quite properly is taken up by a seventy-page comprehensive bibliography of Maryland source materials, arranged on a county-by-county basis. Mr. Peden, however, knows a hawk from a handsaw. In genealogy it very often happens that the best things in life are unpublished, and he conscientiously guides you in right paths to find the civil, religious, and military records where elusive data are likely to be found. Some of these are unique to Maryland; who else has to contend with rent rolls and debt books? But fear not, your cicerone is wise enough to know where to stop and will leave the explanation of mare's nests like quitclaims and ground rents to the specialists.

HOW

In a sense the whole of a book of this kind is an answer to the question "How can I learn what I want to know," but the section on Publishers and Purveyors focuses on how you can come to own copies of the useful works listed in the Bibliography. Used in connection with *Genealogical Books in Print,* published by Baltimore's own Genealogical Publishing Company, the Publishers and Purveyors section makes it possible for the terminally wealthy to put together a private collection of genealogical works which would put most public libraries in the shade or, alternatively, for an individual to satisfy a long-felt want for a given book without having to haul his own weight in quarters to a photocopier. Compact discs, the coming thing in genealogical publishing, are covered as well.

I hope you have imbibed the sense that I like this book, because I do. I can see it reducing the wear-and-tear on Maryland's librarians, of whom I am one, while simultaneously increasing the number of Maryland genealogical researchers, one of whom I suppose you to be. Eventually, it will have to be overhauled by a sixth edition, for the great world spins forever down the ringing grooves of change, but as with any tool useful for a big job let us be glad that we have it when we need it.

> Francis P. O'Neill
> Reference Librarian
> Maryland Historical Society

PREFACE

Mary Keysor Meyer, author of the original *Genealogical Research in Maryland: A Guide* published in 1972, stated that her main purpose was to answer some of the questions asked most frequently by genealogists about research in Maryland. Through the revisions that followed in 1976, 1983, and 1992 she continued to make the *Guide* as accurate a research tool as possible. Her untimely death in 1998 left a void in the Maryland genealogical community. This enlarged and revised fifth edition of the *Guide* is dedicated to her memory.

I have attempted to adhere to the same purposes and principles that Mary Meyer had expressed in her earlier works, and also to make the necessary revisions and additions. Naturally, problems in works such as this are virtually unavoidable and I do apologize for any errors, omissions, or oversights. Every effort has been made to make this as complete a guide to genealogical research in Maryland as possible.

As for changes made, all topical sections found in the former editions of the *Guide* have been completely revised and updated, especially the "Bibliography" and "Public Libraries and Research Centers." Eight new sections cover vital records, probate records, census records, land records, religious records, military records, immigration, ethnic, and African–American research have been added. "Other Genealogical Web Sites" is another category that will be a very useful section for genealogical research in Maryland.

Web sites, e-mail addresses, telephone numbers, and fax numbers for archives, libraries, historical societies and genealogical societies have been included as well. These electronic tools have become the most significant aids for off-site Maryland genealogical research as we enter the next millennium.

I would like to extend my appreciation to the dedicated members and staff of Maryland's historical societies, genealogical societies, libraries, and archives for their support during this compilation. Their replies to my questions and questionnaires were truly the keys to the successful revision of the *Guide*.

Henry C. Peden Jr., F.M.G.S.

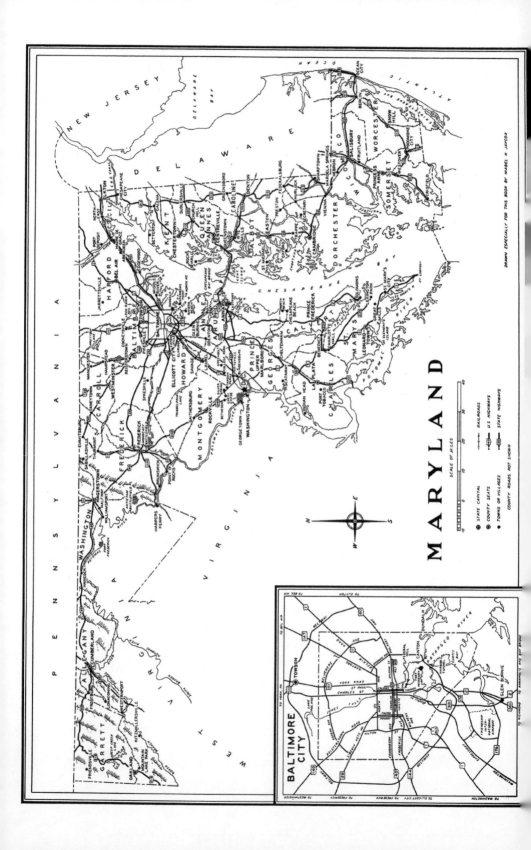

COUNTIES OF MARYLAND

Name	Created	County Seat	Parent County
Allegany	1789	Cumberland	Washington
Anne Arundel	1650	Annapolis	Original
Baltimore	1659	Towson	Original
Baltimore City	1851	Baltimore	Baltimore
Calvert	1654	Prince Frederick	Original
Caroline	1773	Denton	Dorchester, Queen Anne's
Carroll	1836	Westminster	Baltimore, Frederick
Cecil	1674	Elkton	Baltimore, Kent
Charles	1658	LaPlata	Original
Dorchester	1669	Cambridge	Original
Frederick	1748	Frederick	Prince George's
Garrett	1872	Oakland	Allegany
Harford	1773	Bel Air	Baltimore
Howard	1851	Ellicott City	Anne Arundel
Kent	1642	Chestertown	Original
Montgomery	1776	Rockville	Frederick
Prince George's	1695	Upper Marlboro	Charles, Calvert
Queen Anne's	1706	Centreville	Talbot, Kent, Dorchester
St. Mary's	1634	Leonardtown	Original
Somerset	1666	Princess Anne	Original
Talbot	1662	Easton	Original
Washington	1776	Hagerstown	Frederick
Wicomico	1867	Salisbury	Somerset, Worcester
Worcester	1742	Snow Hill	Somerset

INTRODUCTION

Getting Started

The compiler of any family history soon realizes that many questions will remain unanswered, many details are lost to time, and any success in reconstructing family lines is more often luck than skill. The very nature of the work, searching through old family papers and scores of miscellaneous public and private records, can be daunting to the most seasoned researcher. The novice genealogist is easily overwhelmed. This new edition of the *Guide to Genealogical Research in Maryland* is designed to help you, and all family historians, make their way through the sometimes baffling maze of source material and will help you find the ancestors for whom you are searching. Whether you are a beginner or an experienced genealogist, the following thoughts will help you glean the most from this guide and your venture into family history.

Before going to the library or the archives, or even much farther into this book, think carefully about what you hope to discover. Are you trying to identify an immigrant ancestor or one who fought in the American Revolution or the Civil War? Or are you simply trying to fill in the blanks on your family tree? Either way, identifying your long-term goal will help you plan your research strategy and also help you to be efficient with your research time.

The most basic element in your strategy is to begin with yourself and work backward. Even if you are working on a family line that you "know" is yours and has been in the same county for over two centuries, you can waste a lot of time working forward from the past. That person or family whose name appears in an old county history may or may not be related to you; and if they are related it could be a distant connection. The descendents of one couple through five generations can number upward of one thousand people. Therefore, beginning with yourself and working backward can save hundreds of hours of research time.

As you begin with yourself, start by filling in an ancestor chart. You are number one on the chart, your father is number two, your mother is number three, etc. When you write in the information, document your sources. It may seem unnecessary, or even silly, to take the time to write down your own birth certificate number, but future generations will thank you.

Working with the chart should boost your confidence if you are a beginner. You know more than you think you do. When you have exhausted your own paperwork, collect memorabilia from your family. Perhaps your parents, cousins, or even siblings have items that will help identify past generations. In many families there is usually someone every few generations who is the self-appointed caretaker of the family's history; someone who remembers the stories and may also have material clues to the past. Ask if you may borrow, or at least look at and copy, wedding invitations, funeral notices and death certificates, birth announcements, military service papers, insurance policies, cemetery lot deeds, diaries, memoirs, Bibles, letters, photographs, scrapbooks—anything that may provide a link to previous generations. Contact out-of-state family members by reviving the almost lost art of letter writing. Be precise, explain exactly what you are doing and what you hope to find, and always include a self-addressed stamped envelope. Your reply will come back more quickly.

One final point to think about before you actually go the library or the archives is whether someone else has already done this work. Contact the local genealogical society and/or historical society for the family name (surname) lists in the vertical files and for the names of any members who may be working on the same families. Some of these groups do charge a minimal fee for these services and others offer research only to members. Another benefit of society membership is that some publish genealogical queries in their newsletters. The addresses of such organizations are in this guide.

When you go to the library, first check the card catalog for any published histories of your family; also check the "vertical files" for unpublished papers and collections that may contain references to the surname you are researching. For example, many family historians leave copies of their work with the Maryland Historical Society Library and/or with the county organizations. Other sources for information on your family are the genealogical society publications. All of the county societies publish family histories in their journals, and the *Bulletin of the Maryland Genealogical Society* carries genealogies from all parts of the state. Once you arrive at the point where you are ready to begin your research, you should have a fairly clear idea of what you already have and what you still need.

Family history research involves looking through and studying the records presented in this guide. The record groups are organized by topic and described herein with explanations of missing and incomplete files. When using these documents, remember that these sources were not created for genealogical purposes; all of them were generated by a government agency or a private institution for specific reasons. Also, when questioning why your ancestor does not appear, for example, in the 1850 census in Baltimore when you have a deed that states he owned property on Monument Street, keep in mind that the records are only as accurate as the people who did the job. It is likewise valuable to remember that family history is not a science. You can apply the same research strategy to each case, but lost, incomplete, and inaccurate documents will change the outcome of each search. Family history is like detective work in that you are working from the clues each generation left behind.

In addition to this guide, a few basic tools will also help you more clearly understand the world in which your ancestors lived. A good state history (Robert J. Brugger's *Maryland: A Middle Temperament, 1634–1980* is a good example), a county history, and a few good maps are essential. A map of the present locale and others from the time periods in which you are working will orient you to the demographics of the era and the physical domain of the past. The maps will show you boundary changes, the development of the counties, the important waterways, and in some cases may also mark your family's property. If you are using an early-nineteenth-century census, you may find that one of your ancestors served in the armed forces. County histories, especially those written in the late nineteenth century, often contain glorious accounts of the local militia unit's heroic deeds and sometimes include biographical sketches of each soldier and his family.

This mention of local histories prompts a word of caution to new researchers and a reminder to research veterans. When using these secondary sources (records created after the event), be sure to check the documentation cited by the author or compiler. If the footnote cites the information as having come from "Aunt Sarah," check the data for accuracy against the available primary source material. In case of a conflict, the primary source material usually carries the greater weight in determining generation linkage and family relationships. For example, if the county history states that Joseph Smith married Jennifer Jones in 1865, and the citation is Miss Sarah Smith, check for the event in church or county marriage records. If the church record states that Joseph Smith married Jane Johnson in 1865, it is probably correct. Details tend to blur and become distorted as stories pass from one generation to the next, and human memory is not always exact. Again, records created at the time of the event are generally more accurate than those created afterward. Check the date of the record and determine whether it is a primary source.

Some, like Bible records, take a practiced eye. Many pre-twentieth-century families wrote their personal milestones in their Bibles. For those years before mandatory vital registration became law, these carefully written entries are often the only remaining record of the family's history. The births, baptisms, marriages, and deaths may span several generations, and at first glance appear to answer a lot of questions; many, however, are not as reliable as they first appear. When using Bible records, check the title page of the book for the publication date. A publication date later than the first entries tells you that the earlier events were recorded from memory. Also, look at the handwriting and the ink. Are the entries all in the same hand and by the same pen, or do they vary over time? If they are all the same then most of the information was probably put down from memory in one sitting, thus increasing the likelihood of error. Much of the success in putting together accurate family history depends on looking at sources with a critical eye.

Documenting family relationships through past generations should be easier and more logical as you work your way through this guide. Mr. Peden's revisions will help Maryland's genealogists of every caliber. Experienced historians will find new ways to approach familiar sources, and beginners will find their starting points.

Patricia Dockman Anderson
Maryland Historical Society

A GUIDE TO
GENEALOGICAL
RESEARCH IN
MARYLAND

PART I

Maryland's Research Centers

Researchers tracing Maryland's families have a wealth of sources, resources, and repositories, all within a day's drive. From the small county historical and genealogical societies in the far corners of the state to the central libraries and archives in Baltimore and Annapolis, this is a state rich in genealogical material. Many family historians, however, are not in a position to devote an unlimited number of hours to research and must learn to make efficient and productive use of the time available. This section contains a current listing of repositories with their full addresses, phone numbers, web sites, and e-mail addresses, and descriptions of the holdings as well as a few tips for beginning researchers. For example, call ahead to verify the days and hours the facility is open to the public. Do not rely solely on the information printed in a brochure, on a web site, or even in this guide. Bear in mind, hours and days change and sometimes these facilities close unexpectedly. A group bus trip may fill the library or archives and force others to wait for an open table. Museums host special events that may make it prudent to close the library. Libraries also close for inventories and may delay opening when they hold staff meetings. Remember to ask about rules and regulations regarding hand copying and photocopying. Most repositories have a "pencils only" policy. Photocopying machines require different coins; some have bill-changers and others operate with a debit card. It is immensely frustrating to find a piece of family history and then not have the necessary coins to make photocopies.

In addition to learning the basic operating policies of these institutions, know the purpose or mission of the repository. Government records are housed by government agencies, and libraries generally hold books, personal papers, pamphlets, rare books, and manuscripts. Duplication, of course, often occurs. For example, the Maryland Historical Society, which contains large holdings of private papers, also holds some original colonial government records; the Maryland State Archives, official repository of government documents, also houses some private papers and rare books. Both institutions have on-line descriptions of their holdings.

Microfilming has also greatly expanded the quantity and variety of records available to family historians, and it is now possible to find and use federal government records such as census and immigration reports in state and local facilities. Remember, however, that records created at the state level are kept by the state archives, and federal documents are kept by the National Archives and Records Administration. Knowing the function of each institution helps genealogists understand more clearly what they will and will not find on a research trip.

Beginners should avoid abstracting source material, that is hand-copying selected information. They should instead make photocopies of every document and journal article. Abstracting increases the likelihood of error. For example, the researcher might easily make a mistake in transcribing a number onto a note sheet. Additionally, information that may not seem important or relevant at the start of a search can later become important as more family members are identified and more relationships are established. When photocopying, always write the identifying information on the back of the page: the name and date of the record and where it is located. Photocopies made from published works should also include the title page. Genealogists tend to build mountains of copied papers and handwritten notes, and keeping these sheets clearly identified will help organize the work. Creating a research calendar of the materials that have already been searched saves time and repetition.

Major Research Centers

The Maryland Historical Society

201 West Monument Street
Baltimore, MD 21201-4674

Telephone: 410-685-3750
Fax number: 410-385-2105
Web Site: www.mdhs.org

Dennis A. Fiori, Executive Director
David deLorenzo, Deputy Director, Library
Francis P. O'Neill, Reference Librarian

HOURS: Tues.–Sat., 10 a.m.–4:30 p.m. Closed on Mondays, all Federal holidays, and two weeks in January (call for exact dates). Admission charge to non-members. The society's main entrance is at 201 West Monument Street, between Howard Street and Park Avenue.

The Maryland Historical Society is a private organization supported entirely by its members and donors. Founded in 1844, it has occupied its present location since 1919. The library houses 70,000+ books, more than eighty newspaper titles on microfilm, two million manuscripts, thousands of photographs, and 3,000+ items, such as census records, city directories, and manuscript collections on microfilm and microfiche. Most of these holdings are specific to Maryland, or Maryland-oriented, with emphasis on history and genealogy. The society also publishes the quarterly *Maryland Historical Magazine* which, until the early 1940s, carried considerable genealogical material, most of which has been reprinted in recent years by the Genealogical Publishing Company in Baltimore.

Individuals wishing to use the facilities of the Manuscripts Division and the Prints and Photographs Division should contact the staff in advance of their visit to ensure that the materials of interest will be available.

Photocopying of most library books is allowed, but there are exceptions. Readers should check with the reference librarian on duty. Materials too large or unsuitable for copying (such as maps, charts, and photographs) can be sent out for reproduction. Newspapers cannot be copied because of their fragile condition, but copies can be made from those newspapers that have been microfilmed. The society can provide microfilm copies of most holdings upon request. Charges for each process will be quoted on inquiry.

The society's microfilm collection is most likely the largest in Baltimore and includes: all U.S. censuses of Maryland, 1790–1920, Delaware to 1850, Virginia in 1850, and some in Pennsylvania; ship passenger lists for the Port of Baltimore, 1820–1952 (indices only, 1891–1952); the Baltimore City Directories; the Sanborn fire insurance atlases; numerous Maryland newspapers; International Genealogy Index (IGI); and other materials.

The library catalog is now computerized and available on-line. The society's library also maintains numerous special finding aids. These include:

Dielman-Hayward File — index of death, marriage, and biographical items taken from Maryland newspapers dating from the late eighteenth century to the present; also includes some Frederick County marriage licenses and references to biographical notes in some unindexed books. There are about 250,000 entries in this card file.

Filing Case A — a series of files (alphabetized in boxes) of unpublished genealogical materials, manuscripts, and research notes. This is a very useful genealogical tool. It should be noted that there is no "Filing Case B."

Genealogy Index — an all-name index to several library collections and files, including "Filing Case A" and unpublished genealogical charts. This index also contains references to the collections of some of Maryland's most prominent genealogists, including Christopher Johnston, Wilson Miles Cary, Nannie Ball Nimmo, and Mary Turner Layton.

Norris Harris Church Index — index of births, marriages, baptisms, and deaths copied from church registers held by the society. This index, begun in 1969, is incomplete, but is nevertheless an important finding aid for early Maryland vital records.

The Wilkins File — a card index of books published with poor indices or none at all (J. T. Scharf's *History of Western Maryland, History of Delaware, History of Baltimore City and County,* and *History of Maryland*; G. W. Howard's *Monumental City;* T. J. C. Williams's *History of Frederick County*; H. D. Richardson's *Sidelights on Maryland History*; G. Brumbaugh's *Maryland Records: Colonial, Revolutionary, County and Church*; M. Ljungstedt's *County Court Notebook*), plus the Maryland

Census of 1776, Wilkens Genealogical Collection, and the Nimmo Genealogical Collection. All entries are arranged alphabetically by surname.

The society maintains a list of professional researchers (available upon request; various rates; send SASE). Library staff members and members of the Maryland Genealogical Society also conduct genealogical research on an individual, hourly-rate basis.

The Maryland Historical Society receives all books donated to, or reviewed by, the Maryland Genealogical Society (MGS). The MGS maintains an office in the historical society building, but it is not staffed on a regular basis. Persons wishing to contact the MGS, or the editor of its *Maryland Genealogical Society Bulletin*, are encouraged to do so by writing to the society at 201 West Monument Street, Baltimore, Maryland 21201.

Printed descriptions of the manuscript collections, including genealogical collections, can be found in two publications: Avril J. M. Pedley's *Manuscript Collections of the Maryland Historical Society* and Richard J. Cox & Larry E. Sullivan's *Guide to the Manuscript Collections of the Maryland Historical Society*. Both books are available at the Maryland Historical Society, and both are available on the society's website.

The collections of the Archives of the Episcopal Diocese of Maryland, formerly housed in the Maryland Historical Society, were moved in 1991 to the Diocesan Center, 4 East University Parkway, Baltimore, MD 21218. Materials belonging to the Maryland Society, Sons of the American Revolution (records and applications since 1889) were moved in 1994 to the University of Baltimore's Langsdale Library, at 1420 Maryland Avenue, Baltimore, MD 21201-5779.

The Maryland Historical Society is located near the Amtrak Station and the city's Light Rail Transit System, and local buses pass within one-half block. Parking is available at the society, and several parking lots are nearby; a large public parking lot is only two blocks away on the corner of Howard and Centre Streets. Two other major genealogical research centers, the Enoch Pratt Free Library and the George Peabody Library, are within walking distance.

MHS Genealogical Contests

THE PARKER GENEALOGICAL CONTEST

In 1946 Mrs. Sumner A. Parker, a well-known and enthusiastic genealogist, presented the Maryland Historical Society with a sum of money in memory of her late husband. Income generated from this gift, as stipulated by Mrs. Parker, is awarded yearly to the person who publishes the best genealogical work dealing with families of, or originating in, Maryland.

RULES

1. Entries must be typewritten or in printed form and include an index.
2. References to sources from which information was obtained must be cited.
3. Entries for this contest must be received by December 31 of the year in which the publication was produced.
4. Entries must be mailed to the Parker Genealogical Contest, Maryland Historical Society Library, 201 W. Monument Street, Baltimore, MD 21201.
5. Entries will be judged on quality of content, organization, scope, and clarity of presentation.
6. The decision of the judges is final.
7. All entries become the property of the Maryland Historical Society. All rights to publication, etc. remain the property of the entrant.

NORRIS HARRIS GENEALOGICAL SOURCE RECORD CONTEST

Mrs. Norris Harris, a member of the Maryland Historical Society, the Maryland Genealogical Society, and numerous lineage societies, established an annual monetary award for the best compilation of genealogical source records of Maryland. The prize was established in memory of her late husband, who was an ardent genealogist.

RULES

1. All entries must be submitted in typewritten or published form and include an index if not arranged in alphabetical order.
2. Entries are judged on scope, originality of the project, volume, and value to the genealogical researcher.
3. Entries must be original, never before abstracted for public use, or published in any other work, serially or otherwise.
4. Entries should be submitted to the Norris Harris Genealogical Source Record Contest, c/o Maryland Historical Society Library, 201 W. Monument St., Baltimore, MD 21201, and must be received by December 31st of the contest year.
5. All entries become the property of the Maryland Historical Society. Publication rights and/or copyright remain with the entrant.

The Maryland State Archives

Hall of Records Building
350 Rowe Boulevard
Annapolis, MD 21401

Telephone: 410-260-6400
Toll free: 1-800-235-4045
Fax number: 410-974-3895
E-mail: archives@mdarchives.state.md.us
Web Site: www.mdarchives.state.md.us

Dr. Edward C. Papenfuse, State Archivist
Dr. R. J. "Rocky" Rockefeller, Director of Reference Services

HOURS: Tues.–Fri., 8:00 a.m.–4:30 p.m.; Sat., 8:30 p.m.–4:30 p.m (closed 12 noon to 1 p.m. for lunch on Sat. only and patrons must leave the building). Closed Sunday, Monday, and all state holidays. Admission and on-site parking are free.

Formerly known as the Hall of Records, this depository moved from its old location on the campus of St. John's College in Annapolis in 1984. It is now located on Rowe Boulevard, a major access road into the city from Rt. 50.

Founded in 1935, the Maryland State Archives is the official depository for all the state records created by the executive, legislative, and judicial branches of government prior to April 28, 1788, and for all non-current records of those agencies as well as the records of all counties, cities, and towns in the state, not in current use. This includes the probate and land records of the proprietary government, Circuit Courts, and Register of Wills.

Current records of the counties in Maryland are microfilmed under archives' supervision. Consequently, copies of probate, land, marriage, and other county records are available for public use at that facility.

The Maryland State Archives has vital records which are available to the researcher, but there are restrictions mandated by law: death certificates must be at least 10 years old and birth certificates must be at least 100 years old before copies can be made. If requested, an abstract of the information on the certificate can be prepared (for a fee).

Original records of the Washington (D.C.) Diocesan Library, along with originals and microfilm copies of many other church records (primarily Protestant Episcopal, Catholic, Methodist, and Lutheran) are also on deposit there. For further information about these particular holdings, see the "Religious Records," "Religious Archives," and "Bibliography" sections herein.

Since 1966, the Chancery Court and the land patent records in custody of the former land office have been held at the Maryland State Archives. Many of the records of the Chancery Court have been indexed and are available on the Search Room computers.

The archives' staff will furnish copies of any unrestricted material in their custody, but a copy of their cost policy should be obtained and understood. They also have a list of genealogical researchers upon request.

Before writing or visiting the state archives the researcher should study one or more of the various published guides to the holdings of the facility. See the bibliography under "General Sources" or the heading of the county in which you have an interest.

The archives has many indexed finding aids. Some of the most valuable genealogical finding aids are:

Chancery Court Index — formerly a card index, this information has been computerized. Each entry identifies the plaintiffs and defendants in suits heard in the Chancery Court from 1668–1806 and 1817–51. Suits include disputes over boundary lines, estates, pardons, post-mortems, etc. Of particular interest are the many depositions in which the deponent states his age, parentage, or other items of personal history.

Hodges Marriage Reference Index — is a card file index of marriages found in the land records, wills, testamentary, and other court records. This is not a record of marriages performed or licenses issued; it is a record of marriages inferred in other documents. Errors abound, but it remains a helpful resource. Use with care.

Land Grants Index — is a card file index of persons granted land in the province or state from 1634 to the present. A companion file is arranged by the tract name.

Naturalizations Index — is a card file of names found in naturalization records, Provincial Court judgements, 1685–1777; General Court proceedings for the Eastern Shore, Bacon's *Laws of Maryland*; Baltimore County Court and Court of Common Pleas for Baltimore City, 1796–1930 (Baltimore County to 1851, then Baltimore City only to 1930); Brown-Hienton index to approximately 24,000 persons naturalized between 1783 and 1904.

Testamentary Proceedings Index — is a card file of the names that appear in the proceedings of the Prerogative Court of Maryland. The Prerogative Court recorded probate records for all counties in Maryland during the colonial period. A 1777 General Assembly act abolished this court and provided for a Register of Wills and an Orphan's Court for each county. Every name found in the series has been indexed. This is an important finding aid, especially for those counties whose early records have been lost or destroyed by fire.

"Welcome to the Maryland State Archives Web Site" is an informative article written by Vernon L. Skinner and Patricia V. Melville and published in the *Maryland Genealogical Society Bulletin*, Vol. 38, No. 1 (Winter, 1997). The Maryland State Archives has joined numerous other libraries and archives in providing Internet access to portions of their holdings. Access primarily consists of a home page made possible by a grant from the Maryland Department of Education, Division of Library Development and Services.

The Maryland State Archives' home page is divided into the following topics: All about the Maryland State Archives; Maryland and Its Government; Reference Services; Geographical Services; Education and Outreach; and, Preservation and Conservation. This web site can be used to determine what records are available for research and to obtain accession numbers prior to visiting the Maryland State Archives. The web site is constantly being updated to remain current and to add new acquisitions.

The Maryland State Law Library

361 Rowe Boulevard   Telephone: 410-974-3395, 410-260-1430
Annapolis, MD 21401   Web Site: www.lawlib.state.md.us

HOURS: Mon., Wed., Fri. 8:00 a.m.–4:30 p.m.; Tues., Thurs., 8:00 a.m.–9 p.m.; Sat. 9 a.m.–4 p.m. Closed on designated state holidays. The library is located across Rowe Boulevard from the Maryland State Archives.

This facility is principally a law library designed to render legal reference and research to the Court of Appeals, judges, lawyers, various state government departments and officials, and also to serve the public (free admission).

The library holds more than 150,000 books, about 65 percent of which pertain to the law; however, a large number of books, maps, newspapers, and microfilm materials relate directly to Maryland history and genealogy.

Among the important materials to be found here is the most complete file of the *Maryland Gazette* in existence. This file of one of the nation's oldest newspapers dates from 1729 to 1839. The law library also has a complete file of the *Baltimore Sun* from 1837 to date.

The library holds many English records, U.S. federal censuses 1790–1920, and the original Mortality Schedules of the State of Maryland from 1850 to 1880. The library also has a very good, basic collection of Maryland county histories and published source records.

The library's staff is unable to conduct research for individuals, but a helpful pamphlet is available by request: *Sources of Basic Genealogical Research in the Maryland State Law Library, A Sampler.*

The George Peabody Library of the Johns Hopkins University

17 East Mount Vernon Place
Baltimore, MD 21202

Carolyn Smith, Librarian

Telephone: 410-659-8179
Fax number: 410-659-8137
E-mail: carolyn.smith@jhu.edu
Web Site: www.archives.mse.jhu.edui8000

HOURS: Mon.–Fri., 9 a.m.–3 p.m. Closed on all of the Johns Hopkins University holidays. The Peabody is situated on East Mt. Vernon Place, between Charles and St. Paul Streets, three blocks east of the Maryland Historical Society.

The George Peabody Library, formerly the Library of the Peabody Institute of the City of Baltimore, dates from the founding of the Peabody Institute in 1857. In that year George Peabody, a Massachusetts-born philanthropist, dedicated the Peabody Institute to the citizens of Baltimore in appreciation of their "kindness and hospitality."

According to its charter, the institute originally comprised a free public library, a lecture series, a conservatory of music, and an art collection. The Peabody Library building was opened in 1878 and the Peabody Stack Room contains five tiers of ornamental cast-iron balconies that rise to a height of sixty-one feet above the floor.

In 1966 the Peabody was taken over by the Baltimore City Public Library System and, in 1982, it was transferred to the Johns Hopkins University.

It should also be noted that the Peabody has received as a gift from Gary E. Meyer his collection of books and articles in the German language detailing German immigration into the United States. This material has since been completely indexed in the Filby & Meyer series *Passenger & Immigration Lists Index*.

The Peabody houses more than 255,000 volumes, including an exceptional collection of regional history, heraldry, and maps. In 1993 about 5,000 books from its genealogical reference collection, including most of the genealogical material added after World War II, were transferred to the library of the Maryland Historical Society. However, it still has one of the finest collections of British county histories and parish registers in the eastern United States. Photoduplication is available if the condition of the manuscript permits. Peabody staff cannot do genealogical research, but they do welcome independent researchers.

The Peabody was also the repository for files of the Genealogical Council of Maryland. After the publication of the first volume of their *Provincial Families of Maryland* in 1998, the council submitted their original files for retention at the Maryland State Archives.

The Baltimore City Archives

2165 Druid Park Drive   Telephone: 410-396-0306
Baltimore MD 21211-1425

HOURS: by appointment only. Parking is available in the archives' lot or on the street. These archives are located near Druid Hill Park, midway between I-83 and Reisterstown Road.

The archive houses 5,200 feet of municipal documents, delineating the entire history of the Baltimore City government from the 1729 Town Commissioners Survey Book laying out the city to current files of most city agencies. Records relate to public health, taxation, elections, education, law enforcement, and legislative actions.

Among the valuable finding aids is the WPA-HRS index to over 300,000 individuals whose names appear on petitions, licenses, bonds, muster rolls, inquests, police and health reports, correspondence, and applications. There are also census records, and election, health, and tax records.

The archives has a card index to the so-called "City Passenger Lists." These lists of passengers arriving from foreign ports were required to be filed with the Mayor of Baltimore City from 1833 to 1866, as a tax was required to be paid for each foreigner who entered the port. These same lists were microfilmed by the National Archives and a Soundex index was prepared by that institution.

There are no municipal naturalization records among the holdings of the city archives except microfilm copies of the index to Naturalizations for the Baltimore Federal Court, 1797–1906, 1918–23, and 1925–51. However, the Preliminary Voter Registration Books from 1882 to 1889 provide data on naturalization. The volumes in this collection provide the following information: name, whether or not naturalized, age, place of birth, time of residence in Baltimore City, ward and precinct of registration. Voter registration records are available for the years 1838, 1839, 1869, 1877–89. Although not as useful as the Preliminary Voter Registration Books, they still may yield helpful information.

In 1868 the Baltimore City Police Department was charged with taking a census. The resulting record enumerated each resident of wards 3, 6, 8, 9,

13, and 20 with the following statistics: name, address, age, sex, color, country of birth, date of naturalization, occupation, and religion. There are also numerous city tax records; some are arranged alphabetically by surname and others arranged by street address.

Other records located in the city archives are Quarantine Records, Coroners Inquest Reports, and Internment Records, 1834–40, all of which can contribute to the study of families in nineteenth-century Baltimore City.

The Baltimore City Archives is currently open to the public. In spite of staff shortages they will do search requests. Contact them first for details on procedures and costs.

The Enoch Pratt Free Library

400 Cathedral Street   General Telephone: 410-396-5430
Baltimore, MD 21201   Maryland Department: 410-396-5468
                            Fax number: 410-396-9537
               E-mail: jkorman@epf12.epfbalto.org

HOURS: Mon., Tues., and Wed. 10 a.m.–8 p.m.; Thurs. and Sat., 10 a.m.–5 p.m.; and Sunday (October through May), 1–5 p.m. Closed on all federal and state holidays.

The main branch of the Enoch Pratt Free Library is the parent of the Public Library System for Baltimore City. The local history department (in "The Maryland Room") houses a fine collection of Marylandia. In recent years they have taken an increasing interest in genealogical services and have accessioned available federal census records and other materials.

In addition to the standard works of Maryland county histories, *Baltimore City Directories*, the *Archives of Maryland*, the *Maryland Historical Magazine*, and published source records, the Maryland Room houses one of the few every-name indices to the *Maryland Historical Magazine*, an outstanding biographical file, and numerous early Maryland newspapers. It also has some published family histories and genealogies.

The microfilm department holds microfilm copies of the *Baltimore Sun* from its first issue in 1837 to the present. The Reference Section holds numerous directories and phone books of many larger American cities.

The main branch of the Enoch Pratt Free Library is within easy walking distance of the Maryland Historical Society (four blocks) and the George Peabody Library (two blocks) and is readily accessible to public transportation.

Archives of the Archdiocese of Baltimore

Baltimore Catholic Archives   Telephone: 410-547-5443
320 Cathedral Street   Fax number: 410-727-5432
Baltimore, MD 21201   E-mail: archives@archbalt.org
                             Web Site: www.arcbalt.org

Rev. Paul K. Thomas, Archivist

HOURS: Generally open weekdays from 10 a.m.–6 p.m. by appointment.

This archive does not have materials available for genealogical purposes but will point people in the right direction for family research. Each church keeps its own original records. About seventy-five churches have had their records microfilmed for public use at the Maryland State Archives. The Archives of the Archdiocese of Baltimore (established in 1789) is the repository for Catholic diocesan documents. Its holdings include extensive correspondence with the Vatican, acts and decrees of national Catholic councils, original architectural drawings for the first U.S. Catholic Cathedral, multiple letters of Elizabeth Seton (the first U.S. native-born canonized saint), biographies of bishops, and chancery records, etc. Two additional addresses and telephone numbers for Catholic Genealogical Research: Archives of the Diocese of Wilmington, 10 Montchanin Road, P.O. Box 4019, Wilmington, DE 19807-4019 (telephone: 302-655-0597); and, Archives of the Archdiocese of Washington, 5001 Eastern Avenue, P.O. Box 29260, Washington, D.C. 20017 (telephone: 301-853-5316).

The Church of Jesus Christ of Latter Day Saints

1875 Ritchie Highway, Annapolis, MD 21401	410-757-4173
120 Stemmers Run Road, Baltimore MD 21221	410-686-6709
4100 St. John's Lane, Ellicott City MD 21041	410-465-1642
199 North Place, Frederick MD 21701	301-698-0406
18900 Kingsview Road, Germantown MD 20874	301-972-5897
10000 Stoneybrook Drive, Kensington MD 20895	301-587-0042
4560 Padgett Road, White Plains MD 20746	301-423-8294

Also known as the Mormon Church, the LDS Family History libraries hold the International Genealogical Index, Family History Files, and the Social Security Death Benefits Index. There is no charge to use the library. Call ahead for hours of operation and to reserve time at the computer.

The Jewish Museum of Maryland

The Jewish Historical Society
15 Lloyd Street
Baltimore, MD 21202

Telephone: 410-732-6400
Fax number: 410-732-6451
Web Site: www.jhsm.org

Dianne Feldman, Research Associate

HOURS: Tues., Wed., Thurs., Sun., 12 noon–4 p.m.

The Jewish Museum includes the Jewish Historical Society, the Lloyd Street Synagogue (the first in Maryland, built in 1845), and the B'nai Israel Synagogue (Baltimore's oldest operating synagogue, built in 1876). The organization maintains a collection of over one million photographs, papers, and objects. Historical research is available by appointment with the archivist (ext. 18) in the Robert L. Weinberg Library. Guided tours include the two historic synagogues and *The Golden Land: A Jewish Family Learning Place*. For information about group visits, call the Education Department (ext. 13). A newsletter is published three times a year. *Generations* is the Jewish Museum's annual magazine.

United Methodist Historical Society

Lovely Lane Museum
2200 St. Paul Street
Baltimore, MD 21218-5897

Telephone: 410-889-4458

Rev. Edwin Schell, Archivist

HOURS: Mon. and Fri., 10 a.m.–4 p.m.

Lovely Lane Museum is the Archives and History Center of the Baltimore-Washington United Methodist Conference. Queries will be answered by mail or phone from its 7,000 travelling preacher card files and 3,000-plus local preacher card files. They will gladly make referrals to appropriate churches for information being sought. There are fees for research into membership, marriage, or baptismal records in their possession, beginning at a minimum of $10. Would-be users of Methodist records are urged to avail themselves of the large collection on microfilm at the Maryland State Archives. The only records in Lovely Lane Museum are those of closed churches. The merged churches are responsible for records of constituent congregations. The museum maintains files of early Methodist marriages in alphabetical order for both bride and groom. These files may be accessed by telephone or a letter to the archivist. Researchers pay a nominal fee per day unless they are members of the United Methodist Historical Society. The museum also maintains card files: pastoral appointments to circuits or local churches in the Baltimore Methodist Episcopal or Methodist Episcopal Southern Conferences, 1773–1992; pastors, 1773–1998; and local preachers. Some circuit records begin in 1794 (almost all on microfilm at the Maryland State Archives) and there are memoirs of preachers who died in conference connection between 1773 and 1998. Researchers should be aware that despite the often-sought listing of all local church members, there was never any such record except as maintained by each local church.

Public Libraries and Research Centers

Numerous libraries throughout Maryland have local history and genealogical collections. The following libraries replied to a questionnaire sent them in preparation of this guide. The researcher should be aware that these libraries represent a large portion of the library systems in the state, but there are undoubtedly other libraries and research centers. The prospective user of the following facilities should bear in mind that the hours may change, so it would be prudent to contact the library prior to your planned visit.

Baltimore County Public Library System

320 York Road   Telephone: 410-887-6100
Towson, MD 21204

HOURS: vary at each branch.

This library system has twenty-two branches throughout the county. Most branches have some Marylandia, particularly in Catonsville, Reisterstown, and Towson. The Towson branch has some state census records on microfilm. Librarians will attempt to answer some inquiries if material is available, or make referrals to other institutions. The library staff will also borrow materials from other institutions on interlibrary loan. The library also maintains a Community Information Database that contains listings for local clubs, social service agencies, arts and recreational services, and societies. Information on each agency includes the telephone number, address, agency description, contact people, and hours of operation.

Caroline County Public Library

Central Library
100 Market Street
Denton, MD 21629

Telephone: 410-479-1343
Fax number: 410-479-1443
E-mail: info@caro.lib.md.us
Web Site: www.caro.lib.md.us/library

HOURS: Tues., Wed., Thurs., Sat. 10 a.m.–5:30 p.m.; Mon. and Fri. 10–8 p.m.

The library has local Caroline County and Eastern Shore histories, vertical files, area census records, Maryland Room, early newspaper files on microfilm and some cemetery listings. The Reference and Information Services Department will attempt to answer genealogical inquiries and make referrals to further sources.

Carroll County Public Library

50 East Main Street
Westminster, MD 21157

HOURS: Mon.–Thurs., 9:30 a.m.–8:45 p.m.; Fri., 9:30 a.m.–6 p.m.; Sat., 9:30 a.m.–5 p.m.

This library has a sizable local history and genealogy library staffed by volunteers from the Carroll County Genealogical Society. They will answer genealogical inquiries if material is readily available, or refer researchers to the Historical Society of Carroll County.

Cecil County Public Library

301 Newark Avenue
Elkton, MD 21921-5441

Telephone: 410-996-5600
Fax number: 410-996-5604
E-mail: rd0011@mail.pratt.lib.md.us
Web Site: ceci.lib.md.us
E-mail: infobarb@yahoo.com

Barbara Ramsaur, Information Services

HOURS: Mon. through Thurs., 10 a.m.–9 p.m.; Fri. and Sat., 10 a.m.–5 p.m.

The Local History Room contains items related to Cecil County history and history of Maryland; Cecil County census, 1790 to the latest release on microfilm; *Cecil Whig*, 1841 to the present (1841–1994 on microfilm). Librarians cannot do research for individuals. Most requests are referred to the Historical Society of Cecil County.

Charles County Community Center

(see Southern Maryland Studies Center)

Dorchester County Public Library
303 Gay Street
Cambridge, MD 21613

Telephone: 410-228-7331
Fax number: 410-228-6313
E-mail: infodesk@dorchesterlibrary.org
Web Site: dorchesterlibrary.org

Cheryl Michael, Adult Services

HOURS: Mon., Wed., Fri., 10 a.m.–6 p.m.; Tues., Thurs., 10 a.m.–8 p.m.; Sat., 9 a.m–5 p.m.

The library houses the Dorchester County Historical Society collection. This includes land abstracts (1669–1850s), vertical files, marriage records and census record indices, tombstone records, newspapers and censuses on microfilm, and other genealogy resources. Staff will answer inquiries.

C. Burr Artz Central Library

Frederick County Public Libraries
110 East Patrick Street
Frederick, MD 21701

Maryland Room:301-631-3764
Reference Desk:301-694-1630 ext. 8
Fax number:301-631-3789
E-mail: mm0028@mail.pratt.lib.md.us
Web site: co.frederick.md.us/fcpl/md–hist.html

Mary K. Mannix, Maryland Room Manager

HOURS: Mon., Tues., Wed., 1:00 p.m.–4:00 p.m.; Thurs., Fri., Sat., 10:00 a.m.–1:00 p.m.

The library's Maryland Room provides a research collection documenting the state's economic, social, political, and religious history, as well as genealogy and the Civil War. Special emphasis is placed on Frederick County. Approximately 3,000 titles are in this collection. Primary sources such as maps, photographs, newspapers, oral history, prints, ephemera, and government documents and publications relating to Frederick City and County are collected. Of special interest to the genealogical researcher are the collections of original city directories. Its Maryland Collection is heavy in Frederick County materials with some statewide holdings, area census records, cemetery inscriptions, some church records, and some area newspapers (microfilm). The staff will answer genealogical inquiries briefly. The library maintains a list of professional researchers in the area.

Ruth Enlow Library of Garrett County

6 North Second Street
Oakland, MD 21550

Telephone: 301-334-3996
Fax number: 301-334-4152

HOURS: Mon., Wed., 9:15 a.m.–8 p.m.; Tues., Thurs., Fri., 9:15 a.m.–5:30 p.m.; Sat., 9 a.m.–4 p.m.

Collections include books belonging to the Garrett County Historical Society, some area censuses, marriage records, early area newspapers on microfilm, and some family histories. The Grantsville Branch Library has baptismal and marriage records of a few small Methodist churches in the northern part of the county. The staff will answer genealogical inquiries if information is available; many letters are referred to members of the Garrett County Historical Society.

Harford County Public Library, Bel Air

100 East Pennsylvania Avenue
Bel Air, MD 21014

Telephone: 410-638-3151
Fax number: 410-638-3155
Web Site: www.harf.lib.md.us

HOURS: Mon., Tues., Thurs., 10 a.m.–9 p.m.; Wed., 12 noon–9 p.m.; Fri., 12 noon–5 p.m.; Sat., 10 a.m.–5 p.m.; Sun (October–May), 1–4 p.m.

The library has federal censuses for Harford County, 1790–1920, Baltimore City and County federal censuses from 1850 to 1920 (excluding the Soundex indexes), Maryland census indices 1790–1860, and some adjoining state censuses. It maintains a good collection of Maryland genealogy books in the Maryland Room. Internet access is available in the library and their home page "See Worthy Sites" links to genealogical information. They no longer have the obituary file of persons listed in *The Aegis,* which is now held at the Historical Society of Harford County. *The Aegis* newspaper is on microfilm from 1857 to the present. *The Record* newspaper is held for the current six months only (hard copies). The staff refers genealogical inquiries to local professional genealogists and the Harford County Genealogical Society.

The Johns Hopkins University
Milton S. Eisenhower Library

Special Collections Department   Telephone: 410-516-8348
34th & Charles Streets
Baltimore, MD 21218

HOURS: Mon., Tues., Wed., and Fri., 8:30 a.m.–5 p.m.; Thurs., 8:30 a.m.–8 p.m.

The library's Rare Book Collection houses 48,000-plus volumes, and is strongest in the humanities and social sciences. This includes medieval and Renaissance manuscript books as well as many facsimile editions of similar works, the Machen Collection of incunabula (books printed before 1501), and fine printed books. Of its many collections, the two that will most interest genealogists and historians are the Birney Anti-Slavery Collection and the Friedenwald Collection of books on the American Revolution and preceding events. Access to all manuscript collections is provided through finding aids available on the Internet through MSEL Gopher, a card catalog in the department, and RLIN-AMC. Many collections, and all fully cataloged books, are represented on Janus. Photoduplication of materials is available.

The Johns Hopkins University
John Work Garrett Library

4545 North Charles Street   Telephone: 410-516-5571
Baltimore, MD 21210

HOURS: Open by appointment only.

The library has more than 28,000 volumes, primarily in natural history and English literature. They also have a significant collection of exploration and voyage literature. It is complemented by another collection that concentrates on American travel and colonial history; its core is represented by the reference work *Seventeenth Century Maryland: A Bibliography* compiled by Elizabeth Baer. They also have a large collection of Bibles, the autographs of the signers of the Declaration of Independence and other American manuscripts, plus various maps dating from the sixteenth to twentieth centuries.

Montgomery County Public Libraries

Rockville Public Library   Telephone: 301-217-3800
99 Maryland Avenue   Web Site: www.mont.lib.md.us
Rockville, MD 20850

HOURS: Mon.–Thurs., 10 a.m.–8:30 p.m.; Fri., 10 a.m. to 5 p.m.; Sat., 9 a.m.–5 p.m.; and, Sun. (September–June), 1–5 p.m.

The library has a small and basic collection of Maryland county histories with emphasis on Montgomery County, microfilm copies of early local newspapers, U.S. census records for Montgomery County on microfilm (1790–1920), and some church records on microfilm, including Friends, Episcopalians, and Methodists. The staff will answer letters of inquiry that require only standard indices or basic sources. Others are referred to the Montgomery County Historical Society.

Prince George's County Memorial Library

Hyattsville Public Library
6530 Adelphi Road
Hyattsville, MD 20782

Telephone: 301-985-4690
Web Site: www.prge.lib.md.us

HOURS: Mon.–Thurs., 10 a.m.–9 p.m.; Fri., 10 a.m.–6 p.m.; Sat., 10 a.m.–5 p.m.; and, Sun. (September–May), 1–5 p.m.

The Maryland Room collections include the censuses of Maryland 1790–1920, some compiled cemetery records, microfilm copies of Prince George's County historical records (wills, tax assessment books, other county court records) 1698–1963; 1798 Federal Tax Assessment records for Maryland, the *Baltimore City Directories* (1863–81), local histories, and published source records of the area.

St. Mary's County Memorial Library

23250 Hollywood Street
Leonardtown, MD 20650

Telephone: 301-475-2846
Fax number: 301-884-4416
Web Site: www.somd.lib.md.us/stma/libraries
E-mail: stma.ref@somd.lib.md.us

HOURS: Mon.–Thurs., 9 a.m.–8 p.m.; Fri., 12 noon–5 p.m.; and, Sat., 9 a.m.–5 p.m (except summer, 9 a.m.–1 p.m.).

The library has good Maryland and local history collections and houses the collection of the St. Mary's County Genealogical Society. It answers all inquiries.

Southern Maryland Studies Center

Charles County Community College
8730 Mitchell Road
P.O. Box 910
LaPlata, MD 20646-0910

Telephone: 301-934-2251, ext. 7110
Fax number: 301-934-7699
E-mail: smsc@charles.cc.md.us
Web Site: www.charles.cc.md.us

HOURS: Reading Room open when classes are in session (contact college library for hours). Documents Room: Mon. through Fri., 1–4 p.m. Researchers are encouraged to call ahead if they plan to use primary source materials.

The center was founded by the Charles County Community College in 1976 in order to provide a central location for research on this historically important region. Their collection of print materials includes books, unpublished documents, newspapers, photographs, slides, maps, and oral history tapes. This is a reference-only section of the library; items do not circulate. The center has an outstanding collection of local history and genealogical materials. Researchers will find census records and newspapers on microfilm and may explore manuscript collections dating from the late eighteenth century. The Harry Wright Newman Collection of reference notes covering over 1,000 Maryland families is of particular interest to genealogists. Other special collections include the Southern Maryland Today Project highlighting Southern Maryland Folklore, records of the Charlotte Hall School from 1774 to 1976, and the Marshall Hall Collection which includes photographs of the early twentieth-century amusement park.

Talbot County Public Library

(see "Historical Society of Talbot County")

Telephone: 410-822-1626

University of Baltimore, Langsdale Library

Archives and Special Collections   Telephone: 410-837-4268
1420 Maryland Avenue
Baltimore, MD 21201
E-mail: thollowak@ubmail.ubalt.edu
Web Site: www/ubalt.edu/www/archives/collect.html

Thomas L. Hollowak, Archivist

The holdings include records of the American Clan Gregor Society (1909–96); the General Society of Colonial Wars (1892–); the Society of Colonial Wars in the State of Maryland (1893–); the Society of the War of 1812 in the

State of Maryland (1889–); the Maryland Society of the Sons of the American Revolution (1889–); the Sons of Union Veterans of the Civil War, Maryland Division (1886–1916); and Archives of Maryland Polonia (1886–). Also included are records of the Steamship Historical Society of America, plus numerous records on Baltimore neighborhoods, commerce and business, civic groups, unions, housing authorities, planning councils, and politicians in the twentieth century. Contact the library for a complete list and for library hours.

University of Maryland Baltimore County

Albin O. Kuhn Library and Gallery   Telephone: 410-455-2232
Special Collections Department
5401 Wilkens Avenue
Catonsville, MD 21228

HOURS: Vary during school year; call ahead.

The library houses a growing genealogy and heraldry collection, all Maryland censuses, 1790–1920, ships passenger lists for the Port of Baltimore, local histories and published source records.

University of Maryland, McKeldin Library

College Park, MD 20742-7011   Telephone: 301-405-0567
                                Web Site: ww.lib.umd.edu/umcp

HOURS: Mon.–Thurs., 8 a.m.–11 p.m.; Fri., 8 a.m.–6 p.m.; Sat., 10 a.m.–6 p.m.; and Sun., 12 noon–11 p.m.

The Marylandia Department and Historical Manuscripts & Archives Department are part of the Special Collections Division within the University of Maryland College Park Libraries. The collections are predominantly, but not exclusively, related to Maryland and the surrounding region. Its subject strengths include records on late nineteenth- and early twentieth-century politics, land use, Chesapeake Bay studies, labor history, and personal family papers (mainly post-1850) which document aspects of Maryland history and life.

United States Naval Academy

Admiral Chester A. Nimitz Library   Telephone: 410-267-2420
Annapolis, MD 21402

HOURS: Vary during school year; call ahead.

Special Collections include biographical material on U.S. Naval Officers; published genealogies; army registers of English, German, Italian, and other European officers; and, ships' logs of U.S. naval vessels.

Washington County Free Library

100 South Potomac Street   Telephone: 301-739-3250
Hagerstown, MD 21740   Web Site: www.pilot.wash.lib.md.us

HOURS: Mon.–Fri., 9 a.m.–9 p.m., and Sat., 9 a.m.–5 p.m.

Has general reference and genealogical books.

Worcester County Library, Snow Hill

Worcester Room Genealogical Collection
307 North Washington Street   Telephone: 410-632-2600
Snow Hill, MD 21863   Fax number: 410-632-1159
          E-mail: worc@dmv.com
          Web Site: www.worc.lib.md.us/library/home.html

HOURS: Mon., Wed., 10 a.m.–8 p.m.; Tues., Thurs., Fri., 10 a.m.–6 p.m.; Sat., 9 a.m.–1 p.m.

The collections are rich in Worcester County materials and the adjoining counties in Maryland, Delaware, and Virginia. The collection also includes will abstracts, land records, vital statistics, family histories, census records, and microfilm copies of newspapers (1830–1973). The staff will answer genealogical inquiries and volunteer genealogists will answer specific questions and assist patrons on

Tuesday and Saturday mornings. The Snow Hill branch also houses the William D. Pitts Collection of land survey records of 20,000-plus items, including plats, maps, field surveys files, and field books. The branch archives hold collections of photographs, slide/tape programs, scrapbooks, day books, ledgers, and 2,000 35mm slides. These latter are accessible only by appointment. Contact Lisa Harrison (410-632-2600).

Genealogical Societies in Maryland

Only a few genealogical societies maintain their own library and, if indeed they have one, it is generally housed at either the local historical society, public library, society meeting place, or in a private home.

Most of these organizations will answer inquiries as long as in-depth research is not required, in which case researchers will be referred to professional genealogists. The majority of these societies, however, publish newsletters, bulletins, or journals that include queries. One should write the society in their area of interest for details (enclose a SASE). For additional information see Mary K. Meyer's *Directory of Genealogical Societies in the USA and Canada*, 10th edition (Mt. Airy, Md.: Libra Publications, 1994).

Afro-American Historical & Genealogical Society, Baltimore Chapter

P.O. Box 9366
2330 Edmondson Avenue
Baltimore, MD 21229

The society meets on the first Saturday of each month from September to June. For information about membership, contact Jerry M. Hynson at (410) 795-2093.

Afro-American Historical & Genealogical Society, Central Maryland Chapter

P.O. Box 2655   Fax: 410-381-6795
Columbia, MD 21045   E-mail: sylcooke@aol.com

The society meets on the second Saturday of each month and supports its membership in genealogical and historical research of African Americans in Howard County.

Allegany County Genealogical Society

P.O. Box 3103
Lavale, MD 21502

Anne Arundel Genealogical Society

P.O. Box 221   Telephone: 410-760-9679
Pasadena, MD 21123-0221

Library site:
Kuethe Library Historical and Genealogical Research Center
5 Crain Hwy. S.E.
Glen Burnie, MD 21061
        Web Site: www.geocities.com/yosemite/trails/4256/gensoc.html

HOURS: Thurs., Fri., Sat., 10 a.m.–4 p.m.

Founded in 1974 the society publishes a newsletter which evolved into *Anne Arundel Speaks*, a quarterly newsletter tailored to help genealogical researchers and to keep members informed of current happenings in the genealogical community. In January and July the society publishes *Anne Arundel Readings*, a fifty-page journal of genealogical source material on persons who lived in Anne Arundel County. The society meets on the first Thursday of each month at Severna Park Methodist Church on Benfield Boulevard in Severna Park. Their holdings include cemetery records, Bible records, genealogies, extensive material on New England and southern states, Civil War volumes, and Anne Arundel County photographs and ephemera. They have published a number of books over the years. Contact them for a list of the publications still available for sale. They also offer research assistance by experienced genealogists in exchange for a donation plus copy costs.

Baltimore County Genealogical Society

P.O. Box 10085
Towson, MD 21285-0085

Telephone: 410-285-4004

Library location:
8601 Harford Road at the intersection of Hiss Avenue in Parkville
(2nd floor, rear parking lot entrance)
Web Site: www.serve.com/bcgs/bcgs.html

The society meets on the fourth Sunday of each month at 2 p.m. Their library is open 12 noon–2 p.m. on meeting days, second Tuesday (5 p.m.–9 p.m.), and second Thursday and second Saturday (10 a.m.–2 p.m.). They publish *The Notebook* (quarterly) and offer many services to members, including Bible records, vertical files, special publications, cemetery records, and ancestor charts. They also have a Computer Interest Group, an Eastern European Interest Group, and a Baltimore Genealogy Research Group that arranges trips to research centers in adjoining states and Washington, D.C.

Carroll County Genealogical Society, Inc.

P.O. Box 1752
Westminster, MD 21158

Telephone: 410-876-1552

Web Site: www.carr.lib.md.us/ccgs/ccgs.html

HOURS: see Carroll County Public Library

The society's library is located within the Carroll County Public Library building at 50 East Main Street in Westminster. It is maintained by the society with volunteers who assist researchers when available. Researchers and library patrons may use the society's library whenever the public building is open, even if a volunteer is not available for assistance.

Genealogy Section of the Catonsville Historical Society

P.O. Box 21154   Telephone: 410-744-3034
Catonsville, MD 21228

HOURS: Irregular (call ahead).

The society holds monthly meetings at 7:30 p.m. on the first Wednesday of the month (September to May) at the society's headquarters, 1824 Frederick Road, Catonsville. Guests are welcome. They have a small library of "how-to" genealogy books and materials for use of the membership. Local history materials on Baltimore and Catonsville are available for research by appointment.

Cecil County Genealogical Society

P.O. Box 11   Telephone: 410-287-8793
Charlestown, MD 21914
Library location: Tory House, Charlestown

HOURS: 1st Sat. (October–June), 10 a.m.–Noon

This small library's holdings relate primarily to Cecil County families. The society publishes a quarterly newsletter and members will assist in starting family research.

Frederick County Genealogical Society

(FRECOGS)   E-mail: brinlong@erols.com
P.O. Box 234   Web Site: www.zekes.com/ndspidell/fredco.html
Monrovia, MD 21770-0234

FRECOGS meetings are held at 7 p.m. on the fourth Tuesday of the month at the LDS Family History Center, 199 North Place, Frederick (unless notice states otherwise). The society prepares a monthly newsletter every other month, an annual membership list, an annual index to the bimonthly newsletter, an exchange surname database, and holds a Researcher's Reunion Day each year.

Genealogy Club of the Montgomery County Historical Society

111 West Montgomery Avenue   Telephone: 301-340-2974
Rockville, MD 20850-4212   Fax number: 301-340-2871
                                 Web Site: www.montgomeryhistory.org
                                 E-mail: mchistory@mindspring.com

HOURS: Tues. through Sun., 12 noon–4 p.m. (except Christmas and Easter).

The research library is open to members (no fee) and non-members for a small user fee. Staff and volunteers will do research in the collections for copy costs, postage, and a suggested donation. The society maintains published genealogies and family files; Montgomery County will abstracts 1776–1875; Montgomery County probate records and land records, 1776–1865 on microfilm; abstracts of the *Montgomery County Sentinel* newspaper 1855–1945 (as well as original and microfilm copies); census record abstracts 1850–80 for Montgomery County; maps and plats; Montgomery Mutual Insurance papers and other manuscripts; cemetery & church records; marriage licenses; tax assessment records 1783–1840, 1866–67; apprenticeship records 1779–1840 (abstracts); World War I enlistment cards.

Genealogical Council of Maryland

P.O. Box 10096
Gaithersburg, MD 20898-0096
    E-mail: mailgcm@aol.com
    Web Site: www.members.aol.com/mailgcm/gcm.html

The council is a non-profit, tax-exempt genealogical group that serves as a coordinating organization for state projects, speakers, and funding for member societies. The GCM also serves as a state representative for activities sponsored by national societies. Council committees and projects include the Bible Records Committee, Church Records Committee, Cemetery Records Committee, Education Committee, Speaker's Bureau, and Civil War Project. Among the council's publications are the *Directory of Maryland Burial Grounds*, Vol. I (Westminster: Family Line Publications, 1996); Robert W. Barnes, editor, *Inventory of Maryland Bible Records*, Vol. I (Westminster: Family Line Publications, 1989); and Edna Agatha Kanely, *Directory of Maryland Church Records*, (Silver Spring MD: Family Line Publications, 1987).

Harford County Genealogical Society

P.O. Box 15   Web Site: www.rtis.com/reg/md/org/hcgs
Aberdeen, MD 21001

Founded in 1979, the society publishes two books on local genealogical topics each year. These books are available by writing to the above address for a listing, or by using the aforementioned web site. The *Newsletter* is published six times a year. The society meetings are held the third Sunday in January, March, May, July, September, and November (2 p.m.) at Churchville Presbyterian Church, Churchville, Maryland (unless notice states otherwise). The society does not maintain its own library, but donates its books and research materials to the Historical Society of Harford County at 143 East Main Street in Bel Air.

Howard County Genealogical Society

P.O. Box 274   E-mail: bush@worldnet.att.net
Columbia, MD 21045   Web Site: www.users.aol.com/castlewrks/hcgs

The society does not have a separate library but contributes to the genealogical resources at the Howard County Historical Society library, Court Avenue, Ellicott City. It is open on Tuesdays from noon to 8 p.m. and Saturdays from noon to 5 p.m. Telephone 410-750-0370.

Huguenot Society of Maryland

1506 Pine Bluff Way   Telephone: 410-974-0736
Arnold MD 21012-2418   E–mail: tsquared@toad.net
                         Web Site: www. Huguenot.netnation.com
Elizabeth S. Guald, President

The society provides education through books and talks about Huguenots, their principles, virtues, and contributions to the United States of America. They collect and preserve historical data and relics illustrative of Huguenot life, manners and customs, and commemorate the great events of Huguenot history. They have genealogical records on Huguenot families in the United States and some members write and publish books about Huguenot subjects. The national society sells books about Huguenots. See the web page for more information.

Lower Delmarva Genealogical Society

P.O. Box 3602   Telephone: 410-749-6158
Salisbury, MD 21802-3602   410-742-3501
                         E-mail: pegl@shore.intercom.net
                         Web Site: www.bay.intercom.net/ldgs

The society works in conjunction with the Edward H. Nabb Research Center for Delmarva History and Culture at Salisbury State University, assisting with research and maintaining genealogical records. They have many early records and will answer brief questions of genealogical interest and place queries in a newsletter for a small fee. They will also make a surname search, free to members. The society solicits articles on Eastern Shore families and other materials of interest to historians and to genealogists.

Maryland Genealogical Society

201 West Monument Street   Telephone: 410-685-3750
Baltimore, MD 21201

The society maintains an office in the Maryland Historical Society and donates its books and other genealogical materials to the MHS library. They publish a quarterly newsletter and the *Maryland Genealogical Society Bulletin*, a renowned genealogical journal. They also hold an annual genealogical conference that attracts speakers and researchers from around the United States.

Mid-Atlantic Germanic Society (MAGS)

P.O. Box 2642
Kensington, MD 20891-2642
Web Site: www.ourworld.compuserve.com/homepages.ptwinner

The society holds its biannual conference meetings in the spring and fall. For a number of years, they have maintained two significant files of surname data, the "German Locality Index" and the "MAGS Surname Exchange Index," both computerized. *Der Kurier*, the newsletter of the society, is published four times a year (September, December, March, June). They have "Stumped Roots Service" and a professional referral service available for members.

Prince George's County Genealogical Society

Rainwater-Miles Research Center
12219 Tulip Grove Drive
Bowie, MD 20718-0819
Mailing address: PO Box 819
Bowie MD 20718-0819
Web Site: http://www>rootsweb.com/~mdpgeorg/text/pggensoc>html

Telephone: 301-262-2063
E-mail: pgcgs@juno.com

HOURS: Wed., 10 a.m.–7 p.m. (except 1st Wed., 10 a.m.–1 p.m.) and last Sat. of the month, 1–5 p.m.

Founded in 1969 the society holds monthly meetings (7 p.m.) from September through June at the Greenbelt Library, 11 Crescent Road, in Greenbelt. Meetings are free and open to the public. The society publishes ten newsletters a year and operates a research center that is free and open to the public. The center has a photocopier, microfilm and microfiche readers, and two patron computers. The registrar will undertake on-site research for a nominal fee.

The research center has a 4,000-plus volume library that is nationwide in scope with an emphasis on Maryland. It houses more than 400 periodicals, Bible records, surname file maps, selected microforms and CD-Rom, the original records of the Thomas F. Murray Funeral Home of SE Washington DC, all P.G. County censuses 1790–1920 (except 1830 and 1890) and copies of Prince George's County naturalization records.

St. Mary's County Genealogical Society

P.O. Box 1109
Leonardtown, MD 20650-1109

Telephone: 301-373-8458

Web Site: www.bsd.pastracks.com/smcgs

The society publishes ten issues of its newsletter a year. Its collections are housed at the Leonardtown Library and are open to public use. The holdings cover a wide variety of information beyond the scope of St. Mary's County.

Upper Shore Genealogical Society of Maryland

P.O. Box 275   Telephone: 410-754-2785 or 410-778-0931
Easton, MD 21601   (to verify meeting place and schedule)
E-mail: zekejr@home.dmv.com
Web Site: www.geocities.com/heartland/9448/usgs.html

Meetings are held on the third Sunday each month (except June, July, and August) at the Diocesan Center, 305 Goldsborough Street unless otherwise announced. The society serves as the focal point for genealogical activities of the Upper Shore counties of Caroline, Dorchester, Kent, Queen Anne's, and Talbot. The society's journal *Chesapeake Cousins* is published twice a year (spring and fall) and issues periodic newsletters.

Washington County Genealogical Society

c/o Jackie Rogers
122 South Locust Street
Hagerstown, MD 21740

Historical Societies and Museums

Allegany County Historical Society

218 Washington Street　　　　　　Telephone and Fax: 301-777-8678
Cumberland, MD 21502
　　　　　　　　　　Web Site: www.angelfire.com/md/historyhouse

HOURS: (June–October) Tues. through Sun., 11 a.m.–4 p.m.; (November–May) Tues. through Sat., 11 a.m.–4 p.m.

The society has volunteers for research assistance in their library and house museum that provide outside research for a fee. Their genealogical holdings include 129 books, files of family histories, city directories, family Bibles, some cemetery records, photographs, and maps.

Anne Arundel County Historical Society, Inc.

Historical and Genealogical Research Center
5 Crain Highway South　　　　　　Telephone: 410-760-9679
Glen Burnie, MD 21061

HOURS: Thurs., Fri., Sat., 10 a.m.–4 p.m.

The society will answer queries, supply copies at minimal charge, and often refer to professionals or to the Anne Arundel Genealogical Society. The Kuethe Library houses more than 5,000 volumes pertaining to Anne Arundel County, New England, New York, Pennsylvania, Virginia, North Carolina, and several other southern as well as mid-western states. The collections include holdings of the Anne Arundel Genealogical Society, and twelve filing cabinets of genealogical and biographical materials and newspaper clippings, maps, photographs, printed ephemera, census microfilm, and obituary file (computerized).

Baltimore County Historical Society

9811 Van Buren Lane   Telephone: 410-666-1878
Cockeysville, MD 21030
                    Web Site: www.bcplonline.org/branchpgs/bchs

HOURS: Wed. 1–4 p.m.; Sat. 10 a.m.–3 p.m. Closed on Saturdays in August and on major holiday weekends.

Visitors are invited to conduct research in the society's collections, but it is not a lending library. Photocopies are available for a fee. Microfilm and microfiche readers are available as are a scanner and printer for copying photographs. The staff will answer inquiries by mail. The society's collections include a card catalog of 29,000-plus names of persons and historical places and things, sixty letter file drawers of genealogical and historical interest, fifteen map file drawers of family charts, land grants, and historical maps, eighteen atlases, census records (book and microfilm), 1790–1920 (partially indexed), 5,600-plus photographs of persons and places (indexed), 1,300-plus books on genealogy and history of Baltimore County, more than 300 church and family cemetery inscriptions, and local newspapers (paper copies and/or microfilm).

Calvert County Historical Society

30 Duke Street   Telephone: 410-535-2452
P.O. Box 358
Prince Frederick, MD 20639
                    Web Site: www.somd.lib.md.us/calv/cchs
                    E-mail: lcollins@somd.lib.md.us

Linda M. Collins, Curator

HOURS: Tues., Wed., Thurs., 10 a.m.–3 p.m.

The society maintains a library of local history and genealogy, with collections of family papers, genealogical files, copies of Calvert County censuses 1800–1920 (including agriculture censuses 1850–80), and microfilm copies of local newspapers. Two fires in 1882 resulted in the loss of most records prior to that date, but records of the Provincial Court and Prerogative Court help fill some of the records gap prior to the Revolutionary War. Staff will answer inquiries or refer them to professional researchers or local family members.

Calvert Marine Museum

14150 Solomons Island Road   Telephone: 410-325-2042
P.O. Box 97   Fax number: 410-326-6691
Solomons, MD 20688
          Web Site: www.somd.lib.md.us/museums/marine-museum

HOURS: Open daily, except on Thanksgiving, Christmas, and New Year's Eve (call ahead for hours of operation).

The museum has limited genealogical materials, but maintains a vast local history and general reference library and major exhibits.

Caroline County Historical Society, Inc.

P.O. Box 160   Telephone: 410-479-2055
Greensboro, MD 21639

HOURS: Fri., Sat., Sun., 11:00 a.m.–4:00 p.m.

The society's library at this time is very small, but it does house a few donated store ledgers and family Bibles. Its Museum of Rural Life is located on the corner of Second and Gay Streets on the courthouse green in

Denton. The museum in Greensboro, on Sunset Avenue, is open on Founders Day (July 1) and by appointment.

Historical Society of Carroll County

210 East Main Street
Westminster, MD 21157-5225

Jay A. Graybeal, Director

Telephone: 410-848-6494
410-848-9531
E-mail: hscc@carr.org
Web Site: www.carr.org/hscc

HOURS: Tues.–Fri., 9:30 a.m.–12:30 p.m. and 1 p.m.–4 p.m.; Sat., 9 a.m.–12 noon.

The society maintains a library containing local history and genealogy, obituary files, local newspapers, photographs, and vertical files (on genealogical correspondence and various subjects). It also houses the Tracey Collection, one of the outstanding Maryland collections of drawings, surveyors books, and maps of the earliest land patents in Baltimore, Carroll, Frederick, and Washington Counties, Maryland. Family Search will answer queries for a fee. There is also a library user fee for non-members.

The Historical Society of Cecil County

135 East Main Street
Elkton, MD 21921

Telephone: 410-398-1790
E-mail: history@cchistory.org
Web Site: www.cchistory.org

HOURS: Mon., 12 noon–4 p.m.; Tues., 6 p.m.–8:30 p.m.; Thurs., 10 a.m.–4 p.m.; and, 4th Sat., 10 a.m.–2 p.m.

The society maintains a library (regarding local and state history and genealogy), with maps, census records, military records, county newspapers, tax lists, marriage records, church records, immigration records, ships' manifests, commissioner minute books, complete sets of *War of the Rebellion*, the published *Archives of Maryland,* and also maintains museum exhibits. The staff will answer genealogical inquiries.

Charles County Historical Society

P.O. Box 336
Port Tobacco, MD 20677
R. Wayne Winkler, President

Telephone: 301-934-8305
E-mail: wink2410@erols.com

Chesapeake Beach Railway Museum

P.O. Box 783
Chesapeake Beach, MD 20732

Telephone: 410-257-3892

HOURS: Daily (May–September), 1–4 p.m., and Sat. and Sun. only (October–April).

Resources include a railway station, car museum, general references, local history, and technological history materials.

Dorchester County Historical Society

P.O. Box 361
Cambridge, MD 21613

Telephone: 410-228-7953

HOURS: Open daily (call ahead for hours).

The library is housed in the Dorchester Public Library, 303 Gay Street, Cambridge. The collections include about 500 volumes plus ninety reels of microfilm, complete lists of available Dorchester County land abstracts, tombstone records, Bible records, census records, local newspapers, fire insurance maps, *Archives of Maryland*, *Maryland Historical Magazine* and *Dorchester Genealogical Magazine*. The staff will answer genealogical inquiries, but most are forwarded to the *Dorchester Genealogical Magazine*, 1058 Taylor's Island Road, Madison, MD 21648.

Historical Society of Frederick County, Inc.

24 East Church Street
Frederick, MD 21701

Telephone: 301-663-1188
Fax number: 301-663-0526
Web Site: www.fwp.net/hsfc
E-mail: director@fwp.net

Marie Washburn, Librarian

HOURS: Tues.–Sat., 10 a.m.–4 p.m.

The society maintains a museum and a library that houses 4,000-plus volumes of Frederick County history and genealogy, including family genealogies, diaries, manuscripts, and photographs. Research services and photocopies are available for a fee.

Garrett County Historical Museum

107 South Second Street
P.O. Box 28
Oakland, MD 21550

Telephone: 301-334-3226

HOURS: Mon.–Sat., 11 a.m.–4 p.m. Seasonal and subject to change; call ahead.

The library has numerous genealogical resource materials. The staff answers genealogical inquiries.

Historical Society of Harford County, Inc.

143 North Main Street
P.O. Box 366
Bel Air, MD 21014-0366

Telephone: 410-838-7691
E-mail: harchis@aol.com
Web Site: www.harfordhistory.net

HOURS: Tues. (Court Records Section only, 10 a.m.–12 noon, and 1 p.m.–2:30 p.m.); Wed. (Archives Section only, 7:30 a.m.–2 p.m.); Thurs. (Family History and Resource Library Sections only, 9 a.m.–3 p.m.); and 4th

Sat. (Archives and Family History Sections only, 10 a.m.–2 p.m.). The Hays House Museum located at 324 Kenmore Avenue (near the Bel Air High School) is open Sunday from April to December, 1–4 p.m. (and other times by appointment).

The society's headquarters are located in the Old Post Office Building at the corner of North Main and Gordon Streets. It is a center for historical and genealogical research on Harford County's people and places (with its records, manuscripts, documents and archives divided into the four sections noted above). Its genealogical materials include old court records and archives, historical documents, family records and histories, cemetery inscriptions, newspaper obituary files, tax lists, census records, marriage licenses, vertical files, and published and unpublished records and books. The society also houses the collections of the Harford County Genealogical Society. The *Harford County Bulletin* and the society's newsletter are published quarterly.

The Hays House, Bel Air's oldest house (built circa 1788), is owned and operated by the society. It is a museum and site for colonial tea parties, tours, and encampments. Located at 324 Kenmore Avenue near the Bel Air High School, the Hays House is open on Sunday from 1:00 p.m.–4:00 p.m. and other times by appointment. For more information call 410-838-1213.

Howard County Historical Society

8328 Court Avenue　　　　Library telephone: 410-750-0370
P.O. Box 109　　　　　　Museum telephone: 410-461-1050
Ellicott City, MD 21043　　　　Fax number: 410-750-0370
　　　　　　　　E–mail: mkmannix@tibetanmastiffs.com
Mary K. Mannix, Library Director

HOURS: Library open Tues., 12 noon–8 p.m., and Sat., 12 noon–5 p.m. Museum open Tues., 12 noon–5 p.m., and Sat., 12 noon–5 p.m.

Holdings consist of 3,000+ volumes, maps, plats, photographs, ninety-six rolls of microfilm (censuses, newspapers), thirty-three bound volumes of newspapers, vertical files (surnames and subjects), journals, scrapbooks, and printed ephemera, all of which relate to Howard County, its history, people, and businesses. The society also collects material on the surrounding mill communities outside the county, which are closely tied to Howard County. Collections of note include: marriage licenses, 1858–1937; deeds, mortgages (c1850–1950); voters registrations, (c1865–1933); World War II Selective Service records; and microfilm copy of an 1864 slave register. They also maintain an audio-visual collection, including a copy of *Word of Mouth: The Black Experience in Howard County*. The society is especially strong in Civil War material, including manuscript material of the United Daughters of the Confederacy, plus ninety-one volumes of *War of the Rebellion*. The library serves as the archives for several county organizations, including the Daughters of the American Revolution and the Howard County Genealogical Society. The staff will answer simple inquiries; those requiring detailed research are referred to professional genealogists, a list of which will be furnished on request.

The society also has available on computer a database compiled from the records of the Slack Funeral Home of Ellicott City. Another very useful collection consists of materials such as research notes, clippings, and institutional histories on the religious communities that have existed in the county throughout its history. Related items include a listing of all religious individuals who have practiced in the county and recent photographs of all standing religious structures.

Jefferson Patterson Park & Museum

10515 Mackall Road   Telephone: 410-586-8500
St. Leonard, MD 20685   Appointments: 410-586-8550
      Web Site: www.ari.net/mdshpo/museum.html

HOURS: Museum is open Apr. 15–October 15, Wed.–Sun., 10 a.m.–5 p.m. The library is open Mon.–Fri., 8:00–5:00 by appointment only.

The Jefferson Patterson Park & Museum is a Maryland state museum of history and archeology whose mission is to preserve, research, and interpret the diverse cultures of the Chesapeake Bay region. Located on a 544-acre property along the Patuxent River in Calvert County, JPPM contains over seventy documented archeological sites spanning 9,000 years. The park is listed on the National Register of Historic Places. The archeological, agricultural, and historical resources of the property are interpreted to the public through a wide range of exhibits, educational programs, and services.

The JPPM research library has one of the region's largest collections of references about archeology and the history of Maryland and the eastern United States. Although it is not a lending library, museum staff encourage its use by scholars and the general public. The library has over 3,000 books dealing with topics such as Native American life, archeology, history, agriculture, historic architecture, the identification and conservation of artifacts and antiques, the Chesapeake Bay environment, and museum studies. Many of the southern Maryland reference materials are obscure and would be hard to find in other libraries. The library also has a collection of historic maps depicting various portions of southern Maryland.

Historical Society of Kent County, Inc.

P.O. Box 665   Telephone: 410-778-3499
Chestertown, MD 21620   Fax number: 410-778-3747
Society location: Geddes-Piper House
101 Church Alley, Chestertown, MD 21620
                          E-mail: hskcmd@friend.ly.net
                  Web Site: www.kentcounty.com/historicalsociety
Mary K. Myer, Executive Director

HOURS: Tues., 3–5 p.m.; Wed., Thurs., Fri., 10 a.m.–4 p.m. Weekend hours: May 1 to November 1, Sat. and Sun., 1–4 p.m.

The society's house and museum is open to promote heritage tourism and education about the people and history of Kent County. The society possesses a research library and conducts a winter lecture series and an Annual Candlelight Walking Tour of over a dozen private homes in the historic district. Their holdings include documentation of the county's history, nineteenth-century maps, records of county families (including Hope Barroll's legal practice) and account books relating to nineteenth- and early twentieth-century commercial businesses, plus religious history, hymnals, eighteenth- and nineteenth-century Chinese export teapots, Victorian era fans, furnishings from the eighteenth and nineteenth centuries, an extensive collection of iron cooking utensils and food processing devices, and pottery and glass artifacts, as well as genealogical research tools. The staff will provide genealogical services for a fee.

Montgomery County Historical Society, Inc.

111 West Montgomery Avenue   Telephone: 301-340-2974
Rockville, MD 20850

E-mail: mchistory@mindspring.com
Web Site: www.montgomeryhistory.org

HOURS: Tues.–Sun., 12 noon–4 p.m.

The library holds numerous volumes of published genealogies; state and local histories; will abstracts, 1776–1875; marriage licenses, 1796–1896; church records; pension applications; deed abstracts, 1777–94; tax lists, 1783–1840; cemetery records; oaths of fidelity, 1778; census records 1776 (state), 1790–1900 (1830 and 1890 are missing); slave census, 1868; newspaper abstracts and original newspapers; maps, plats, photographs, and ephemera. The staff answers genealogical inquiries and also maintains a list of professional researchers and genealogical family files.

Prince George's County Historical Society

Frederick S. DeMarr Library of County History
P.O. Box 14   Telephone: 301-464-0590
Riverdale, MD 20737
(staff available Saturday from 12 noon–4 p.m.)

Library location:
5626 Bell Station Road
Glenn Dale, MD 20679

HOURS: Sat., 12 noon–4 p.m.

The society has extensive books, papers, and library resources about Prince George's County, plus limited but unique materials from other Maryland areas. They hold some genealogical materials but refer most callers to the Prince George's County Genealogical Society. The staff is frequently able to provide local geographical and cultural background of families. The society maintains an extensive vertical file covering the past forty-five years of local news, family papers, and manuscript research materials.

Queen Anne's County Historical Society

P.O. Box 296
Centreville, MD 21617

St. Mary's County Historical Society, Inc.

P.O. Box 212
Leonardtown, MD 20650

Telephone: 301-475-2467
301-475-9455
Web Site: www.somd.lib.md.us/smchs

HOURS: Administrative Office open Mon.–Fri., 12 noon–4 p.m.; Research Center open Wed.–Fri., 12 noon–4 p.m. and Sat., 10 a.m.–4 p.m. Research Center closed most of December for holidays. Old Jail Museum and Tudor Hall Research Center (contact the society for additional information).

The library houses 1,200+ volumes of published genealogies and state and local histories, plus the *Maryland Historical Magazine* (since 1906), *Archives of Maryland* (72 vols.), *The Chronicles of St. Mary's* (since 1953), local newspapers (microfilm), probate records, rent rolls, debt books, abstracts of deeds, county assessment records, church records, vital records, an index to all tombstones in the county, U.S. censuses, 1790–1920 (1830 and 1890 do not exist), slave schedules, mortality schedules, and a selection of research records on various county families. The staff will answer queries. Research is done on an hourly rate.

Somerset County Historical Society

Teackle Mansion
11720 Mansion Street
Princess Anne, MD 21853

Telephone: 410-651-2238

HOURS: Sun., 1–3 p.m.; Wed. & Sat., 1–3 p.m. from April through 2nd weekend in October.

The society offers free genealogical service, but its holdings of genealogical interest are minimal. Call ahead for information.

Steamship Historical Society of America

Web Site: www.ubalt.edu/www/archives/ship.html
[see "U. of Baltimore, Langsdale Library"]

The society is dedicated to preserving artifacts and memories from the steamship days of the past. Their mission is to make steamship information available and to encourage conservation efforts. The society offers a research service and maintains an online photograph catalog.

Historical Society of Talbot County

25 South Washington Street   Telephone: 410-822-0773
P.O. Box 964   Fax number: 410-822-7911
Easton, MD 21601

HOURS: Library & Archives by appointment only. Museum & Gallery, Tues.–Sat., 11 a.m.–3 p.m.

The society has a limited staff and refers all genealogical researchers to the Maryland Room of the Talbot County Public Library.

Washington County Historical Society

Jamieson Genealogy Library   Telephone: 301-797-8782
135 West Washington Street   E-mail: washcohist@erols.com
P.O. Box 1281
Hagerstown, MD 21740

Mary J. Rogers, Librarian

HOURS: Tues. through Sat., 9 a.m.–4 p.m.

The society maintains a collection of numerous books on state and local history, Hagerstown directories, county church records, Hagerstown newspapers index (1790–1824), maps, and vertical files regarding genealogy and various historical subjects. Genealogical inquiries will be referred to professional genealogists.

Wicomico Historical Society, Inc.

106 West Main Street
P.O. Box 573
Salisbury, MD 21803-0573

Telephone: 410-860-0447
Fax number: 410-860-1441

Web Site: www.skipjack.net/le.shore/whs
E-mail: history@shore.intercom.net

HOURS: Wed., Thurs., Fri., 10 a.m.–2 p.m. Also open by appointment (tours of Wicomico Heritage Centre Museum at Pemberton Park).

The society provides rotating exhibits featuring various interpretive themes portraying the history of Wicomico County; portions of their collections (numbering 5,000) are used in exhibitions; it also sponsors special events. The society houses artifacts relating to Wicomico County history such as farm and household implements (eighteenth- to early twentieth-century), toys, dolls, photographs, wearing apparel, political memorabilia, and furniture.

Worcester County Historical Society

P.O. Box 111
Snow Hill, MD 21863

Web Site: www.dol.net/~ebola/ftown.html

HOURS: Mon. and Wed., 10 a.m.–8 p.m.; Tues., Thurs. and Fri., 10 a.m.–6 p.m.; and Sat., 9 a.m.–1 p.m. Volunteer genealogists on Tues. and Sat. a.m.

The society will answer some general inquiries, but they do not have a physical site. The genealogical collection was donated to the Worcester Room at the Worcester County Library (see information under separate heading herein).

Other Web Sites of Genealogical Interest

Allen County Library: www.acpl.lib.in.us (major genealogical library in Indiana)

Census Film Images (Southern States) and Genealogical Pointers: www.moobasi.com

Church of Jesus Christ of Latter Day Saints (Mormon Library) 400+ Million Surname Records (Ancestor Files) Available on Internet: www.familysearch.org

Cyndi's List of 26,800+ Genealogical Sites on Internet: www.oz.net/ ~cyndihow/sites.html

GenConnect RootsWeb: Connecting Families through Genealogy: www.rootsweb.com

GenForum.genealogy.com

Library of Congress: www.lcweb.loc.gov

National Archives and Records Administration: www.nara.gov (catalogs: www.nara.gov/nara/menus/genealog.html)

Social Security Administration: www.ssa.gov

U.S. Genealogical Web: www.usgenweb.com

U.S. Internet Genealogical Society (USIGS): www.usigs.org

U.S. National Park Service: www.npt.gov

World Genealogical Web: (for Maryland) www.usgenweb.com/md

PART II

Record Groups

This section contains descriptions of the record groups most valuable to family historians and an account, per jurisdiction, of available documents. One of the first lessons genealogists learn once they are out "in the field" is that significant numbers of primary source documents no longer exist. Many have been lost over the course of two or three centuries, others have been destroyed by fire—the Calvert, St. Mary's, and Dorchester County courthouses suffered devastating fires in the nineteenth century. Still others have simply deteriorated over time. Those documents that have survived are now carefully preserved and protected by state law and institutional policy. Again, these documents were not created as genealogical sources. All were produced by government agencies or private institutions with a specific purpose—the census to determine congressional representation, and land records to protect property ownership.

Maryland's laws and customs have changed, in many ways dramatically, over the past three and a half centuries. Slavery and indentured servitude are relics of a distant past. Women now enjoy the same property-holding and voting privileges as men. Children usually outlive their parents, and for many the power of religion in everyday life is not as strong a force as it was in the pre-twentieth-century Western World. People, however, were still people, concerned with their families, homes, and livelihoods.

Researchers who take the time to familiarize themselves with past laws and customs will develop an understanding of how record groups are organized. They will also have more success reconstructing family lines than those who do not understand the legal, political, and social systems of the period in which their ancestors lived. For example, if John Jones died in 1825 in Frederick County and no will is present, either because he did not leave one or because it is lost, there may still be probate records that will help piece together family relationships. Distribution accounts list those who received a share of the estate; inventories provide an account of the deceased's property; and accounts of sale are records of items sold that are part of an estate. A more thorough look through the general court records might yield apprenticeship agreements between neighbors and the minor children of John Jones. Land records might show a division of the family property among the heirs, some of whom might have sold their interest to their siblings. These transactions sometimes include a plat of the property. All of this additional information is lost to the person who gives up the search when the document they hope to find, in this case a will, does not exist.

Civil Vital Records

Vital records are among the most valuable documents family historians use to connect generations. Taken from the Latin word for life, vivere, these are literally the most basic records of one's life—birth, marriage, and death. There are two categories of vital records: the civil records generated by state and local government and church records.

Civil vital records are almost as old as the Maryland colony itself, but the system we know today originated in the nineteenth century. Prior to that time, the colonial assembly had tried to monitor births and deaths from as early as 1650 in order to protect property rights, but these laws proved ineffective for several reasons. The colonial court charged a fee to register births, and people had to travel considerable distances to get to the courts. Only a few of these seventeenth-century books remain, and the records are scattered for Charles (1654–1706), Somerset (1649–1720), and Talbot (1657–1681) Counties. These births and deaths are included in the general business dockets of the courts and are recorded with cattle marks, conveyances, and attachments. Many of these colonial births, marriages, and deaths have been abstracted and published.

The 1692 Act of Establishment made the Anglican Church the official church in the Province of Maryland, and church vestrymen assumed the role of recording births, marriages, and deaths. The law applied to all colonists, regardless of their religion. Researchers may find parallel entries for a person or family in the books of more than one denomination. In the late eighteenth and early nineteenth centuries, the population of the new United States grew at an astoundingly rapid rate, and with this growth came an increased need to protect public health. Epidemics swept through the seaport cities following outbreaks of deadly diseases in Europe. Residents of Philadelphia and Charleston suffered through several epidemics of small pox and yellow fever, and thousands of New England children died of diphtheria. American doctors knew disease arrived by ship, but it would be another full century before health officials identified the mosquito as the carrier of malaria. Municipal officials in the large East Coast cities began to keep track of the causes of death.

Yellow fever epidemics in Baltimore prompted the Maryland General Assembly to open the state's first health office, in 1792, and after the city's incorporation five years later municipal leaders organized the health department. Health department physicians inspected ships, buried paupers, transported the poor to the almshouse, staffed a hospital, and vaccinated against small pox as early as 1802. They also maintained mortality tables listing the age of the deceased and the cause of death. Two surviving record groups from the early years of the Health Department are the Interment Records of those persons buried in city churchyards and cemeteries from 1834 to 1840, and the Coroner's Inquest Reports 1827, 1835–60, and 1867. Both are available at the Baltimore City Archives. Typed copies of these records are also available to researchers at the Maryland Historical Society and those from 1834-1840 have been published.

The same year the city doctors began vaccinating, the General Assembly chartered the Medical and Chirurgical Faculty of Maryland as the watchdog of state health conditions. The faculty's investigations confirmed that people living outside of Baltimore enjoyed better health than those living in the densely populated port city. All of these efforts came out of the need to protect Maryland's citizens from disease, but it would be another seventy-three years before Baltimore enacted an effective vital registration law.

The city's ordinance requiring its citizens to register their births and deaths went into effect January 1, 1875, and it proved to be the beginning of an effective system. The state did not find success collecting vital statistics until 1898. Both the state and city vital registration offices underwent periodic reorganizations and operated separately of each other until 1972 when they merged into what is today the Department of Health and Mental Hygiene.

The information required by the city and state has changed in the hundred-plus years that these agencies have been collecting vital statistics. Early birth certificates, for example, contain the names of the parents but not the name of the child; only the date of birth and sex of the child are on the certificate. Nineteenth-century death certificates do not contain the names of the deceased's parents. It is particularly disappointing to work back through several generations of twentieth-century death certificates that do contain these names only to get to the record of an immigrant ancestor and find that the city did not require that information at that time.

One way to step around this problem is to keep track of all of the ancestor's siblings. Additional information may appear on the death record of one who passed away later when more data was collected by the agencies. For example, Mary Lorenz emigrated from Baden to Baltimore in 1847 with her parents, John and Catherine, and two brothers, Anthony and Phillip. Mary died in 1882, a time when Baltimore City did not ask for the names of the deceased's parents. Her brother Anthony lived until 1916. By that year the city health department requested the names of the parents, and their mother's maiden name is on his death certificate. Keeping the search wide enough to include all of the siblings often yields family names and clues to relationships that would otherwise be lost.

Vital record groups are used frequently by family historians; as with any other source they should be approached with a critical eye. The information in these certificates is only as reliable as the memory of the persons who supplied it, and only as accurate as those who recorded it. Birth certificates, marriage licenses, and marriage certificates are less prone to error than death certificates. The former records document the events of living people. Death certificates, however, are often littered with mistakes. Grieving family members and friends are often unable to remember dates of birth, maiden names, middle names, places of birth, parents' names, and parents' places of birth. The information should be checked against as many additional sources as possible.

Births and deaths occurring in the counties of Maryland have been recorded from January 1, 1898, and in the City of Baltimore from January 1, 1875 (with a few deaths in December, 1874). On January 1, 1973, the Vital Records of the City of Baltimore were placed under the management of the Maryland State Department of Health and Mental Hygiene.

Birth records are restricted for 100 years. Copies are available only to the person registered, to the parent or guardian of the person registered, to the legal representative of the person registered, or to an individual who can provide the proof of the death of the person registered either by a death certificate or a newspaper obituary. Certified copies of birth records are also available from Division of Vital Records, 4210 Patterson Ave., Baltimore, MD 21215.

The Maryland State Archives has microfilm copies of birth records for Baltimore City from 1875 to 1978 and for the various counties of Maryland from 1914 to 1978, but the indices to the records of Baltimore City end in 1941 and for the counties in 1950. The indices for the counties from 1898 to 1913 may provide the date of birth and the parents names, but there are no "certificates" to provide additional information. Certificates are available only from the Division of Vital Records, as noted.

Death records are restricted for a period of ten years except to a surviving relative or authorized representative of the deceased's estate (who must produce that proof). As with birth records, certified copies of death certificates after 1969 are available from the Division of Vital records, 4201 Patterson Avenue, Baltimore, MD 21215.

The Maryland State Archives staff will respond to your request for a search of their indexed records only. There is a non-refundable fee for each name searched and for each additional record copy of the same record. For non-restricted death records (if located), you will receive a copy of the record, and for any restricted record you will receive a "genealogical abstract" of the record. Contact the archives beforehand regarding their policies.

The earliest records of birth/death were kept by Somerset County beginning in 1649. The information was kept in Deed Book No. IKL and has been published in Torrence's *Old Somerset on the Eastern Shore of Maryland* (as well as other publications). Some early birth records of Kent County were also recorded among the land records and have been published in Volume 54 of the *Archives of Maryland*.

The majority of Maryland's counties kept some birth and/or death records prior to the effective date for statewide records. However, the records they kept were not complete. The tables below (prepared by Mary Meyer in 1992) will be helpful in locating birth and death records, but should be used with caution:

Counties	Births	Deaths
Allegany	1865–1884	—
Anne Arundel	1865–1877	1865–1880
Baltimore City	—	—
Baltimore	—	—
Calvert	1882–	—
Caroline	1865–1884	1865–1884
Carroll	1865–1885	1865–1902
Cecil	—	—
Charles	1865–1870	1865–1866
Dorchester	1864–1867	—
Frederick	—	—
Garrett	—	—
Harford	—	1865–1867
Howard	—	—
Kent	1865–	1865–1871
Montgomery	—	—
Prince Georges	1865–1867	—
Queen Anne's	1865–1881	—
St. Mary's	—	—
Somerset	1865–1894	1865–1877
Talbot	1865–1873	1865–1871
Washington	1865–1876	—
Wicomico	1868–1875	1869 (1 entry)
Worcester	1865–1869, 1889	—

Marriage records of most counties are available in the various counties from the late eighteenth century. The exceptions are those counties not formed until the nineteenth century (Carroll, Howard, Garrett, and Wicomico) and counties that have lost their records through fire, etc., such as Calvert, Dorchester, and St. Mary's. Marriage records for Kent County do not exist prior to 1796. Many marriage records have been published over the years (see the "Bibliography" under the county of interest). Extant marriage records are available at the Maryland State Archives and are indexed either in book form or on file cards.

There were no divorces in Maryland prior to the Revolutionary War. From that time until the mid-nineteenth century, decrees of divorce were granted by an act of the state legislature and adjudicated by the High Court of Chancery. An abstract of these records was published in Mary K. Meyer's *Divorces and Names Changed in Maryland by Act of the Legislature, 1634–1867.*

Historically, authority was granted in 1829 for the county courts to take evidence in divorce proceedings. In a series of later laws enacted between 1841 and 1853, jurisdiction in divorce proceedings was ceded to the chancellor and finally to the county Court of Equity. Records of divorce complaints may be obtained from the clerk of the circuit court in the county in which the divorce was adjudicated.

Probate Records[*]

Probate records are official records that relate to the disposition of an estate after a person's death. They include, among other things, wills, administration bonds, inventories, distributions, and orphan's court proceedings. The probate court of Maryland during the colonial period was called the Prerogative Court, and many of its features came from the English Prerogative Court. The following brief history explains the development of Maryland probate records and the various types of these records available to genealogists.

In 1632 Lord Baltimore's charter gave him complete control of the Maryland colony; including probate matters. Unable to govern the colony from abroad, Cecil Calvert (Lord Baltimore) appointed his brother Leonard Calvert to look after his interests. Governor Calvert appointed the first commissioner in 1648 to prove wills, grant administrations, handle testamentary matters, take inventories and accounts, and administer the oath to witnesses, executors, and administrators.

---

[*]Henry Peden, "Probate Records in Maryland," *Maryland Genealogical Society Bulletin,* 33 (1992): 3–22. Reprinted with permission.

Although the chief officer for probate matters had been called a judge as early as 1642, he did not preside over a court until 1670, when Sir William Talbot became Secretary of the Province. The secretary had full authority in all matters relating to estate administrations and inventories. In 1671 the name Prerogative Court first appeared in Maryland court records.

In 1672 Phillip Calvert was commissioned Judge or Commissary General for Probate of Wills, but as time passed, the ordinary probate work fell to the Chief Clerk and Register of the Prerogative Court. There is a list of the probate records Philip Calvert received from the clerk in 1637, but unfortunately the actual documents are not extant. By 1692 the register acquired a deputy. The number of commissions had increased to such an extent that the Commissary General was authorized by law to appoint responsible people (deputy commissaries) in every county in the province of Maryland to take probate of wills, take letters of testamentary, and grant letters of administration.

When a will, an inventory, or an account was brought to the Deputy Commissary he took the appropriate actions and recorded the matter in his books. Periodically, up to 1695, he would then send the papers to the prerogative office in St. Mary's and then Annapolis, where they would be entered in the testamentary proceedings.

The state constitution of 1776 provided for the appointment of an Orphan's Court and a Register of Wills in each county. The Prerogative Court was abolished in 1777. The Register of Wills in Prince George's County maintained its records and then sent them to Anne Arundel County in 1823. The books rested in Anne Arundel County's fireproof offices until 1904, when they were moved to the care of the commissioner of the land office. The old probate case files have been maintained by the Hall of Records, now the Maryland State Archives, since 1935.

When the Prerogative Court was abolished in 1777 and the Orphan's Court was established in its place, the Register of Wills served as the clerk and recorded proceedings and all papers filed in probate matters. The various records of the Register of Wills office in Baltimore City and the twenty-three counties are of great importance to genealogists. The Maryland State Archives has accessioned many of these records.

At the Maryland State Archives in Annapolis, probate record indices are available in the Search Room. New indices are added from time to time, and others are available on microfilm. The indices to probate records are divided into two categories: central agency records and county records, because (theoretically) two sets of probate records existed in the colonial period. As previously noted, the chief probate officer of the province was located in the capital. During the earliest years of the province, the Secretary of the Province served in this capacity and later the Commissary General filled the post. Papers were filed in the counties with the deputy commissioners, who then forwarded them to the capital where they were recorded in the Prerogative Court.

It is assumed that the deputy commissioners kept some sort of docket in the county, but no record has been found. After the American Revolution, matters of probate became a county function and remain so today. Subsequently, the General Assembly ordered the original documents of the Prerogative Court sent to the counties to be recorded by the registers of wills. This accounts for most of the duplicate probate records for the colonial period.

Central agency probate records exist for all of the counties created before 1777, namely Anne Arundel, Baltimore, Calvert, Caroline, Cecil, Charles, Dorchester, Frederick, Harford, Kent, Prince George's, Queen Anne's, St. Mary's, Somerset, Talbot, and Worcester. The other seven counties and Baltimore City formed later from one or more of these counties. The researcher is advised to check the files' parent county.

The Maryland State Archives card indices to the central agency records are filed together, except for the Testamentary Proceedings. The names on the cards are those of decedents. The accounts include the names of executors and administrators. The index to the proceedings of the Prerogative Court is called the Index to Testamentary Proceedings and it contains every name found in the record.

The Maryland State Archives has probate records for most counties to 1850 and for many counties to 1980 and later. Indices are available in the Search Room on file cards and on microfilm, and many are being computerized.

Obviously, it is not the intent of this guide to discuss every conceivable aspect of researching probate records, nor to list every record series held at the county and/or state level. Many colonial records have been copied and published (see the bibliography). The following list of records at the Maryland State Archives, although incomplete, should be helpful to researchers:

Allegany County: Administration Accounts, 1792–1961; Administration Bonds, 1791–1899; Equity Dockets, 1868–1902; Guardian Accounts, 1797–1848; Inventories, 1791–1962; Orphans Court Proceedings, 1791–1963; Wills, 1790–1963.

Anne Arundel County: Administration Accounts, 1777–1967; Administration Bonds, 1780–1945; Equity Dockets, 1787–1886; Guardian Accounts, 1791–1871; Inventories, 1777–1966; Orphans Court Proceedings, 1777–1980; Wills, 1777–1980.

Baltimore City: Administrations Accounts, 1666–1974; Administration Bonds,

1667–1852; Estate Dockets, 1772–1950; Guardian Accounts, 1786–1851; Inventories, 1664–1976; Orphans Court Proceedings, 1777–1970; Wills, 1666–1970.

Baltimore County: Administration Accounts, 1674–1969; Administration Bonds, 1666–1852; Guardian Accounts, 1786–1969; Indentures, 1794–1916; Inventories, 1666–1969; Orphans Court Proceedings, 1777–1965; Wills, 1666–1979.

Calvert County: (Records prior to 1882 were destroyed in a fire); Administration Accounts, 1882–1982; Estate Dockets, 1882–1979; Equity Records, 1882–1923; Guardian Accounts, 1882–1983; Inventories, 1882–1960; Orphans Court Proceedings, 1882–1983; Wills, 1882–1958.

Caroline County: Administration Accounts, 1695–1970; Administration Bonds, 1679–1865; Equity Dockets, 1868–1898; Guardian Accounts, 1787–1973; Indentures, 1794–1865; Inventories, 1680–1972; Orphans Court Proceedings, 1785–1955; Wills, 1688–1981.

Carroll County: Administration Accounts, 1837–1963; Administration Bonds, 1837–1853; Estate Dockets, 1909–1962; Guardian Accounts, 1837–1852; Inventories, 1837–1961; Orphans Court Proceedings, 1837–1962; Wills, 1837–1975.

Cecil County: Administration Accounts, 1678–1976; Administration Bonds, 1674–1976; Estate Papers, 1790–1850; Guardian Accounts, 1784–1976; Inventories, 1675–1976; Orphans Court Proceedings, 1798–1955; Wills, 1675–1976.

Charles County: Administration Accounts, 1673–1972; Estate Papers, 1799–1933; Guardianship Accounts, 1788–1972; Inventories, 1673–1972; Orphans Court Proceedings, 1777–1964; Wills, 1665–1981.

Dorchester County: (Records prior to 1852 were destroyed in a fire); Administration Accounts, 1852–1961; Distributions, 1852–1930; Guardian Bonds (Index), 1852–1935; Inventories, 1852–1949; Orphans Court Proceedings, 1852–1961; Wills, 1852–1955.

Frederick County: Administration Accounts, 1750–1963; Administration

Bonds, 1799–1853; Estate Dockets, 1815–1952; Guardian Accounts, 1811–1965; Indentures, 1794–1931; Inventories, 1749–1963; Orphans Court Proceedings, 1777–1963; Wills, 1744–1963.

Garrett County: Administration Accounts, 1873–1979; Equity Dockets, 1875–1904; Guardianship Accounts, 1874–1909; Inventories, 1873–1971; Orphans Court Proceedings, 1873–1979; Wills, 1873–1981.

Harford County: Administration Accounts, 1801–1974; Administration Bonds, 1774–1973; Estate Dockets, 1774–1966; Guardian Accounts, 1801–1970; Inventories, 1777–1973; Orphans Court Proceedings, 1800–1973; Wills, 1774–1976. (It must be noted that the Harford County Register of Wills sent most all of their old probate records to the state archives over the past five years, so this list is inherently incomplete).

Howard County: Administration Accounts, 1840–1976; Administration Bonds, 1840–1976; Estate Dockets, 1908–57; Guardian Accounts, 1844–1975; Inventories, 1840–1973; Orphans Court Proceedings, 1840–1976; Wills, 1840–1976.

Kent County: Administration Accounts, 1673–1966; Administration Bonds, 1664–1866; Estate Dockets, 1644–1963; Guardian Accounts, 1787–1966; Inventories, 1668–1966; Orphans Court Proceedings, 1803–1963; Wills, 1669–1977.

Montgomery County: Administration Accounts, 1777–1858; Administration Bonds, 1858–1969; Estate Records, 1777–1907; Guardian Accounts, 1858–1972; Inventories, 1777–1858; Orphans Court Proceedings, 1779–1966; Wills, 1777–1953.

Prince George's County: Administration Bonds, 1698–1975; Administration Accounts, 1696–1976; Estate Dockets, 1858–1961; Guardian Accounts, 1789–1977; Inventories, 1697–1976; Orphans Court Proceedings, 1777–1977; Wills, 1697–1984.

Queen Anne's County: Administration Accounts, 1741–1979; Administration Bonds, 1774–1978; Estate Papers, 1707–1855; Guardian Accounts, 1784–1981; Inventories, 1739–1977; Orphans Court Proceedings, 1778–1963; Wills, 1667–1984.

St. Mary's County: Administration Accounts, 1674–1976; Administration Bonds, 1799–1974; Equity Dockets, 1808–1976; Guardian Accounts, 1787–1965; Inventories, 1795–1972; Orphans Court Proceedings, 1777–1964; Wills, 1658–1975.

Somerset County: Administration Accounts, 1685–1977; Administration Bonds, 1777–1911; Estate Dockets, 1855–1964; Guardian Accounts, 1789–1850; Inventories, 1678–1977; Orphans Court Proceedings. 1778–1960; Wills, 1664–1977.

Talbot County: Administration Accounts, 1674–1966; Administration Bonds, 1664–1966; Estate Dockets, 1777–1949; Guardian Accounts, 1790–1966; Inventories, 1668–1966; Orphans Court Proceedings, 1787–1946; Wills, 1665–1974.

Washington County: Administration Accounts, 1776–1963; Administration Bonds, 1799–1856; Estate Dockets, 1777–1942; Guardian Accounts, 1786–1852; Inventories, 1777–1964; Orphans Court Proceedings, 1786–1964; Wills, 1749–1977.

Wicomico County: Administration Accounts, 1868–1963; Administration Dockets, 1869–1947; Estate Dockets, 1869–1961; Inventories, 1867–1964; Orphans Court Proceedings, 1867–1959; Wills, 1867–1983.

Worcester County: Administration Accounts, 1687–1963; Administration Bonds, 1667–1850; Estate Dockets, 1742–1957; Guardian Accounts, 1787–1854; Inventories, 1688–1962; Orphans Court Proceedings, 1777–1963; Wills, 1665–1983.

Also, for more detailed information about the availability of probate and other records, consult these guides published by the Maryland State Archives:

Guide to the Finding Aids of the Maryland State Archives;

Records on Microform: A Guide to the Maryland State Archives Holdings;

A Guide to Government Records at the Maryland State Archives: A Comprehensive List by Agency and Record Series; and,

Census Records

Governor Nathaniel Blakiston wrote in 1700 that the population returns he had forwarded to the Board of Trade in London were "not so perfect as they ought to be," and that the census was "so dark and confused . . . [that he was] ashamed to send it in." He had been instructed to count the number of free men eligible to bear arms in the Maryland colony. The frustration expressed by the governor three hundred years ago echoed through the centuries with the collection of the 1990 census, and will undoubtedly be present in the current drive to count the number of people in the United States today.

The census is one of the most popular records used by family historians. Line by line the distant names, ages, and places of birth glide through the light of the microfilm reader in perfect nuclear family order. Father, mother, son, daughter, daughter, son, etc., with the man listed as the head of the household. Women also headed households of small children and aged relatives. Single men and women resided with these families as laborers and laundresses. Is this another branch of the family neatly recorded in an old government document, waiting to be found by a curious and devoted descendent? This may not be the case. If the census was taken between 1850 and 1870 this combination of people with the same surname in the same dwelling may not be the family they first appear to be.

The 1850, 1860, and 1870 censuses are rife with these illusions. Prior to 1850, the census-taker collected only the name of the head of the household. All other persons in the house were listed by a mark in an age, race, and sex category. The 1850 census was the first that collected the names, ages, occupations, and places of birth of everyone in the household. It does not ask the relationship of everyone in the house to the head of the household. The woman who appears to be the wife and mother may actually have been a second wife, sister, or sister-in-law of the head of the household. The children may be his, hers, theirs, or some combination of theirs and other members of the larger clan. Not until 1880 did the census-taker begin to note the relationships of everyone in the house to the head of the household, and since that time establishing relationships based on census reports has been easier.

Consider also that many census-takers did not talk directly with some of the families they counted. For example, if the family was not at home, the census-taker would collect the information from a neighbor or a servant. The enumerators often missed large parts of country districts and dozens of city streets. Others were counted twice. Add phonetic and irregular spelling patterns to this process, and it becomes all the more critical that one use these records carefully.

As with every other document used by genealogists, the census was generated for practical purposes that had nothing to do with family historians. All censuses counted the population of a given area. The colonial censuses, like the one of which Blakiston was so ashamed, were collected for military purposes, as were the censuses collected during the American Revolution. Those rolls of men who took the oath of fidelity and those bachelors who had to pay a tax filled an immediate need for manpower and money. After state delegates ratified the Constitution, the new United States had the responsibility of sending representatives to Congress. The population is still counted every ten years (Article I, Section 2) in order to determine the number of representatives each state sends to Washington. In the broader concerns of building a nation, family relationships did not matter.

The content of the census has changed over the years and each enumeration contains a bit more information than the one before. Each piece helps genealogists put the pieces of the past together. These records remain, as they should, one of the most valuable sources of family history research.

The first censuses taken in Maryland of any practical use to the genealogist are those of 1776 and 1778. Although these censuses are commonly assumed to be the same, they are in fact two different records.

The Census of 1776 was taken pursuant to a resolution of the Continental Congress for ascertaining the population of the United States. In 1778 a census was taken in Maryland of all males above the age of eighteen years (except clergymen) to determine which persons had failed to take the Oath of Allegiance and Fidelity. The extant 1776 census records for Anne Arundel, Caroline, Charles, Dorchester, Frederick, Harford, Prince George's, Queen Anne's and Talbot Counties have been published in Gaius M. Brumbaugh's *Maryland Records: Colonial, Revolutionary, County and Church* (1928). The 1776 Census for Fells Point (Deptford Hundred in Baltimore) was published in the *Maryland Historical Magazine*, 25 (1930): 271–75.

These censuses supply varying categories of information from only the names of individuals to names and ages of all individuals in a household. It should be noted that they are not complete for all the counties in Maryland. There is a card index to the extant records at the Maryland State

Archives and a partial card index in the Wilkins File at the Maryland Historical Society.

The Maryland Historical Society also has microfilm copies of all extant census records of the State of Maryland, 1790–1920 inclusive; 1880, 1900, and 1920 Soundex indices; the 1890 census of Union Veterans and widows; 1850 and 1860 slave schedules; and, mortality schedules from 1850 to 1880. (The original mortality schedules are located at the Maryland State Law Library in Annapolis.) Censuses are also available at large libraries such as the Allen County Public Library, Fort Wayne, Indiana, and the Family History Library in Salt Lake City.

The Maryland Historical Society Library, Enoch Pratt Free Library, the George Peabody Library, and the Maryland State Law Library all have copies of the published census indices, 1790–1860. It should be noted that the majority of these published indices have a high rate of error and should, therefore, be used with caution. There are also omissions in these published indices, so it may be necessary for the researcher to turn to the original census to find the information sought.

Some of these decennial indices have been transcribed and published by different individuals on both a statewide and a county-by-county basis. Researchers should avail themselves of the various versions, because some are notorious for errors. See the bibliography under the county in which you are interested.

Several federal censuses have been lost or destroyed: the 1800 census for Baltimore County was never taken; the 1830 censuses for Montgomery, Prince George's, Queen Anne's, St. Mary's, and Somerset Counties have been lost; and the 1890 census for Maryland (along with virtually the rest of the country with few exceptions) was destroyed by fire early in the twentieth century.

The original Mortality Schedules for the State of Maryland for 1850 and 1860 and the original 1880 census are at the Maryland State Law Library in Annapolis. The original 1850 Census of Harford County (from which the copy held by the National Archives was made) is located at the Historical Society of Harford County, 143 North Main Street, Bel Air, Maryland 21014–0366.

Users of the 1800 Census of Frederick County should be aware that the National Archives, while in the process of microfilming the original, inadvertently omitted two pages. These pages, however, were included in a transcription made by Helen W. and Frank H. Seubold that was published in the *Maryland Genealogical Society Bulletin*, Vol. 18, No. 2 (1977).

Researchers should also be aware that the 1890 Census of Maryland's Union Veterans and Widows includes the names of several Confederate veterans with lines drawn through the entries to indicate that they were mistakenly enumerated.

Religious Records

Maryland's church and synagogue records are often the only source of recorded births, marriages, and deaths that exist for genealogists working on pre-twentieth-century family lines. This section of the guide contains an accounting of the state's extant religious documents and their locations. Many of these church books and papers have been microfilmed through the generosity of the Maryland Genealogical Society. Copies of many of these films are available at the Maryland Historical Society and the Maryland State Archives.

Church and synagogue collections are made up of more than registers of baptisms, marriages, and burials, and researchers should conduct a thorough search of collateral records from the same period for clues and additional family information. For instance, baptisms are sometimes recorded in the vestry or session minutes. These minutes may also hold the record of a dispute between family members or neighbors in which church or synagogue leaders mediated the outcome. Financial records may reveal the names of ancestors who donated money or land to the organization. Items labeled "miscellaneous" or "loose papers" may hold letters, Sunday school class lists, missionary reports, Bar Mitzvah and Bas Mitzvah records, and receipts. Again, taking the time to learn how the organization functioned and operated will suggest additional research possibilities.

One of the most valuable finding aids for using religious records is Edna Agatha Kanely's *Directory of Maryland Church Records* (Westminster, Md.: Family Line Publications, 1987). This book is a comprehensive list of Maryland's churches, their existing records, and where those records are located. Miss Kanely's later work, *Directory of Ministers and the Maryland Churches They Served, 1634–1990* (Westminster, Md.: Family Line Publications, 1991) works as a complement to the church directory. For example, a Bible entry that states Hamilton Janney Coffroth, baptized March 17, 1857, by the Reverend John Grammer, may not contain a notation of Grammer's church. Prior to the publication of these guides, identifying Grammer's church and the location of additional family records may have taken many hours of random searching. With these books, it takes only a few minutes to locate Reverend Grammer in the ministers' directory and to note which church he served in 1857. The church directory then states where the church's records are held.

Church records sometimes hold valuable genealogical information. Baptismal records may provide the place of birth for the parents and sponsors (godparents) as well as for the child. For example, Mary Lorenz, daughter of John and Catharine Pfad Lorenz, was born in Baden in 1837. This information is found in the census records. The St. James Church records provided additional detail with the name of the town, Neckengarach, entered in the register when Mary married Martin Epple in 1853. Catholic priests baptized the Epple's ten children at St. James over the course of almost twenty years, and in noting the names of the sponsors, additional relationships became clear. Mary's sister Elizabeth and brother Anthony served as sponsors for half of these children. These records also offer detail that is not often found elsewhere. The decennial census misses children who are born and then die in the ten-year periods between enumerations. Church records offer the event-to-event detail of births, marriages, and burials that is often impossible to collect elsewhere.

Because the state failed to enforce various acts of the legislature requiring recordation of vital records until the late nineteenth century, researchers must rely heavily on extant church records for dates of birth, death, and marriage. A brief summary of some of the major church records follows. For a detailed list of Maryland churches, church records, locations, and the availability of their records, see the Bibliography and Religious Archives herein.

Protestant Episcopal Records

Records of the Protestant Episcopal Church in Maryland have been well preserved for the most part since the early days of settlement. The Protestant Episcopal Church was also referred to as the Church of England, or the Anglican Church. Original records and/or copies of the extant records can be found at the Maryland State Archives and the Maryland Historical Society. The majority of these early records are also available in published form. (See the bibliography under the county of interest.) The Diocesan Center is located at 4 East University Parkway, Baltimore, MD 21218. It does not house early church records, but they do have a few nineteenth- and twentieth-century records.

Catholic Records

Maryland is divided among three Catholic dioceses. The Archdiocese of Baltimore covers the city, surrounding counties, and Western Maryland. The Archdiocese of Washington covers the District of Columbia, its surrounding counties, and Southern Maryland. The Diocese of Wilmington covers all of Delaware and Eastern Maryland. Original records of parishes in all three dioceses are kept at the churches themselves rather than in the diocesan archives. These records have never been centrally indexed or computerized.

In 1977 the Archbishop of Baltimore gave permission to the Maryland State Archives to microfilm all baptism, marriage, and death records of about seventy-five churches within the archdiocese, mostly from Baltimore City, and to make these records available for research to the public with certain restrictions. Microfilm records are available at the state archives, and a partial set may be used at the Maryland Historical Society. Records housed at the Archives of the Archdiocese of Baltimore are not available to genealogists. Microfilmed records of two churches within the Washington archdiocese are available at the state archives, namely St. Mary's in Laurel and St. Peter's in Waldorf. Microfilmed records of all Maryland churches within the Wilmington diocese are available not only at the Maryland State Archives, but also at the Wilmington Diocesan Archives, at the Easton Public Library, and through the LDS Family History Centers. Researchers may view and copy records of communions, confirmation, marriage, and burial records without restriction, but access to Catholic baptismal records is limited to coincide with access to federal census records. To see restricted reels of baptisms (i.e., after 1920 as of 1992, and after 1930 as of 2002) researchers can obtain permission from the applicable pastor or curator after affirming in written form a promise to respect other people's right to privacy.

There is a paucity of Catholic records prior to the Revolutionary War, the result of limited religious toleration in some periods or fires and other catastrophes at other times. Prior to the firm establishment of parish churches, missionary priests, mainly Jesuits, ministered throughout the area, and some of their records can be found at the Georgetown University library. However, through the efforts of a number of dedicated individuals, some of the old records have been found and transcribed for use by the public. (Refer to the Religious Archives section herein).

Quaker Records

The Society of Friends, or "the people called Quakers," were in Maryland by 1658, and many of their records are extant. For a better understanding of the available records and their location, refer to Phebe R. Jacobsen's *Quaker Records in Maryland*.

Original records of the Third Haven (or Tred Avon) and Northwest Fork Meetings on the Eastern Shore have been deposited at the Maryland State Archives in Annapolis. The archives also has a microfilm copy of the Baltimore Yearly Meeting records and the Sandy Spring Meeting in Montgomery County. Quaker records through 1800 for counties on Maryland's Western Shore have been compiled by Henry C. Peden Jr. in two volumes, Northern and Southern Maryland.

Records of the Third Haven, Cecil, and Marshy Creek Meetings have been published as an appendix to Kenneth Carroll's *Quakerism on the Eastern Shore of Maryland*. These records as well as other miscellaneous records are available at the Friends Historical Library, Swarthmore College, Swarthmore, Pennsylvania 19801.

Methodist Records

Methodism found fertile soil in Maryland at an early date. The Maryland State Archives has an extensive collection of the Methodist records on microfilm. A few original records are held at the United Methodist Historical Society of the Baltimore Annual Conference (Lovely Lane Museum), 2200 St. Paul Street, Baltimore, MD 21218. Lovely Lane does, however, maintain a large collection of records of "traveling preachers" and clergymen, 1773 to date, and the circuits that they served. Records of the First (Light Street) Methodist Church in Baltimore are available at the Maryland Historical Society. They are unique in that records kept by clergymen in various locations in the area were entered in the books of the First Methodist Church. Refer to page 15.

Lutheran Records

In Western Maryland, German settlers established Lutheran, Reformed, Evangelical, Moravian, and Brethren churches. With the exception of the Brethren, Mennonite, and Amish, German sect churches were excellent record-keepers. For the most part the records are extant and the greater share of them have been translated and transcribed and are available in either manuscript or published form. Many German records of Frederick County have been translated and published by Frederick S. Weiser and C. T. Zahn.

Military Records

Military records and their content have evolved over time like all of the other record groups previously discussed in this guide. Researchers will glean the most possible information from these documents by following that evolution through the wars and subsequent legislation drafted to benefit Maryland's veterans and their families. Since many of these veterans both fought for and benefited from both the state and federal governments, this section makes frequent references to the National Archives and its holdings. Again, records generated by the federal government are held at the federal level, and records generated by the state are held at the state level.

Although it may seem obvious, it is important to remember that no colonial war records exist at the national level. The United States did not exist. Colonial military records are found at the colonial (state) and county levels. Several militia lists and notations about commissioned officers offer information about Maryland's colonial soldiers.

The American Revolution generated the first documents at the national level as well as the state level. No military action of any consequence was seen in Maryland during the war, but Maryland soldiers fought in practically every major battle elsewhere in the colonies; both on land and at sea. About 28,000 Marylanders served in the Continental Army or the militia from 1775 to 1783. Thousands more men and women rendered material aid or other patriotic service by working on state and county committees and subscribing to the Oath of Allegiance and Fidelity to Maryland between 1777 and 1781. Hundreds of Marylanders fought and served as seamen and privateers. The names and service of soldiers who served in the Continental Army are found at the National Archives, as are their pension records. The service of Maryland's Revolutionary War soldiers has been meticulously documented in a series of Family Line publications. The titles are in the Bibliography.

Pension records often hold more genealogical information than service records, and researchers are advised to familiarize themselves with the federal government's laws relating to veterans' benefits. These laws changed and became more inclusive in the forty years following the war. Men who may not have qualified for benefits in 1792 could have become eligible by 1818, and their widows may have applied for their husbands' pensions by 1836.

The first pension law, passed in 1792, paid veterans with a proven disability. An act passed in 1818 granted payment to veterans who may not have been disabled but had served nine months and now demonstrated need. By 1836 the law allowed widows to claim a pension if they had been married to the soldier before the end of the war. These applications contain a wealth of family information since the widow had to prove her relationship. Some of these women even tore out and sent the family record pages from their Bibles.

As with all other sources, look critically at these documents and remember why they exist. A veteran or a widow in desperate need of assistance may have exaggerated the size of a family or moved a wedding date to comply with the law. If possible, check these findings against another source.

Some privates and non-commissioned officers also received bounty land warrants of fifty acres in lieu of payment. For a detailed discussion of Maryland's bounty land warrant holders and their travels through the new United States, see Larry A. Peskin, "A Restless Generation: Migration of Maryland Veterans in the Early Republic," *Maryland Historical Magazine,* 91 (1996): 311–28. A detailed account of Maryland's Revolutionary War records is found in Henry C. Peden, "Searching for your Revolutionary

War Ancestors in the Records of Maryland," *Maryland Genealogical Society Bulletin,* 37 (1996): 154-168.

Colonial Wars

Extant muster rolls and pay rolls are card-indexed at the Maryland State Archives in Annapolis. Various references to soldiers in the seventeenth and eighteenth centuries are found throughout the seventy-two volumes of the published *Archives of Maryland.* No militia lists can be found until the 1740s and 1750s for troops in Maryland counties. A list of some soldiers stationed at Ft. Frederick during the Seven Years' War (French and Indian War) was published under the title of "Maryland Muster Rolls, 1757–1758" by Mary Keysor Meyer in the *Maryland Historical Magazine,* 70 (1975): 104–9. Also, information was published in *Western Maryland Genealogy,* 10 (1994): 12–18, 62–63, 115–17 by Everett B. Ireland, in articles titled "Maryland Colonial Militia Service Records" and "Capt. Peter Butler's Muster Roll." One should consult Murtie June Clark, *Colonial Soldiers of the South, 1732–1774* (Baltimore: Genealogical Publishing Company, 1983) 1–123 for information on the service of many Maryland soldiers during the colonial period. Also see the lists in the *Blue Books* at the Maryland State Archives (which have been indexed in card file 45).

Revolutionary War

The muster rolls of Maryland troops in the Continental service during the Revolutionary War have been published in the *Archives of Maryland,* Volume 18, which is available in many libraries throughout the United States and can be purchased from the Maryland State Archives. It has also been reprinted by the Genealogical Publishing Company in Baltimore, Maryland. Also consult volumes 11, 12, 16, 21, 45, 47, and 48 of the *Archives of Maryland* for information on many soldiers from 1775 to 1783.

The pension records for Marylanders who served in the Continental Line are available from the National Archives and Record Administration, Pennsylvania Avenue and 8th St., N.W., Washington, D.C. 20408. These same pension records may be available at various libraries throughout the United States on microfilm. Pension files for soldiers throughout the United States have also been abstracted and published in three volumes (with a one-volume index) by Virgil D. White in *Genealogical Abstracts of Revolutionary War Pension Files* (Waynesboro, Tenn.: National Historical Publishing Company, 1990).

A great many Marylanders served only in the Maryland militia during the conflict. Many of the muster rolls of the Maryland militia were deposited at the

Maryland Historical Society but have since been transferred to the Maryland State Archives. Copies of original rolls are also available to the public for research at the Maryland Historical Society.

The six-volume typescript "Unpublished Revolutionary Records of Maryland" by Margaret Roberts Hodges in 1941 (which is available at the Maryland Historical Society and the National Society of the Daughters of the American Revolution (NSDAR) Library in Washington, D.C.) was largely copied from the original muster rolls described above. It is by no means a complete listing.

The State of Maryland, by resolution and later by legislative act, granted pensions to certain veterans and/or widows and children of veterans. A list of these pensioners has been published in the *Maryland Genealogical Society Bulletin*, 4 (1963): 32–33, 43; 5(1964): 2–3, 27–28, 39, 53–54, 74–75; 6 (1965): 6–7, 16–17, 34–35, 37, 52–53, 62, 96–98; and in Gaius Brumbaugh's *Maryland Records*, Vol. II (Baltimore: Genealogical Publishing Company, 1967), 314–411.

The various counties of the state also granted financial aid to certain veterans or widows who were, for the most part, indigent. Such records can be found in the Order Books of the General Court of the county in which the veteran lived.

In 1781 the General Assembly passed a law by which land was to be appropriated "westward of Fort Cumberland" in Washington County (now in Allegany and Garrett Counties) in order to discharge the engagement of lands made to the officers and soldiers of the state. Officers were assigned four lots of fifty acres each and enlisted men one lot of fifty acres each. A list of officers and soldiers to whom land was granted was first published by John M. Brewer and Lewis Mayer in *The Laws and Rules of the Land Office of Maryland* (Baltimore: Kelly, Piet and Co., 1871). It was later published by J. Thomas Scharf in his *History of Western Maryland* (repr. 1968) and by Bettie S. Carothers in her *Maryland Soldiers Entitled to Lands Westward of Fort Cumberland* (1973). This latter work was copied directly from the original publication. A map of these lands is available at the Maryland State Archives as well as at the Maryland Historical Society.

In no case are records of Maryland soldiers comparable to the pension records held by the National Archives. Muster rolls and pay rolls held by the state generally reveal little or nothing more than a man's name, rank, and the company in which he served. The county-by-county series of *Revolutionary War Patriots of Maryland* was researched by Henry C. Peden Jr. and published by Family Line Publications between 1985 and 1999. These books should be consulted for the men and women who served in the military or who rendered other patriotic service in Maryland.

Maryland, of course, had its share of British sympathizers, and a number of Tories served with the loyalist forces. A few published sources like Meyer and Bachman's "First Battalion of Maryland Loyalists" can be found in the *Maryland*

Historical Magazine, 68 (1973): 199–210. For a general discussion of Maryland's loyalists see Christopher New, "Plain Truth vs. Common Sense: James Chalmers for the Loyalists, 1776," *Maryland Historical Magazine*, 91 (1996): 53–64. Additional sources may be found in "A Checklist of Loyalist Manuscripts in the Maryland Historical Society," 196–98. Some of these manuscripts are copies of records in the Canadian Archives. Also, the *Orderly Book of the Maryland Loyalists Regiment, June 18, 1778 to October 12, 1778* was kept by Capt. Caleb Jones and published in 1891 (reprinted by Clearfield Press in 1996).

War of 1812

Listings of soldiers who participated in the War of 1812 have been published, but none are as complete as the seven volumes compiled by F. Edward Wright entitled *Maryland Militia, War of 1812*. Also refer to the bibliography for books by William Marine, Nathaniel Hickman, and Thomas Huntsberry.

Veterans of the War of 1812 also received bounty land for their service by laws enacted in 1850 and 1855 Federal pensions were not granted until 1871 and 1878. Applications for pensions and bounty land are located at the National Archives in Washington, D.C. At the Maryland State Archives consult card index 52 (Pension Records, 1867–89). At the Maryland Historical Society consult manuscript MS.1846 (War of 1812 Collection).

Membership applications and other records of the Society of the War of 1812 in the State of Maryland, the Maryland Society of the Sons of the American Revolution, and the Society of Colonial Wars in the State of Maryland are housed at the University of Baltimore, Langsdale Library, 1420 Maryland Avenue, Baltimore, Maryland 21202.

Civil War

Although Maryland never seceded from the Union, large numbers of Marylanders served in the Confederate army in their own units or in companies from various states in the Confederacy. Maryland has few records of these soldiers. Such records (if they do indeed exist) are to be found in the state where the soldier enlisted. The National Archives has collected some of these records and they are available to the public on microfilm at that facility as well as at the Maryland Historical Society.

At the cessation of the fighting, most Confederate soldiers returned to their homes in Maryland. However, a considerable number remained in the South and many went to South America, particularly to Brazil, where they established a "colony." The names of many of this latter group can be found in Filby and Meyer's *Passenger and Immigration Lists Index*. During the Civil War many Confederate soldiers were killed in battle or died in prison camps in Maryland. A typescript work located at the Maryland Historical Society, "Confederate Hill, Loudon Park Cemetery, Baltimore, Maryland" by Samuel H. Miller (1962) lists the names of those buried in the National Cemetery in Baltimore. The Maryland Historical Society also holds some records of the Confederate Old Soldiers Home (now the site of a Maryland State Police barracks) in Pikesville, Baltimore County, Maryland.

After the Battle of Antietam (1862) and the retreat of Lee's army across Maryland from Gettysburg (1863), many Confederate soldiers were buried where they fell. The Antietam National Cemetery was chartered in 1864; not until a number of years later were the bodies of Confederates reinterred there. A small and very rare work entitled *A Descriptive List of Burial Places of the Remains of Confederate Soldiers Who Fell in the Battles of South Mountain, Monocacy, and Other Points in Washington and Frederick Counties, Maryland* (Hagerstown, MD: Free Press Print, 1868) was published by Board of Trustees of the Antietam National Cemetery from lists compiled by Moses Poffenberger and Aaron Good. The Maryland Historical Society library has a copy of this book.

The St. Mary's County Historical Society, in their publication *Chronicles of St. Mary's*, beginning with volume 16 (December, 1968), has published a list of Confederate prisoners who died at Point Lookout prison camp. More detailed information about these men can be found at the National Archives. This is also the case with both Confederate and Union soldiers who died at Camp Parole and were buried in Oakwood Cemetery in Annapolis, Maryland. Records of organizations like the United Daughters of the Confederacy and the Daughters of Union Veterans should not be overlooked in research. Ten volumes of the former are located at the Maryland Historical Society and are available for research. The researcher should also use the 1890 census of Union veterans and widows (widely available on microfilm) and bear in mind that often a listing will appear for a Confederate veteran with a line drawn through it.

Many service and pension records of Union veterans are housed at the National Archives as well as some large libraries. There are twenty-two microfilm rolls of compiled service records of Confederate soldiers who served in organizations from Maryland available at this facility as well as at the Maryland Historical Society. The latter records are copies of those kept at the National Archives.

Also of value is Special Collection 5102 at the Maryland State Archives, entitled "Civil War Soldiers System Indexing Collection." This collection includes copies of the general index cards found in the National Archives, indicating the name, rank, and unit of each soldier who served in the Union and Confederate armies during the Civil War, 1861–65. This database will eventually be available at all Civil War sites, including Antietam and Monocacy.

World War I

A published work compiled by the Maryland War Records Commission (Baltimore, 1933) lists all personnel who served in World War I from Maryland. It is available in many libraries, but does not contain any detailed genealogical data (i.e., names of parents, wives, or children). However, it does give the full name, residence, date of birth, military unit, and highlights of the service record of each soldier.

Original records of the soldiers in World War I are housed at the Army (Navy) Records Center, 9700 Page Boulevard, St. Louis, Missouri, but a fire in 1974 destroyed many of them. Those records that survived are not available for research but are available only to the veteran, the undertaker who is arranging the funeral, or the legal representative. Contact them in case of any policy changes.

World War II

The names of all persons from Maryland who served in this conflict have been published in a five-volume work, *Maryland in World War II, Register of Service Personnel*, by the War Records Commission (Maryland Historical Society, 1965). The books can be purchased from the society. They are also widely available in numerous libraries.

Discharge records of all Maryland service personnel are in the custody of the War Memorial Commission, Gay and Lexington Streets, Baltimore, Maryland 21202. However, copies of these discharges are available only to the veteran, surviving spouse, or the funeral director.

Additional War Records

Compiled service and pension records of World War I, World War II, the Korean War, and the Vietnam War, as well as peace-time military personnel, are housed at the Army Records Center in St. Louis, Missouri, but these records are restricted and not available to the general public for research. Write to them in case of any recent policy changes under the Freedom of Information Act.

Service and/or pension records of Marylanders in the Mexican War, Spanish-American War, Indian Wars, and the Boxer Rebellion are located at the National Archives. There may be miscellaneous records in the Manuscript Department at the Maryland Historical Society. Also, see the "Bibliography" section for published works on some of these wars or conflicts.

One should not overlook any locally kept records of veterans. Many Maryland veterans had their discharges recorded in the courthouse of their home county.

Land Records

Maryland's land records often hold invaluable genealogical data. Land records are among the earliest documents created by the colonial government, and the fact that they existed in an era when few other government papers did makes them all the more valuable to family historians. They establish residence in a given place and time and often hold information about family relationships. The colonial, state, and county land records are voluminous and make up some of the largest record groups in archival collections.

Lord Baltimore's (George Calvert's) charter for the Maryland colony contained guidelines for land distribution, many of them based on ancient feudal custom and law. The proprietor could set up manors and lease or grant parcels of land. The 1636 "Conditions of Plantation" outlined land allotment instructions to the governor that he might distribute and oversee the colony's settlement according to the proprietor's plan. These "conditions" included Calvert's obligation to pay the crown two Indian arrows per year and one-fifth of all gold and silver ores.

Early settlers fell into two categories: "adventurers" and the people they transported. Under this headright system, men who paid the transportation costs of other settlers received land grants based on the number of persons they brought into the colony. Those transported by the "adventurers" worked off their passage. When they completed their terms of service they were then eligible for their own fifty acres until Lord Baltimore abolished the headright system in 1680.

The colonial land grant process involved four steps: the petition, the warrant, the survey, and the patent. The settler first petitioned the governor for a specific piece of land. Once the governor approved the petition, he issued a warrant to lay out the tract. Surveyors then measured off the tract and drew the plat. Plats (or surveys) are detailed drawings of the property lines and often include the names of adjoining tracts and neighboring landholders. The last step was the patent awarded to the landowner that secured title to the property. Most of these early tracts had names that not only make them easier to identify in the land record book indices, but may also offer a glimpse into the settler's experience in the new colony. Consider the tract names Wilson's Folly, Richard's Adventure, Thompson's Regret, Moore's Hope, Steven's Delight—all of which suggest how the landowner may have viewed his colonial investment.

Property ownership, and the transfer of that property from one generation to the next, was of critical importance to early Marylanders. Deeds were often the only legal instrument in which settlers could leave the names and relationships of their heirs and thereby provide a clear transfer of title. Consequently, the older the record, the more genealogical data it may contain. For example, William Brooks of Baltimore County inherited the tract "Bellfast" from his father, Charles, in 1824. Several branches of the Brooks family lived in northern Baltimore County by these early years of the nineteenth century, and sorting out the children of the third and fourth generations became difficult.

A systematic search of all of the Brooks land transactions turned up a deed recorded in 1852 by which two of William Brooks's sons transferred property, including part of "Bellfast," that they had inherited from their father. The deed stated that the property was part of the "real estate of William Brooks, Sr. . . . [who had died] sometime in September 1830 and left the following children to wit: Elizabeth Brooks, since married Thomas Morford, Sarah Brooks since married Amos Gooding, Charles Brooks, Abraham Brooks, Nimrod Brooks, John Brooks, Mary Brooks, Daniel Brooks, William Brooks, and Thomas Brooks." This example also illustrates the importance of collecting all of the references to the surname since it cannot be determined beforehand what relationships the search will yield. Only after all the names are gathered can they be sorted and put in the correct family groups.

Records about land transactions are very useful in genealogical research because they include names of persons, identification of their lands, and family relationships, as well as information about persons other than the principals. An excellent article by the late S. Eugene Clements, entitled "Land Records of Colonial Maryland," appeared in the *Maryland Genealogical Society Bulletin*, 33 (1992): 653–91. He rendered a full accounting of the land-owning process in early Maryland, plus a detailed listing of available land records at the Maryland State Archives from 1636 to the present. Researchers will be well advised to consult this article. The land records themselves can be found either in the original records or in microfilm copies at the Maryland State Archives in Annapolis:

Provincial and State Records: Land Office Patent Records, 1637–current; Eastern Shore, 1796–1842; Index, 1636–1844; Card Indices 54, 55; Certificates for patented and unpatented lands by county; Land Office Warrant Records 1661–1967; Index 1636–1842; Eastern Shore, 1781–1843.

Allegany County: Land records, 1791–1987; Land abstracts, 1806–46, Index, 1806–74; Plats, 1792–1954; some of the land records were lost in the 1893 fire. The county was established from Washington County in 1789.

Anne Arundel County: Land records, 1653–1851 (first fifty years' records were lost in 1704; partial reconstitution); Land records index, 1653–1839; Land abstracts index, 1806–74; Plats, 1799–1850, 1839–1967; Plats Indices, 1839–1929, and 1925–67 (original county, established in 1650).

Baltimore County: Land records, 1659–1851; Land abstracts, 1816–21, Index 1806–74; Land commissions, 1727–1851; Plats, 1729–1830, 1835–46, Plat Index, 1835–1952 (Original county, established circa 1659).

Baltimore City: Land records, 1851–1981; Land Commission papers, 1852–1908; Dockets, 1852–1922; Plats, 1851–68, 1785–1900, 1881–1922 (separated from Baltimore County in 1851).

Calvert County: Land records were saved from a fire in 1748 and then lost when the British burned the courthouse in 1814; a fire in 1882 destroyed all records; partial reconstruction of deeds, 1840–82; Land records index, 1851–1958; and, Plat books, 1883–1948, 1930–88. (Original county, established in 1654.)

Caroline County: Some land records were lost "from moves and neglects" but not from fire; Land records, 1774–1986; Land commissions, 1774–1851; Land abstracts, 1824–49, Index 1816–74; Plats, 1774–1955, and Indices, 1790–1937. (County established in 1773 from Queen Anne's and Dorchester Counties.)

Carroll County: Land records, 1837–1960, 1851–1988, Indices, 1851–1951; Plats, 1842–1951, 1880–1937, and Plats Index, 1842–1951. (County established from Baltimore and Frederick Counties in 1837.)

Cecil County: Land records, 1674–1792, 1674–1851, 1851–1984, and Indices, 1674–1851, 1851–97, 1651–1946; Land abstracts, 1824–50, Index, 1806–74. (County established in 1674 from Baltimore and Kent Counties.)

Charles County: Land records, 1658–1844, 1658–1851, 1851–1984, Indices 1658–1832, 1851–1948; Grantees, 1899–1971; Grantors, 1899–1971; Land commissions, 1716–21; Land abstracts, 1815–31, and Index 1806–74. Some records were lost in the fires of 1746 and 1892. (County established in 1658 from St. Mary's; it is a different county from old Charles County, 1650–54, no extant detailed records).

Dorchester County: All records except the land records, 1669–1851, were lost in a fire in 1852; land records, 1669–1984, Indices to Grantees, 1669–1818, 1669–1951; and Grantors, 1669–1818, 1669–1951; Land commissions, 1669–1878; Land abstracts, 1824–40, and Index, 1806–74. (County established in 1669 from Somerset and Talbot Counties.)

Frederick County: Courthouse fire in 1861, but land records were left in good condition. Land records, 1748–1986, Indices, 1748–1959. (County established in 1748 from Prince George's and Baltimore Counties.)

Garrett County: Land records, 1872–1984, with Grantee/Grantor Indices, 1872–1971; Plat book, 1852–1932, 1894–1942. (County established in 1872 from Allegany County.)

Harford County: Courthouse fire in 1858, but land records were saved in a vault-like wing; Land records, 1774–1989, Indices, 1774–1960; Land abstracts index, 1806–74; Plats, 1790–1851; Survey records, 1658–1894. (County established from Baltimore County in 1773.)

Howard County: Land records, 1839–51; Land commissions, 1852–99; Land records index, 1855–78, and indices to Grantees/Grantors, 1840–51, 1851–1964; and Plats, 1840–1931. (County established from Anne Arundel in 1851 and known as the Howard District, 1840–51.)

Kent County: Some land records lost in a fire in 1720 and some lost "due to neglect"; Land records, 1648–1986, Indices 1648–1962; Land commissions 1716–21, Index 1806–74; Land record abstracts, 1824–50; Plats, 1703–1946. (Original county, established in 1642.)

Montgomery County: Land records, 1777–1986, Indices, 1777–1927; Grantees, 1777–1951, and Grantors, 1777–1951; Land record abstracts, 1806–25, Index 1806–74; Plats, 1882–1949. (County established from Frederick County in 1776.)

Prince George's County: Land records, 1696–1851, 1851–1983, Indices 1696–1851, 1851–84; Grantees and Grantors, 1884–1949; Land commissions, 1716–21; Land record abstracts, 1806–11, Index, 1860–74; and Plats, 1773, 1835–1972. "No fires, British respected records." (County established in 1695 from Calvert and Charles Counties.)

Queen Anne's County: Land records, 1707–1887, 1852–1987; Index to Grantees/Grantors, 1706–1854; Land commissions, 1716–1801, 1769–1852; Land record abstracts, 1786–99, 1827–49, Index, 1806–74; Plats, 1831–1950. (County established in 1706 from Dorchester, Kent and Talbot Counties.)

St. Mary's County: Many land records lost in fires in 1768 and 1831 (only one volume saved); Land records, 1777–1831 (reconstitution poor), 1851–1927; Indices 1827–51, 1851–1948; Land commissions, 1858–84; Land record abstracts and index, 1806–74; Plats, 1828–1948, 1912–19. (Original county, established in 1634.)

Somerset County: Land records, 1665–1987, and indices, 1665–1851, 1851–95; Indices to the Grantees and Grantors, 1665–1851, 1851–1970; Land commissions, 1717–21; Land abstracts, 1825–50, Index 1806–74; Plats, 1828–1948. (Original county, established in 1666.)

Talbot County: Some losses "due to neglect." Alienation records, 1662–1740; Land records, 1662–1984, and Indices, 1662–1833, 1833–73, 1851–1951; Land commissions, 1702–93; Land record abstracts, 1786–1822; Plats, 1721–1949. (Original county established in 1662.)

Washington County: Most records survived a fire in 1871; Land records, 1777–1985, and Indices, 1776–1851, 1851–1962; Land records abstracts, 1806–15; and, Plats, 1786–1948. (County established from Frederick County in 1776.)

Wicomico County: Land records, 1867–1988, and Indices, 1867–1932, 1867–1947; Land abstracts, 1827–49, Index, 1827–74; Plats, 1867–1950. (County established in 1867 from Somerset and Worcester Counties.)

Worcester County: Most records survived a fire in 1834; Land records, 1742–1987; Indices to Grantees/Grantors, 1742–1844, 1751–1959; Land abstracts, 1827–49, and Index, 1827–74. (County established in 1742 from Somerset.)

Tax Lists

The Tax List of 1783 for Maryland is the most complete of extant tax records for the state and province. It is important as a bridge between the 1776–78 and 1790 censuses, and because of the information it provides.

The originals of many of these tax lists are housed at the Maryland State Archives and are available to the public for research purposes. They are also available on microfilm at the Maryland Historical Society. The lists for Baltimore and Harford Counties have been published. Refer to the Bibliography for details and other published tax lists.

A number of miscellaneous assessment records and tax lists are also available in the individual counties or the Maryland State Archives. For additional information, consult Edward C. Papenfuse, *A Guide to Government Records at the Maryland State Archives,* and also Avril Pedley's *The Manuscript Collections of the Maryland Historical Society* for lists held at that institution.

The Direct Tax of 1798 for Maryland and the District of Columbia was a federal assessment levied to assist in paying indebtedness created during the Revolutionary War. This resulting record series consists of three parts. The first part is a general assessment list containing the names of owners of dwelling houses, lands, wharves, and slaves on October 1, 1798; property subject to valuation, property exempted from valuation as determined by the principal assessor, and valuation revised by the Tax Commissioners.

The second part consists of a "Particular Assessment List" which is a descriptive list giving dimensions of dwelling houses, outbuildings, and land as of October 1, 1798. The third part is a general Tax Book or List giving names of persons by whom the tax is payable, amount of valuation, rate per centum, and amount of tax due.

The originals are now in possession of the Maryland State Law Library in Annapolis. Microfilm copies are available for research at the Maryland Historical Society. Lists for part of Baltimore County (and the part that became Carroll County) have been published.

Rent Rolls and Debt Books

Under the Royal Charter of Maryland, the proprietor was in effect a feudal lord. He granted/patented land to individuals but continued to receive an annual quit rent as well as an alienation fee when the land was sold by one individual to another. Records of these annual quit rents were kept in two separate sets of books, the Rent Rolls and the Debt Books.

The Rent Rolls consist of lists of land holdings arranged by county, entered first under the name of the tract of land as given in the patent, its acreage, date of survey, name of original grantee, location of tract, and usually the possessor of the tract at the time the Rent Roll was compiled.

The Debt Books, which were compiled in the eighteenth century, list the name of each landowner, acreage, name of the tract, and the amount of rent due.

Not all of the Rent Rolls and Debt Books have been located, since many have been lost or destroyed over the years. The Maryland Historical Society has five Debt Books and twenty-nine Rent Rolls, the latter of which are fully described in the *Maryland Historical Magazine*, 19 (1924): 341–69.

The Maryland State Archives maintains forty-nine volumes of Rent Rolls in addition to microfilm and photostatic or xerographic copies of those held by the Maryland Historical Society.

Ethnic Family History*

Baltimore ranked as the second largest port of entry for European immigrants during most of the nineteenth century, second only to New York and rivaling Boston and Philadelphia. Estimates range from hundreds of thousands to nearly two million people who entered the United States through this port, accounting for approximately one-third of the total immigrant population. Most of the people who came through the port of Baltimore, or across state lines from the South, moved on, but many stayed to make Maryland their home. Their stories can sometimes be pieced together by looking at the private and/or government organizations that helped them along their way.

Traditional genealogical tools such as census reports, passenger lists, and naturalization records provide answers to many genealogical questions, but beyond the governmental structure that generated these documents, private organizations offered assistance through local benevolent societies. The records of these societies sometimes provide valuable family information.

Most immigrants who shared an ethnic background drew together as minorities in America. Prominent local citizens of the same ethnic background recognized the need to coordinate relief for the new arrivals and founded these societies. They offered food, clothing, housing, medical care, employment, and when necessary, legal help.

The first of these benevolent groups was the German Society of Maryland. The German population of Maryland had been a positive and productive force since the early years of the eighteenth century when the Palatines settled in Frederick County. By 1747 more than one thousand

Germans lived and worked in the Monocacy Valley. Maryland Germans also worked as shopkeepers, bookbinders, bakers, saddlers, carpenters, shoemakers, bricklayers, weavers, musicians, and locksmiths. In May 1754 Governor Horatio Sharpe's report to Lord Baltimore mentioned the Germans as the "best element among the inhabitants of Baltimore." By the last quarter of the eighteenth century, acts passed by the General Assembly were translated into German, and on the order of the House of Delegates, Frederick's printer translated the proceedings of the Committee on the Federal Constitution.

As the German population grew, so did cases of mistreatment and abuse of immigrants. "Redemptioners," emigrated for a better life and signed work contracts in exchange for their passage—contracts written in English. On the long voyages across the Atlantic, food and water became scarce and medical care was nonexistent. Ship captains sometimes withheld these basic necessities in order to extort additional service time or money. When family members died during the crossing, the survivors were charged with the work time of the deceased. If a wife lost her husband and/or children, she had to serve her time plus additional five years terms for each of their contracts.

Reports of these horrors appeared in the seaport newspapers, and America's long-established German families and community leaders organized relief societies and petitioned state legislatures for immigrant protection laws. The first record of the German Society of Maryland, a call to organize for the protection of redemptioners, is dated 1783. The society elected Dr. Frederick Weisenthal as their president and the group began meeting ships and securing legal assistance for those immigrants caught in unjust contracts. The Maryland General Assembly incorporated the society in 1818, and that status gave them the power to bring suit against ship captains. Two weeks after their incorporation, the assembly passed immigrant protection laws. The law stated that all work contracts had to be executed by an appointee of the governor who was skilled in both languages. Other laws limited terms of service to four years, forbade splitting families, and guaranteed that children would be educated at the expense of the person hiring the redemptioner.

Thus established, the German Society of Maryland provided assistance to immigrants, aided the construction of churches, schools, and orphanages, and kept an ever-watchful eye on the ships that unloaded new immigrants on the docks at Locust Point. The society is still active today and occasionally receives requests for financial assistance. They also offer college scholarships to students who can prove descent from a German ancestor.

The records of this organization have not fared well over the last two hundred years. The papers prior to the incorporation do not exist and

---

*Reprinted from Patricia Dockman Anderson, "Maryland's Ethnic Organizations," *Maryland Genealogical Society Bulletin,* 34 (1993): 263–69.

many of the later records were destroyed in the Great Fire of 1904. What does survive are twenty-two boxes of material that until recently remained in the society's care. The society turned the collection over to the Maryland State Archives, and the papers have been microfilmed. The surviving documents include case books, minutes, correspondence, membership lists, and passenger lists.

Baltimore's Irish population also took care of their own and formed the Hibernian Society in 1803. An advertisement appeared in the *American Patriot and Fells Point Advertiser* for a meeting at Bryden's Inn on Light Street to "formulate a plan . . . to organize relief . . . for emigrants arriving daily . . . many are friendless and forlorn." Unlike the German Society that operated primarily as a legal and political group, the Hibernian Society was strictly a relief agency.

In their own country, the Irish people as a whole had suffered invasions for centuries that culminated with Cromwell's victory in the seventeenth century and the resulting penal laws. Under these laws, Irish Catholics could not vote or hold office, practice law, teach or attend university, nor could they own property. Catholic children could not attend school and Catholic churches were not permitted to operate. These laws subjugated the Irish and left them struggling in desperate poverty, working menial labor jobs, and living with high disease and death rates. The penal laws remained in effect until 1829. More than one million people died during the Great Famine of the 1840s and more emigrated. By 1914 the population of Ireland was only half of what it had been in 1840. Consequently, most of the Irish who arrived in America came as refugees and needed immediate physical assistance. The Hibernians provided money, food, clothing, and medical care.

Unlike other ethnic societies, the Hibernians accepted members regardless of whether they could afford to pay their dues. The most important function of the society was to coordinate relief, and more valuable than the dues was a willingness to work. As a result of their subjugated and impoverished lives under the penal laws, the Irish became great grassroots organizers. The society had representatives in every ward of the city collecting money and members. Money collected went to the aid of the immigrants. Funds also went to pay the passage of most of the Irish who emigrated in the 1840s. Between 1848 and 1864 Irish Americans sent sixty-five million dollars to Ireland, much of it squeezed from very low incomes.

In 1834 the Associated Friends of Ireland in Baltimore turned over their remaining funds to the Hibernians, and their ledger is part of the society's collection. This political group supported Irish freedom from 1831 to 1834 and their ledger lists hold the member's name and their Irish county of birth. Larry Sullivan abstracted these lists and published them in an article entitled "The Records of Ethnic Political Associations as a Genealogical

Source: The Associated Friends of Ireland in the City of Baltimore," *Maryland Magazine of Genealogy*, 5 (1982): 23–33.

The Hibernian Society went on, as did the German Society, to help their poor in Baltimore and Maryland. They also established the Hibernian Free School in 1824 to educate children with Irish parents. The school closed in 1937, but the society still awards a scholarship to students who can claim an Irish ancestor.

The records of the Hibernian Society are virtually complete; only the years 1803–15 are missing. The records from 1815 to 1978 have been preserved and are in the care of the Maryland Historical Society library, MS. 2029. There is a wealth of genealogical data in these boxes, but since the collection is not indexed, it is tedious to research. There are no case books, but the minutes and membership lists include mention of deaths, marriages, place of origin, and in some cases, assistance given by the society.

The third major ethnic society that formed in Maryland was the Hebrew Benevolent Society, in 1856. The Jewish people had experienced centuries of minority status in other countries and they reached America prepared to take care of themselves and those who followed.

A small number of Jews lived in colonial Maryland, and by 1820 only 120 lived in Baltimore. By 1856 the Jewish population had grown to over 4,000, and with that growth came the need for assistance. The society organized around the objective that they would "provide relief to indigent Israelites," and they elected Dr. Joshua Cohen as their first president. These early immigrants were primarily German Jews, and they organized the benevolent efforts. These same programs later aided thousands of Eastern Europeans fleeing pogroms in the last quarter of the nineteenth century until immigration was slowed by the enactment of quota laws in 1921 and 1924.

The records of the Hebrew Benevolent Society are extensive and of great genealogical value. They are preserved by the Jewish Historical Society and are available to researchers by appointment with the archivist. The collection includes the minutes of the society, two volumes of donations, and fifty volumes of case files from the years 1900–1930. The papers of the Hebrew Immigrant Aid Society (HIAS) make up a large collection that includes a card file of those who applied for assistance. The cards have the name of the immigrant, the ship on which they arrived, their destination, and their relationship to the person with whom they would be staying.

The society also holds the records of the Hebrew Orphan Asylum that housed approximately seventy to 130 children a year from 1885 to 1915. By 1906 the orphanage accepted children directly from Eastern Europe. These ledger books are open to researchers, but the case files are restricted. Another record group of interest to family historians is the midwives' records that span the years 1895 to 1920. These include Italian as well as Jewish births (because the Italian community bordered the Jewish community). The original Hebrew Benevolent Society evolved, with other organizations, into the Jewish Family and Children's Bureau. Today it is part of the Associated Jewish Charities of Baltimore.

These are just a few of Baltimore's benevolent societies. Organizations also formed to help the Italians, the Poles, the Czechoslovakians, and other immigrants who made their way to Maryland. For information about these societies, check the current telephone directory; many of them are still in existence. The best one-stop source for leads on private organizations is John T. Guertler and Adele M. Newberger, *The Records of Baltimore's Private Organizations* (New York: Garland publishing, 1981.)

After the Civil War, Baltimore and Maryland underwent profound changes that affected immigrants and their respective benevolent societies. The industrial age that had attracted so many people to America in the first half of the nineteenth century exploded in the second half. Tens of thousands of European immigrants came to this state, working for their share of the American dream. Their labor helped Maryland to lead the nation in the canning and textile industries. The expanding rail lines of the B&O Railroad carried Maryland goods westward and linked the state to the growing agricultural centers in the Midwest. New immigrants boarded trains and went to Wisconsin, Illinois, and Nebraska. In 1869 the B&O struck a deal with the North German Lloyd Lines whereby emigrants could purchase a combination steamship and rail ticket. The railroad opened a new receiving station on piers 8 and 9 at Locust Point and many new immigrants were in Baltimore only a few hours before they boarded the train and headed West.

This era also saw the rise of urban poverty in the immigrant neighborhoods that housed the workers of the industrial age. Laissez-faire government and social Darwinism allowed the squalid conditions to multiply unchecked until they were addressed by progressive reformers in the late nineteenth and early twentieth centuries. The growth of social services and charitable groups under the guidance of the Charity Organization Society eventually assumed the primary role of caring for the immediate needs of the poor.

Immigration and Naturalization

Over two million immigrants are estimated to have come through the Port of Baltimore in the nineteenth and early twentieth centuries. Most moved on to other cities, towns, and farming communities across the country. Others stayed and made Maryland their home. This wide dispersal means that people from across Maryland and the nation can trace their American roots to Baltimore.

The federal government enacted laws creating passenger lists in 1818 to keep track of the growing number of European immigrants entering the country. This first law required the ship's captain to submit a list of the passengers to customs officials at all of the major ports. These "customs lists" exist for Baltimore for the years 1820–91, but many of the pre-1833 lists were destroyed by a fire in 1897. The lists give the name of the passenger, his/her age, sex, occupation, country (and sometimes locality) of origin, and destination. The list also contains the name of the ship, the captain, port of departure, and date of arrival. If an individual died on board, the date and cause are noted.

Baltimore's lists are supplemented by a second set collected as the result of an 1833 law that required the captains to turn over a duplicate passenger manifest to the city government. This latter series, known as the "city lists," are identical in form and content to the federal customs lists. When the National Archives filmed the customs lists, the city lists were used to fill in the gaps. Both the microfilmed copies and the original lists are arranged chronologically by the date the vessel arrived. The passenger lists for the Port of Baltimore are available to researchers on microfilm at the Maryland Historical Society and the National Archives.

The city lists exist because of an effort to restrict, and then provide for, indigent immigrants. The large numbers of German and Irish coming into Baltimore placed a tremendous drain on the Trustees of the Poor and on city services. Anti-immigrant sentiment ran high and included fears that the newcomers were lunatics or criminals. Most were poor and needed assistance (see Ethnic Research). Some Americans were suspicious of foreign ways and customs, and others worried about competition for their jobs.

The resulting pressure on the Maryland General Assembly led to the above-mentioned law requiring the second list. The ships' captains also had to pay a $1.50 head tax per immigrant that was collected by the city and divided among the benevolent societies and the Trustees of the Poor. Hopes that the tax would discourage immigration faded quickly. Other cities charged a higher rate and in so doing made Baltimore an even more appealing port of entry.

Passenger lists are crucial in determining when people arrived in Maryland from abroad. This information is rarely found elsewhere. The lists, as with all other sources, have their problems. Many lists are missing. Those that survive are littered with inaccuracies. Consider the language barrier between foreign arrivals and American customs officials. Spelling errors were impossible to prevent; names were recorded as they were heard. Poor handwriting and carelessness on the part of the recorder multiply the problems. Indexers who abstracted the names and data from the lists also made errors.

The microfilmed index is a card file prepared according to the Soundex method that lists passengers alphabetically by the first letter of their last name followed by a three-digit numerical code. The system was designed to bring all similar sounding names together. All of the major repositories in Maryland have a Soundex instruction sheet available to researchers. Inexperienced users of the system should ask the librarian, archivist, or a volunteer to double-check the code assigned to the immigrant's name. If the name does not appear in the index, look through the preceding and following names for about five pages each way. The card may have been placed out of order in the microfilming process.

Naturalization—becoming an American citizen—was an important event for many immigrants. These records also hold valuable information for genealogists. Naturalization took place in the local as well as the federal courts and began with a petition for naturalization in which the immigrant stated his intention to become a citizen. The most valuable document in this process, the Declaration of Intention, contains the most genealogical information. The applicant not only gave his name and date and place of birth, but also gave his occupation and a physical description. These statements may also include the testimony of witnesses who verified the immigrant's information; many of these are family members. Unfortunately these declarations were considered preliminary paperwork, and many were destroyed after the naturalization certificate was issued. This final certificate, the permanent record, usually contains only the name and place of origin of the new American citizen and a sworn statement that he has renounced his allegiance to the "King of . . . ." Naturalization records and their indices are available at the Maryland State Archives.

African American Family History

A generation ago, Alex Haley's epic *Roots* sent thousands of African Americans searching for their ancestral past. This sudden and widespread interest sent novice black researchers and scores of professional genealogists to the same sources used by white Americans. What they found is that black families can usually be traced, without too much difficulty, back to the years of the Civil War. "Resources for African American History at the Maryland State Archives," a publication of the Maryland State Archives, contains a complete description of the holdings that relate to black history.

Descendents of free blacks will find their pre–Civil War ancestors documented in the same sources described in this guide: vital, church, military, land, and probate records. Other records, like manumission papers, freedom certificates, and other sources related directly to color may also provide information about antebellum generations. These ancestors are coded [B]lack, [M]ulatto, or listed as free men of color to distinguish them from white Americans. Other nuances in record-keeping may reflect the social attitudes of the times. For example, researchers should look closely at sources like city directories in which blacks are either listed separately in the back of the book, or are noted by an asterisk before their names. Without this information about how the directories were compiled, black families would be overlooked. Also, the company that prepared the 1850 Maryland Census Index did not pull the names of any free blacks. These people will only be found by searching the film page by page. This will be slightly less time consuming if the person can first be located in the city directory.

Researchers who are descendents of slaves face different data problems and have to think in terms of property rather than people when searching through government records. One of the most effective methods is to identify the slave owner's landed property. Focus on the slave owner and his/her family for clues such as the names of slaves in estate inventories. Even though most slaves only had one name, most owners did not have more than one slave with the same name. Chattel (property) records in the general court books and chancery (equity) court cases also handled property disputes of all kinds. Oral history is also of critical importance in establishing family history. Many relationships and traditions were handed down in this way.

The very nature of nineteenth-century African American genealogy makes a broad understanding of black history and the American slave system imperative. There are many publications that will help researchers investigating Maryland's African American families understand the world in which their ancestors lived. Christopher Phillips, *Freedom's Port: The African American Community of Baltimore, 1790–1860* (Urbana and Chicago: University of Illinois Press, 1997); T. Stephen Whitman, *The Price of Freedom: Slavery and Manumission in Baltimore and Early National Maryland* (Lexington: The University Press of Kentucky, 1997); and Barbara Jeanne Fields, *Slavery and Freedom on the Middle Ground* (New Haven: Yale University Press, 1985) are just a few of the dozens of titles that offer important insights into black life.

In addition to the archives' finding aids, several other collections may also help researchers. The Maryland Colonization Society Papers at the Maryland Historical Society include minutes, manumissions, censuses, deeds, and the returns of "Negroes to Liberia." The names of these travelers were abstracted and published by Jerry M. Hynson in "Marylanders to Liberia," *Maryland Genealogical Society Bulletin* , 39 (1998): 169–82. William D. Hoyt Jr. "The

Papers of the Maryland State Colonization Society," *Maryland Historical Magazine,* 32 (1937): 247–71 offers a description of the collection.

The papers of the Baltimore Association for Moral and Educational Improvement of Colored People, also housed at the Maryland Historical Society, is described in Richard Paul Fuke, "The Baltimore Association for Moral and Educational Improvement of Colored People, 1864–1870" *Maryland Historical Magazine,* 66 (1971): 369–404; Mary Carroll Johnansen, "'Intelligence Though Overlooked': Education for Black Women in the Upper South, 1800–1840," *Maryland Historical Magazine,* 93 (1998): 443–66; James H. Whyte, "Activities of the Freedmen's Bureau in Southern Maryland, 1865–1870," *Chronicles of St. Mary's* 7 (1959): 11–18. This is just a sample of the available literature and scholarship for those researching Maryland's African American families. Researchers working on black families also have the advantage of African American genealogical societies, web sites, and publications.

BIBLIOGRAPHY

T he following bibliography contains many important published works on Maryland source records and county histories. Some of these works may contain errors and should be used with caution. Always consult the primary source. It should be noted that this is not just a listing of books currently for sale, since many of the books listed are out of print and can only be purchased as used editions. Nevertheless, most of these books may be found in various libraries throughout the state and nation.

The following list is not comprehensive. It does not include the many unpublished compilations, published genealogies, or references to the thousands of articles published in various genealogical periodicals. For the latter, researchers should consult the *Genealogical Periodical Annual Index* published by Heritage Books in Bowie, Maryland.

Allegany County

(also see Western Maryland)

Albright, Eleanor L. and Mary A. Dye. *Naturalized in Cumberland: A City in Celebration 1787–1987*. Cumberland, Md.: Mayor and City Council, 1987.

Crosby, Anthony E. Jr, and Michael R. Olson. *Commemorating Frostburg's Percy Cemetery: Restoration and Research*. Frostburg, Md.: By the authors, 1995.

Cupler, Mary D. *Allegany County, Maryland 1800 Census*. 1971. Reprint, Westminster, Md.: Family Line Publications, 1992.

Fair, Patricia Stover and T. J. C. Williams. *Every Name Index to History of Allegany County, Maryland*. [By Thomas and Williams.] Oklahoma City, Okla.: Fair Printing Company, 1991.

Feldstein, Albert L. *Gone but Not Forgotten: A Bibliographical Graveside Tribute to Historical Allegany Figures*. 2 volumes. Cumberland, Md.: Cumberland Press Print Company, 1988–89.

Gatewood, Gloria. *Marriages and Deaths from the Cumberland Alleganian, 1864–1867*. Westminster, Md.: Family Line Publications, 1986.

Genealogical Society of Allegany County. *Allegany County, Maryland, Rural Cemeteries*. Cresaptown, Md.: By the Society, 1991.

———. *Old Pike Post*. LaVale, Md.: By the Society, since 1983.

————. *Rose Hill Cemetery, Cumberland, Maryland: An Inventory*. LaVale, Md.: By the Society, 1995.

A Guide to Maryland State Archives Holdings of Allegany County Records on Microform. Annapolis: Maryland State Archives, 1989.

Historical Records Survey, WPA. *Inventory of the County Archives of Maryland, No. 1, Allegany County*. Baltimore, 1937.

Hume, Joan, ed. *Maryland: Index to the Wills of Allegany County, 1784–1960*. Baltimore: Magna Carta Book Co., 1970.

Lowdermilk, William Harrison. *History of Cumberland. Maryland From the Time of the Indian Town, Caiuctucuc, in 1728, up to the Present Day*. 1878. Reprint, Baltimore: Regional Publishing Company, 1971.

Michael, D. O, comp. and ed. *Western Maryland Materials in Allegany and Garrett County Libraries*. Cumberland, Md.: Allegany County Local History Program, 1977.

Scharf, J. Thomas. *History of Western Maryland, Being a History of Frederick, Montgomery, Carroll, Washington, Allegany and Garrett Counties*. 2 volumes. 1882. Reprint, Baltimore: Regional Publishing Company, 1968. [For index see "Western Maryland."]

Thomas, James W. and T. J. C. Williams. *History of Allegany County, Maryland*. 2 volumes. 1923. Reprint, Baltimore: Regional Publishing Company, 1969.

Volkel, Charlotte A., Lowell M. Volkel, and Timothy Q. Wilson. "An Index to the 1800 Census of Allegany, Anne Arundel, Calvert Counties and the City of Baltimore, State of Maryland." 1967. Maryland Historical Society Library, 1967. [Typescript.]

Wright, F. Edward. *Newspaper Abstracts of Allegany & Washington Counties, Maryland, 1811–1815*. Westminster, Md.: Family Line Publications, 1989.

————. *Newspaper Abstracts of Allegany & Washington Counties, Maryland, 1820–1830*. Westminster, Md.: Family Line Publications, 1993.

————. *Marriages and Deaths from the Newspapers of Allegany & Washington Counties, Maryland, 1820–1830*. Silver Spring, Md.: Family Line Publications, 1987.

Anne Arundel County

Anne Arundel County Genealogical Society. *Cemetery Inscriptions of Anne Arundel County, Maryland*. 2 volumes. Pasadena, Md.: By the Society, 1982, 1987.

Anne Arundel Speaks. Pasadena, Md.: Anne Arundel County Genealogical Society. Quarterly publication since 1974.

Arps, Walter E. Jr. *Heirs & Orphans: Anne Arundel County Distributions, 1788–1838*. Silver Spring, Md.: Family Line Publications, 1985.

Barnes, Robert W. *Colonial Families of Anne Arundel County, Maryland.* Westminster, Md.: Family Line Publications, 1996.

Bradford, James C., ed. *Anne Arundel County, Maryland: A Bicentennial History of Annapolis, Maryland.* Annapolis, Md.: Anne Arundel and Annapolis Bicentennial Commission, 1977.

Bagby, Audrey M. and Betty L. deKeyser. *Cedar Hill Cemetery Gravestone Inscriptions,* Vol. 1, *Interment Records,* Vol. 2. Pasadena Md.: Anne Arundel County Genealogical Society, 1999.

Clark, Raymond B. Jr. *Index to Anne Arundel County, Maryland, Wills, 1650–1777.* Arlington, Va.: By the author, 1981.

Dallam, Edith Stansbury. *Old Herring Creek Parish: A History, 1663–1799.* Lothian, Md.: St. James Parish, 1978. [Contains a register of baptisms.]

Daughters of the American Revolution in State of Maryland, Marlborough Towne Chapter. *Tombstone Inscriptions of Southern Anne Arundel County.* Baltimore: Gateway Press, Inc., 1971.

Dodd, Rosemary B. and Patricia M. Bausell. *Abstracts of Land Records Anne Arundel County, Maryland, 1653–1728.* 4 volumes. Pasadena, Md.: Anne Arundel County Genealogical Society, 1991–1998.

Eason, Ruth P. *History of the Town of Glen Burnie.* Glen Burnie, Md, n.d.

Green, Karen Maurer. *The Maryland Gazette, 1727–1761: Genealogical and Historical Abstracts.* Galveston, Texas: Frontier Press, 1990.

A Guide to Maryland State Archives Holdings of Anne Arundel County Records on Microform. Annapolis: Maryland State Archives, 1989.

Gurney, John T. III, ed. *Cemetery Inscriptions of Anne Arundel County, Maryland.* 2 volumes. Pasadena, Md.: Anne Arundel County Genealogical Society, 1982, 1987.

Heiss, Willard. *Maryland Quaker Records.* Ft. Wayne, Ind.: Ft. Wayne Public Library, 1976, 159. [Contains some records of West River Meeting.]

Historical Records Survey, WPA. *Inventory of County and Town Archives of Maryland, No. 2, Anne Arundel County.* Baltimore, 1941.

Hopkins, G. M. *Atlas of Anne Arundel County, Maryland.* 1878. Reprinted by the Greater Glen Burnie Jaycees, 1969.

Hynson, Jerry M. *Maryland Freedom Papers.* Vol. 1, *Anne Arundel County.* Westminster, Md.: Family Line Publications, 1996.

Jones, Barbara and Avlyn Conley. *Index to 1860 Census of Anne Arundel County, Maryland.* Riva, Md.: Anne Arundel County Genealogical Society, 1986.

Kelly, J. Reaney. *Quakers in the Founding of Anne Arundel County, Maryland.* Baltimore: Maryland Historical Society, 1963.

Maryland Genealogical Society. *1800 Census of Anne Arundel County.* Baltimore: By the Society, 1959. Reprint, Westminster, Md.: Family Line Publications, 1992.

McIntire, Robert H. *Annapolis, Maryland Families.* 2 volumes. Baltimore: Gateway Press, Inc., 1979, 1990.

Maryland Rent Rolls: Baltimore and Anne Arundel County, 1700–1707, 1705–1724. Baltimore: Genealogical Publishing Company, 1976; reprinted 1996. [From the *Maryland Historical Magazine*, 1924–1931.]

Molter, Nelson J. *An Illustrated History of Severna Park, Anne Arundel County, Maryland*. Severna Park, Md. 1969.

Moss, James E. *Providence, Ye Lost Towne at Severn in Maryland*. Washington, 1976.

Nelker, Gladys. *Town Neck Hundred of Anne Arundel County: The Land*. Westminster, Md.: Family Line Publications, 1990.

Newman, Harry Wright. *Anne Arundel Gentry; A Genealogical History*. Baltimore, 1933. Reprint, Baltimore: Genealogical Publishing Company, 1991.

———. *Anne Arundel Gentry: A Genealogical History, Revised and Augmented*. Vol. 1. 1970. Reprint, Westminster: Family Line Publications, 1990.

———. *Anne Arundel Gentry: A Genealogical History*. Vol. 2. 1971. Reprint, Westminster, Md.: Family Line Publications, 1990.

———. *Anne Arundel Gentry: A Genealogical History*. Vol. 3. Annapolis, Md.: By the author, 1980.

O'Malley, Katherine. *Odenton, The Town a Railroad Built*. Odenton, Md: Reprint, c1990.

Peden, Henry C. Jr. *Revolutionary Patriots of Anne Arundel County, Maryland, 1775–1783*. Westminster, Md.: Family Line Publications, 1992.

Powell, John W. *1850 Anne Arundel County, Maryland Census*. Pasadena, Md.: Anne Arundel County Genealogical Society, 1991.

———. *Anne Arundel County Wills Index, 1778–1918*. Pasadena, Md.: Anne Arundel County Genealogical Society, 1985.

———. *Anne Arundel County, Maryland Marriage Records, 1777–1877*. Pasadena, Md.: Anne Arundel County Genealogical Society, 1991.

Riley, Elihu S. *"The Ancient City," A History of Annapolis, in Maryland, 1649–1887*. 1887. Reprint, Annapolis: Annapolis Bicentennial Committee, 1976.

Volkel, Charlotte A., Lowell M. Volkel, and Timothy Q. Wilson. "An Index to the 1800 Census of Allegany, Anne Arundel, Calvert Counties and the City of Baltimore, State of Maryland." Maryland Historical Society Library, 1967. [Typescript.]

Warfield, J. D. *The Founders of Anne Arundel and Howard Counties, Maryland*. 1905. Reprint, Baltimore: Regional Publishing Company, 1967, and Westminster, Md.: Family Line Publications, 1990, 1995.

Williams, Elsie. "1800 Anne Arundel Census." *Maryland Genealogical Society Bulletin*, 19:243–91. Reprint, Westminster: Family Line Publications, 1992.

Wright, F. Edward. *Anne Arundel County, Maryland Church Records of the 17th and 18th Centuries*. Westminster, Md.: Family Line Publications, 1989.

———. *Maryland Militia, War of 1812.* Vol. 4, *Anne Arundel & Calvert Counties.* Silver Spring, Md.: Family Line Publications, 1981.

Baltimore City and County

A Guide to Maryland State Archives Holdings of Baltimore City Records on Microform. Annapolis: Maryland State Archives, 1989.

A Guide to Maryland State Archives Holdings of Baltimore County Records on Microform. Annapolis: Maryland State Archives, 1989.

Anderson, Patricia Dockman. *Abstracts of the Ridgely Papers.* Westminster, Md.: Family Line Publications, 1991.

Annotated Finding List of Genealogy and Heraldry Reference Material in the Baltimore County Public Library. Towson, Md.: Baltimore County Public Library, 1965.

Arps, Walter E. Jr. *Departed this Life: Death Notices from the Baltimore Sun.* 4 volumes [1851–1860]. Silver Spring, Md.: Family Line Publications, 1985.

———. *Maryland Mortalities, 1876–1915.* [Originally printed in the *Baltimore Sun Almanac.*] Silver Spring, Md.: Family Line Publications, 1983.

Baltimore City Directories. 121 volumes. 1796–1964. [Titles vary; some on microfiche; available at Baltimore City Archives and the Maryland Historical Society Library.]

Baltimore County Genealogical Society. *Abstracts of the Baltimore County Land Commissions, 1727–1762.* Westminster, Md.: Family Line Publications, 1989.

———. *Baltimore County Cemeteries.* Vol. 5, *St. Mary's Cemetery.* Silver Spring, Md.: Family Line Publications, 1985.

———. *Baltimore County Cemeteries.* Vol. 6, *Mt. Olive United Methodist Church Cemetery.* Westminster, Md.: Family Line Publications, 1989.

———. *Mt. Carmel Cemetery Records, 1854–1905,* 3 volumes. Baltimore County Genealogical Society: Published for the Society by Family Line Publications, 1998.

———. *Notebook.* Published by the Society, 1979– .

———. *Tombstone Inscriptions of Govans Presbyterian Church Cemetery.* Westminster, Md.: Family Line Publications, 1996.

———. *Tombstone Inscriptions at St. James Protestant Episcopal Church, My Lady's Manor, Monkton, Maryland.* Towson, Md.: Published by the Society, 1992.

Baltimore County Cemeteries Collected by the Baltimore County Historical Society. 6 volumes Reprint, Westminster, Md.: Family Line Publications, 1985–1986. [Vol. 1, Northern Baltimore County; Vol. 2, Eastern Baltimore County;

Vol. 3, Western Baltimore County; Vol. 4, various cemeteries in Baltimore County; Vol. 5, St. Mary's Cemetery; Vol. 6, Mt. Olive United Methodist Church Cemetery.]

Baltimore Town and Fell's Point Directory of 1796. Silver Spring, Md.: Family Line Publications, 1983. Supplement contains Baltimore County naturalizations, 1796–1803.

Barnes, Robert W. *Baltimore County Marriage References, 1659–1746.* Silver Spring, Md.: Family Line Publications, 1986, 1998.

———. *Guide to Research in Baltimore City and County.* Westminster, Md.: Family Line Publications, 1989, revised 1993.

———. *Baltimore County Families, 1659–1759.* Baltimore: Genealogical Publishing Company, 1989, 1996.

———. *Index to the Marriages and Deaths in the Baltimore County Advocate, 1850–1864.* Silver Spring, Md.: Family Line Publications, 1985.

———. *Index to Baltimore County Wills, 1659–1850.* Lutherville, Md.: Published by Bettie S. Carothers, 1979.

———. *Abstracts of Baltimore County Administration Accounts,* Libers 6, 7, 8. Lutherville, Md.: Published by Bettie S. Carothers, 1975.

———. *Marriages and Deaths from Baltimore Newspapers, 1796–1816.* Baltimore: Genealogical Publishing Company, 1978.

———. *Baltimore County Deed Abstracts, 1659–1750.* Westminster, Md.: Family Line Publications, 1996.

Barnes, Robert W. and Bettie S. Carothers. *1783 Tax List of Baltimore County, Maryland.* Lutherville, Md.: Bettie S. Carothers, 1978. Reprint, Silver Spring Md: Family Line Publications, 1987. [Includes maps by George Horvath.]

Bell, Annie Walker Burns. *Baltimore County, Maryland, Guardian Bonds, No. 8, 1799–1809, Liber W. B. 2 1777–1875,* 2 volumes. Annapolis: n.p., 1929, 1939.

———. *Maryland Land Records: Baltimore County Deeds, 1659–1725.* Annapolis: By the author, 1933.

———. *Baltimore County, Maryland: A Registry of Administrations, 1776–1805.* 3 volumes. Annapolis, Md.: n.p., 1939.

Burns, Annie Walker. *Abstracts of Wills of Baltimore County, Maryland, 1782–1850.* 23 volumes. Washington, D.C.: By the author, 1954–67.

———. *Index to Guardians Accounts, Baltimore County, Maryland, 1777–1875.* 6 volumes. Annapolis, Md.: By the author, n.d.

———. *Index to Persons in Baltimore County, Maryland, 1658–1723.* Annapolis, Md.: By the author, n.d.

———. *Marriage Records of Baltimore County, Maryland, 1823–1826.* Washington, D.C.: By the author, 1956.

Churches of Baltimore County by Area. 3 volumes. Baltimore: Maryland Council of Churches, Department of Planning and Research, 1968–69.

Clark, Raymond B. Jr. *Index to Baltimore County, Maryland Wills, 1660–1777*. Arlington, Va.: By the author, 1983.

Clark, Sara Seth and Raymond B. Clark Jr. *Baltimore County, Maryland, Tax List, 1699–1706*. Washington, D.C.: By the authors, 1964.

Clayton, Ralph. *Black Baltimore, 1820–1870*. Bowie, Md.: Heritage Books, Inc., 1987.

Clemens, S. B. and C. E. Clemens. *From Marble Hill to Maryland Line: An Informal History of Northern Baltimore County*. n.p., 1976. Revised by the authors, 1983.

Cochran, William C, et al., eds. *Memoirs of the Dead, and Tomb's Remembrancer, 1806*. Baltimore: By the Editors, 1806. Reprinted with added appendix and index by Martha Reamy. Westminster, Md.: Family Line Publications, 1989.

Cox, Richard J. *A Name Index to the Baltimore City Tax Records, 1798–1808, of the Baltimore City Archives*. Baltimore City Archives, 1981.

————. *Resources & Opportunities for Research at the Baltimore City Archives*. Baltimore City Archives, 1981.

Davis, John. *Baltimore County, Maryland, Deed Records, 1659–1775*. 4 volumes. Bowie, Md.: Heritage Books, Inc., 1996–97.

Forbes, Marie. *Speaking of Our Past: A History of Owings Mills, Maryland, 1640–1988*. Bowie, Md.: Heritage Books, Inc., 1988.

Genealogy and Biography of Leading Families of the City of Baltimore and Baltimore County, Maryland. Chicago, 1897.

Gibbons, Mrs. Edwin C. Jr. *Vital Records of the First Independent Church, Baltimore, Maryland, 1818–1921*. Silver Spring, Md.: Family Line Publications, 1987.

Hall, Clayton C., ed. *Baltimore, Its History and Its People*. 3 volumes. New York, 1912.

————, ed. *History of Baltimore, Maryland from Its Founding as a Town to the Current Year, 1729–1898*. 2 volumes. Baltimore, 1898.

Hayward, Mary Ellen and R. Kent Lancaster. *Baltimore's Westminster Cemetery and Westminster Prebyterian Church: A Guide to the Markers and Burials, 1775–1943*. Baltimore: Westminster Preservation Trust, Inc., 1984.

Heiss, Willard. *Maryland Quaker Records*. Ft. Wayne, Indiana: Ft. Wayne Public Library, 1976.

Hollowak, Thomas L. *Index to Obituaries in the Jednosc–Polonia, 1926–1946*. Chicago: Polish Genealogical Society, 1983.

————. *Index to the Marriages and Deaths in the Baltimore Sun, 1837–1850*. Baltimore: Genealogical Publishing Company, 1978.

————. *Longevity List of Baltimore City, 1880–1889: Deaths of Persons Who Were Aged 70 or Older*. Silver Spring, Md.: Family Line Publications, 1986.

————. *Index to Marriages in the Baltimore Sun, 1851–1860*. Baltimore: Genealogical Publishing Company, 1978.

————. *Polish Heads of Household in Maryland: An Index to the 1910 Census*. Baltimore: By the author, 1990.

————. *Births from the Baptismal Record of Saint Stanislaw Kostka Church, 1879–1889*. Baltimore: Historyk Press, 1992.

Hopkins, G. M. *Atlas of Baltimore County, Maryland*. 1877. Reprint, Towson, Md.: Courthouse Archives and Museum Section, 1968.

Horvath, George J. Jr. *Particular Assessment Lists for Baltimore and Carroll Counties, 1798*. Silver Spring, Md.: Family Line Publications, 1986, 1989.

Howard, George W. *The Monumental City, Its Past History and Present Resources*. Baltimore, 1873. [This volume includes many biographical sketches.]

Howard, Louise O. and M. McK. Trice. *Guardianships and Indentures Involving Orphans: Orphans Court of Baltimore County, Libers WB No. 1 and WB No. 2, 1778–1792*. 2 volumes. Lutherville, Md.: Bettie S. Carothers, 1975–76.

LeFurgy, William E. *The Records of a City: A Guide to the Baltimore City Archives*. Baltimore: Baltimore City Archives and Records Management Office, 1984.

McElroy, Dorothy E. and Charles A. Earp. *The History and Roster of the First Christian Church. Disciples of Christ of Baltimore, Maryland, 1810–1996*. Bowie, Md.: Heritage Books, Inc., 1996.

McHenry, James, ed. *Baltimore Directory and Citizen's Register for 1807*. Silver Spring, Md.: Family Line Publications, 1985.

Maguire, Joseph C. Jr. *Index of Obituaries and Marriages in the [Baltimore] Sun, 1861–1865*. Westminster, Md.: Family Line Publications, 1992.

Mallick, Sallie A, ed. *Sketches of Citizens of Baltimore City and Baltimore County*. Westminster, Md.: Family Line Publications, 1991.

Maryland Rent Rolls: Baltimore & Anne Arundel Counties, 1700–1707, 1705–1724. A Consolidation of Articles from the Maryland Historical Magazine, 1924–1931. Baltimore: Genealogical Publishing Company, 1976. [Reprinted with a complete index.]

Maryland Tax List 1783, Baltimore County: From the Collection of the Maryland Historical Society. Philadelphia, 1970.

Meyer, Mary K. *Baltimore City Birth Records, 1865–1894*. Mt. Airy, Md.: Pipe Creek Publications, 1998.

Morrison, Hugh A. and G. T. Ritchie. *Index to Marriage Notices in the Baltimore Sun, 1837–1838*. Washington, D.C., 1905.

Neal, Margaret. *Tax List of Tax Assessments for Baltimore City, Maryland, 1798, 1799, 1800*. Daughters of American Colonists, Cecilius Calvert Chapter, 1988.

Obert, Rowene T. *Baltimore City and County, Maryland Marriage Licenses,*

1777–1799. Salt Lake City, Utah: The Genealogy Shoppe, 1974.

O'Neill, Francis P. *Index to Obituaries and Marriages in the [Baltimore] Sun, 1866–1870.* 2 volumes. Westminster, Md.: Family Line Publications, 1996.

———. *Index to Obituaries and Marriages in the [Baltimore] Sun, 1871– 1875.* 2 volumes. Westminster, Md.: Family Line Publications, 1995.

Oszakiewski, Robert A. *Maryland Naturalization Abstracts.* Vol. 1, *Baltimore County and Baltimore City, 1784–1851.* Westminster, Md.: Family Line Publications, 1995.

Peden, Henry C. Jr. *Baltimore City Deaths and Burials, 1834–1840.* Westminster, Md.: Family Line Publications, 1998.

———. *Historical Register of the Sparrows Point Police Department, 1901– 1986.* [Commissioned policemen at Bethlehem Steel Corporation in Baltimore County.] Bel Air, Md.: By the author, 1986.

———. *St. John's & St. George's Parish Registers, 1696–1851.* Baltimore and Harford Counties. Silver Spring, Md.: Family Line Publications, 1987.

———. *Revolutionary Patriots of Baltimore Town and Baltimore County, Maryland, 1775–1783.* Silver Spring, Md.: Family Line Publications, 1988.

———. *Inhabitants of Baltimore County, 1763–1774.* Westminster, Md.: Family Line Publications, 1989.

———. *Methodist Records of Baltimore City, Maryland, 1799–1839.* 2 volumes. Westminster, Md.: Family Line Publications, 1994.

———. *Baltimore County Overseers of Roads, 1693–1793.* Westminster, Md.: Family Line Publications, 1992. [This volume includes a map.]

———. *Presbyterian Records of Baltimore City, 1765–1840.* Westminster, Md.: Family Line Publications, 1995.

———. *Quaker Records of Baltimore and Harford Counties, 1801–1825.* Westminster, Md.: Willow Bend Books, 2000.

Piet, Mary A. and Stanley G. *Early Catholic Church Records in Baltimore, Maryland, 1782 through 1800.* Westminster, Md.: Family Line Publications, 1989.

Quinan, John R. *Medical Annals of Baltimore, 1608–1880.* Baltimore, 1884.

Reamy, Bill and Martha Reamy. *Records of St. Paul's Parish: Volume 1, Early 1700's to 1800; Volume 2, 1801–1825.* Westminster, Md.: Family Line Publications, 1988, 1989.

———. *St. Thomas' Parish Register, 1732–1850.* Westminster, Md.: Family Line Publications, 1987.

———. *St. James' Parish Register, 1787–1815.* Silver Spring, Md.: Family Line Publications, 1987.

———. *1860 Census of Baltimore City.* Vol. 1, *1st and 2nd Wards.* Silver Spring, Md.: Family Line Publications, 1987.

———. *1860 Census of Baltimore City.* Vol. 2, *3rd and 4th Wards.* Westminster, Md.: Family Line Publications, 1989.

————. *Scharf's History of Baltimore City and County: The Index.* Finksburg, Md.: Pipe Creek Publications, 1991.

Records of the First Reformed Church of Baltimore, 1768–1899. [From the *Maryland Genealogical Society Bulletin.*] Westminster, Md.: Family Line Publications, 1995.

Records of Old Otterbein Church, Baltimore, Maryland, 1785–1881. [From the *Maryland Genealogical Society Bulletin.*] Westminster, Md.: Family Line Publications, 1995.

Richards, Lewis. *Marriage Records, Rev. Lewis Richards, Pastor of the First Baptist Church, Baltimore, Maryland.* Copied by Margaret Neal. Daughters of American Colonists, Cecilus Calvert Chapter, n.d.

Riordan, Rev. Michael J. *Cathedral Records from the Beginning of Catholicity in Baltimore to the Present Time.* Baltimore, 1906.

St. Thomas' Parish Deaths and Burials, Owings Mills, Maryland, 1728–1995. Westminster, Md.: Family Line Publications, 1995. The name of the author is not indicated.

Scharf, J. Thomas. *History of Baltimore City and County.* 1881. Reprinted in 2 volumes by Regional Publishing Company, Baltimore. 1971, 1997.

Scharf, J. Thomas. *The Chronicles of Baltimore: Being a Complete History of Baltimore Town and Baltimore City from the Earliest Period to the Present Time.* Baltimore: Turnbull Brothers, 1874. Reprint, Bowie, Md.: Heritage Books, Inc., 1989.

Scisco, Louis Dow. *Baltimore County Land Records, 1665–1687.* [From the *Maryland Historical Magazine.*] Baltimore: Genealogical Publishing Company, 1992, 1995.

Seitz, R. Carlton. *Maps of Land Patents in Northern Baltimore and Carroll Counties.* Westminster, Md.: Family Line Publications, 1995.

Slattery, Bradleigh V. *Lord Baltimore's Gunpowder Manor, Baltimore County, Now the Long Green Valley.* Baldwin, Md.: By the compiler, 1976. [This volume includes maps.]

Smith, Dawn Beitler. *Baltimore County Marriage Licenses, 1777–1798.* Westminster, Md.: Family Line Publications, 1989.

————. *Index to 1850 Map of Baltimore County and City.* Westminster, Md.: Family Line Publications, 1989.

Suspicious Deaths in Mid-19th Century Baltimore: A Name Index to Coroner Inquest Reports at the Baltimore City Archives. Baltimore: Baltimore City Archives in cooperation with Family Line Publications, 1986.

Thomas, Dawn and Robert W. Barnes. *The Greenspring Valley, Its History and Heritage.* 2 volumes. Baltimore: Maryland Historical Society, 1978.

Volkel, Charlotte A., Lowell M. Volkel, and Timothy Q. Wilson. "An Index to the 1800 Census of Allegany, Anne Arundel, Calvert Counties and the City of Baltimore, State of Maryland." Maryland Historical Society Library, 1967. [Typescript.]

Watring, Anna Miller, E. Charles Miller, and R. Scott Johnson. *Loudon Park Caretakers Records, A–B, 1853–1986*. Westminster, Md.: Family Line Publications, 1993.

Weidmeyer, Carleton L. *Baltimore County's Second District Inhabitants During the Emerging Thirties: Hebbville, Woodlawn*. Clearwater, Fla.: By the author, 1990.

Weiser, Frederick S. *The Earliest Record Book of St. James Evangelical Lutheran Church: Liberty Road, Randallstown, Maryland*. Gettysburg, Pa.: By the author, 1967.

Wilkins, William N. *Baltimore County Court Records, Joppa, Maryland, Levy Allowances and Lists of Taxables by Hundreds, 1739*. Baltimore: By the author, 1949.

———. *Baltimore County Indentures, 1794–1799*. Baltimore: By the author, 1949.

Wilson, Jane B. *The Very Quiet Baltimoreans: A Guide to the Baltimore Cemeteries and Burial Sites of Baltimore*. Shippensburg, Pa.: White Mane Publishing Company, 1991.

Winterbottom, John J. *Mt. Olivet Cemetery: The Caretaker Records*. 3 volumes. Westminster, Md.: Family Line Publications, 1989.

Wright, F. Edward. *Inhabitants of Baltimore County, Maryland, 1692–1763*. Silver Spring, Md.: Family Line Publications, 1987.

———. *Maryland Militia, War of 1812*. Vol. 2, *Baltimore County*. Silver Spring, Md.: Family Line Publications, 1979.

———. *Baltimore Directory of 1807*. Silver Spring, Md.: Family Line Publications, 1985.

Wright, Holly G. *Baltimore Directory of 1799, Containing the Names, Occupations, and Places of Abode of the Citizens*. Silver Spring, Md.: Family Line Publications, 1984.

Wust, Klaus. *German Zion Church in Baltimore, 1755–1955: The Bicentennial History of the Earliest German-American Church in Baltimore, Maryland*. Baltimore: Zion Church of the City of Baltimore, 1955.

Yates, Dean K. *Forged by Fire: Maryland's National Guard at the Great Baltimore Fire of 1904*. Westminster, Md.: Family Line Publications, 1992.

Zimmerman, Elaine Obbink and Kenneth Edwin. *Records of St. Paul's Cemetery, 1855–1946*. Westminster, Md.: Family Line Publications, 1992.

———. *Interment Records, Lorraine Cemetery and Mausoleum, 1883–1929*. Westminster, Md.: Family Line Publications, 1995.

Calvert County

(also see Southern Maryland)

Atlas of Calvert County, Maryland. College Park, Md.: University of Maryland, 1969.

Carothers, Bettie Stirling. *1783 Tax List of Maryland*. Lutherville, Md.: By the author, 1977. [This volume includes the lists of Cecil, Talbot, Harford, and Calvert Counties.]

Clark, Sara Seth and Raymond B. Jr. *Calvert County, Maryland Wills,* Vol. 1, *1654–1700;* Vol. 2, *1700–1777*. St. Michaels, Md.: By the authors, 1974, 1981.

Gatewood, Gloria. *Marriages and Deaths from Calvert Journal, 1876–1879*. Huntingtown, Md., 1988.

A Guide to Maryland State Archives Holdings of Calvert County Records on Microform. Annapolis: Maryland State Archives, 1989.

Hutchins, Ailene W. *Calvert County, Maryland Early Land Records*. Prince Frederick, Md.: By the author, 1982.

Keen, Gladys, et al. *Calvert County, Maryland 1800 Census*. 1965. Reprint, Westminster, Md.: Family Line Publications, 1992.

O'Brien, Mildred Bowen. *Calvert County, Maryland Family Records, 1670–1929*. Baltimore: Gateway Press, Inc., 1978.

Peden, Henry C. Jr. *Revolutionary Patriots of Calvert & St. Mary's Counties, Maryland, 1775–1783*. Westminster, Md.: Family Line Publications, 1996.

Stein, Charles F. Jr. *A History of Calvert County, Maryland*. 2nd ed. Baltimore: By the author, 1960, rev. 1976.

Volkel, Charlotte A., Lowell M. Volkel, and Timothy Q. Wilson. "An index to the 1800 Census of Allegany, Anne Arundel, Calvert Counties and the City of Baltimore, State of Maryland" Maryland Historical Society Library, 1967. [Typescript.]

Wright, F. Edward. *Maryland Militia, War of 1812,* Vol. 4, *Anne Arundel and Calvert County*. Silver Spring, Md.: Family Line Publications, 1981.

Caroline County

(also see Eastern Shore)

Bell, Annie Walker Burns. *St. John's Parish Register. Hillsboro, Caroline County, Maryland*. Annapolis, Md.: By the author, 1939.

Beneath These Stones: Cemeteries of Caroline County. 3 volumes. Easton, Md.: Upper Shore Genealogical Society of Maryland, 1985, 1996.

Clark, Sara Seth and Raymond B. Jr. *Caroline County, Maryland Marriage Licenses 1774–1825, and a Short History of Caroline County*. St. Michaels, Md.: By the authors, 1969.

Cochrane, Laura C., et al. *History of Caroline County from Its Beginning.* 1920. Reprinted with an index by Regional Publishing Company, Baltimore, 1971, 1994.

Cranor, Henry D. *Marriage Licenses of Caroline County, 1774–1815.* 1904. Reprint, Baltimore: Genealogical Publishing Company, Baltimore, 1975, 1994.

A Guide to Maryland State Archives Holdings of Caroline County Records on Microform. Annapolis: Maryland State Archives, 1989.

Harper, Irma. *Heirs & Legatees of Caroline County.* [1774–c1864]. Westminster, Md.: Family Line Publications, 1989.

Hooper, Debbie A. *Caroline County 1850 Census.* Westminster, Md.: Family Line Publications, 1990.

Horsey, Eleanor F. *Origins of Caroline County from Land Plats,* 2 volumes. Denton, Md.: By the compiler, 1974.

Isler, John B. *1875 Map of Caroline County, Maryland.* Reprint, Westminster, Md.: Family Line Publications, 1987.

Merriken, Ellenor R. *Herring Hill. Federalsburg.* Denton, Md.: Baker Printing Company, 1969.

Peden, Henry C. Jr. *Revolutionary Patriots of Caroline County, Maryland, 1775–1783.* Westminster, Md.: Family Line Publications, 1998.

Saulsbury, M. L. *Map of Caroline County, Maryland.* Denton, Md.: George Herbert Fooks, 1969.

Skinner, Vernon L. Jr. *Caroline County, 1680–1817: An Index to Wills and Administrations in the Hall of Records.* Brookeville, Md.: By the compiler, 1980.

Stenley, Virginia D. *Chancery Books of Carroll County, Maryland, 1837–1889.* 2 volumes. Westminster, Md.: Family Line Publications, 1994, 1996.

Volkel, Charlotte A., Lowell M. Volkel, and Timothy Q. Wilson. "An Index to the 1800 Federal Census of Caroline, Cecil, Charles, Frederick, and Kent Counties, Maryland." Maryland Historical Society Library, 1967. [Typescript.]

Winterbottom, John J. *Caroline County 1800 Census.* Maryland Genealogical Society, 1972. Reprint, Westminster, Md.: Family Line Publications, 1992.

Wright, F. Edward. *Caroline County 1850 Census.* 1972. Reprint, Westminster, Md.: Family Line Publications, 1981.

———. *Caroline County Marriages, Births, Deaths, 1850–1880. Abstracts of Newspapers. Federal Mortality Schedules and Court Records.* Silver Spring, Md.: Family Line Publications, 1981.

———. *Caroline County, Maryland, 1860 Census.* By the compiler, 1973. Reprint, Westminster, Md.: Family Line Publications, 1973.

———. *Caroline County 1820 Census.* Puerto Rico: By the compiler, 1973.

Carroll County

Bates, Marlene S., Martha Reamy and Bill Reamy. *Abstracts of Carroll County Newspapers, 1831–1846.* Westminster, Md.: Family Line Publications, 1988.

Bell, Annie W. Burns. *Index to Zion Lutheran Church Register, Carroll County, Maryland.* Baltimore: By the author, 1940.

Carroll County Genealogical Society. *Carroll County Cemeteries,* Vol. 1, *Southeast.* Westminster, Md.: By the Society, 1989.

―――. *Carroll County Cemeteries,* Vol. 2, *East Central.* Westminster, Md.: By the Society, 1990.

―――. *Carroll County Cemeteries,* Vol. 3, *Southwest.* Westminster, Md.: By the Society, 1992.

―――. *Carroll County Cemeteries,* Vol. 4, *Northeast.* Westminster, Md.: By the Society, 1995.

―――. *Carroll County, Maryland 1860 Census Index.* Westminster, Md.: By the Society, 1990.

―――. *Carroll County, Maryland, Marriage Licenses, 1837–1899.* Westminster, Md.: By the Society, 1987.

Carroll County, Maryland, Marriage Licenses, 1837–1899. 2nd edition. Westminster, Md.: Genealogy Department Volunteers, Carroll County Public Library, 1995.

The Carrolltonian. Westminster, Md.: Carroll County Genealogical Society, 1982– .

A Guide to Maryland State Archives Holdings of Carroll County Records on Microform. Annapolis: Maryland State Archives, 1989.

A Guide to Genealogical Research in Carroll County. Westminster, Md.: Carroll County Genealogical Society, 1984; 2d edition, revised, 1991.

Historical Records Survey, WPA. *Inventory of the County and Town Archives of Maryland. No. 6, Carroll County.* Baltimore, 1940.

Holdcraft, Jacob Mehrling. *More Names in Stone: Cemetery Inscriptions from the Peripheral Areas of Frederick County, Maryland.* Ann Arbor, Michigan: n.p., 1972.

Horvath, George J. *The Particular Assessment Lists for Baltimore and Carroll Counties, 1798.* Silver Spring, Md.: Family Line Publications, 1986, 1989.

Index to 1850 Census of Carroll County, Maryland. Westminster, Md.: Carroll County Public Library, 1978.

Lake, Griffing & Stevenson. *Illustrated Atlas of Carroll County, Maryland.* Philadelphia: Lake, Griffing & Stevenson, 1877.

Martenet, Simon J. *Martinet's Map of Carroll County, Maryland.* Baltimore: Martinet, 1862. Reprinted by Noodle-Doosey, Manchester, Maryland. 1984. An index of names on the map is available from the publisher.

Polk's Westminster. Carroll County, Maryland City Directories. Richmond: R. L. Polk & Company, various years.

Purman, James. *A Rescue from Oblivion.* [Holy Trinity Church.] n.p., n.d.

Robertson, Harold J., and Cemetery Trustees. *Deer Park Methodist Cemetery, Smallwood, Maryland.* Westminster, Md.: Family Line Publications, 1996.

Scharf, J. Thomas. *History of Western Maryland being a History of Frederick, Montgomery, Carroll, Washington, Allegany and Garrett Counties.* 2 volumes. 1882. Reprint, Baltimore: Regional Publishing Company, 1968.

Schildknecht, C. E. *Monocacy & Catoctin: Some Early Settlers of Frederick and Carroll Counties, Maryland.* 2 volumes. Gettysburg, Pa.: By the compiler, 1985.

Warner, Nancy M. et al. *Carroll County, Maryland: A History, 1837–1976.* Westminster, Md.: Carroll County Bicentennial Committee, 1976.

Weiser, Frederick S. *Records of St. Mary's Reformed Church and St. Mary's Lutheran Church, Silver Run, Carroll County, 1820–1850.* Manchester, Md.: Noodle-Doosey Press, n.d.

Weiser, Frederick S. editor and translator. *Maryland German Church Records.* Vol. 7, *Saint Mary's Church, Silver Run, Carroll County, Lutheran Records, 1784–1863, and Reformed Records, 1812–1866.* Manchester, Md.: Noodle-Doosey Press, 1987.

———. *Maryland German Church Records.* Vol. 8, *Saint Luke's Church. "Winter's Church", near New Windsor, Carroll County, 1784–1884, Trinity Evangelical Luth. Church, Taneytown, Carroll County, 1788–1841, Emanuel Church. "Baust's Church", near Tyrone, Carroll County, Lutheran and Reformed Records, 1792–1849.* Westminster, Md.: Historical Society of Carroll County, 1994.

Weiser, Frederick S. and C. T. Zahn, editors and translators. *Maryland German Church Records,* Vol. 9, *The Pipe Creek Church. Benjamin's, St. Benjamin's or Krider's Church, near Westminster Carroll County, Reformed Records, 1766–1835, Lutheran Records, 1767–1837, Jerusalem, Bachman's. or Bauer's Church, Bachman Valley, Carroll County, Lutheran Records, 1799–1881.* Westminster, Md.: Historical Society of Carroll County, 1993.

———. *Maryland German Church Records.* Vol. 10, *Zion Church. "The German Church," Manchester, Carroll County, Trinity United Church of Christ Records, 1760–1836, and Immanuel Lutheran Church Records, 1760–1853.* Westminster, Md.: Historical Society of Carroll County, 1995.

Cecil County

Alexander, Lorain E. and Darlene M. McCall. "Genealogical Research Guide for Cecil County." Charlestown, Md.: 1982. [available MHS library]

Beard, Alice. *Births, Deaths, and Marriages of the Nottingham Quakers, 1680–1889.* Westminster, Md.: Family Line Publications, 1989.

Bell, Annie Walker Burns. *Index, Cecil County, Maryland, Rent Rolls, 1658–1724.* Baltimore: By the author, 1940.

Bicentennial of the Brick Meeting House, Calvert, Cecil County, Maryland. Lancaster, Pa.: Society of Friends, Brick Meeting House, 1902.

Biographical Record of Harford and Cecil Counties, Maryland. 1897. Reprinted with a new index by Harford County Genealogical Society. Westminster, Md.: Family Line Publications, 1989.

Brinkley, John J. *1800 Census of Cecil County.* 1972. Reprint, Westminster, Md.: Family Line Publications, 1992.

Brown, June D. *Abstracts of Cecil County Land Records, 1673–1751.* Westminster, Md.: Family Line Publications, 1998.

Burns, Gary L. *Bible Records: Genealogical Society of Cecil County.* Charlestown, Md.: By the Society, 1990.

———. *Naturalization Records of Cecil County, Maryland.* Charlestown, Md.: Cecil County Genealogical Society, n.d.

Cann, Joseph C. *History of St. Francis Xavier Church and Bohemia Plantation, now known as Old Bohemia, Warwick, Maryland.* Old Bohemia Historical Society's History Committee, 1976.

Carothers, Bettie S. *1783 Tax List of Maryland, Part 1: Cecil, Talbot, Harford, Calvert Counties.* Lutherville, Md.: By the compiler, 1977.

Cecil County: A Reference Book of History, Business and General Information. Baltimore: The County Directories of Maryland, Inc., 1956.

Cecil County Genealogical Society. *Index of the History of Cecil County, Maryland, by George Johnston.* Charlestown, Md.: By the Society, 1980.

———. *Newsletter.* Charlestown, Md.: By the Society, 1977–.

———. *Land Patents of Cecil County.* Silver Spring, Md.: Family Line Publications, 1986.

———. *Cecil County, Maryland Tombstone Inscriptions, Districts 7, 8 & 9.* Charlestown, Md.: By the Society, 1992.

———. *1860 Census of Cecil County.* Charlestown, Md.: By the Society.

———. *1752 Tax List of Cecil County.* Charlestown, Md.: By the Society.

———. *Index of Cecil County Wills and Administrations, 1674 to 1953.* Charlestown, Md.: By the Society.

Clark, Raymond B. Jr. *Index to Cecil County, Maryland, Wills, 1674–1777.* Arlington, Va.: 1981.

Daughters of the American Revolution in the State of Maryland, Captain

Jeremiah Baker Chapter. *Cecil County, Maryland Marriage Licenses 1777–1840*. Published by the DAR, 1928. Reprint, Baltimore: Genealogical Publishing Company, 1974.

Daughters of the American Revolution in the State of Maryland, Head of Elk Chapter. *Marriage Licenses of Cecil County, Maryland, 1840 to 1863*. By the DAR, 1955.

Gifford, George E. Jr. *Cecil County, Maryland, 1608–1850*. Rising Sun, Md.: Calvert School, 1974.

A Guide to Maryland State Archives Holdings of Cecil County Records on Microform. Annapolis: Maryland State Archives, 1989.

Hovermill, Harry A. *Indices to Cecil County, Maryland, Marriage Licenses, 1865–1885*. Charlestown, Md.: Cecil County Genealogical Society, 1982.

Johns, J. H. *A History of the Rock Presbyterian Church in Cecil County, Maryland*. Oxford, Pa.: Oxford Press & Job Office, 1872.

Johnston, George. *History of Cecil County, Maryland*. 1881 Reprinted by Regional Publishing Company in Baltimore. 1967, 1972, and 1989 with new index.

Lake, Griffing, & Stevenson. *An Illustrated Atlas of Cecil County, Maryland*. 1877 Reprint, Perryville, Md.: Lorain E. Alexander-Porter, 1982.

McCall, Darlene M, and Lorain E. Alexander-Porter. *Genealogical Research Guide for Cecil County, Maryland*. Charlestown, Md.: By the compilers, 1983.

Miller, Alice Etta. *Cecil County, Maryland, A Study in Local History*. Elkton, Md.: n.p., 1949. Reprint, Port Deposit, Md.: Port Deposit Heritage, Inc., n.d.

Peden, Henry C. Jr. *Early Anglican Church Records of Cecil County*. Westminster, Md.: Family Line Publications, 1990.

————. *Revolutionary Patriots of Cecil County, Maryland, 1775–1783*. Westminster, Md.: Family Line Publications, 1991.

————. *Inhabitants of Cecil County, 1649–1774*. Westminster, Md.: Family Line Publications, 1993.

Polk's Elkton – North East. Cecil County, Maryland City Directories: Including Cecil County Rural Residents. Richmond, Va.: R. L. Polk & Company, various years.

Portrait and Biographical Record of Harford and Cecil Counties, Maryland. New York, 1897. [The biographical portion was reprinted in 1994, with an index, by the Harford County Genealogical Society.]

Ragan, Nathan M. *Patent List: 7th District of Cecil County, Maryland, or North Susquehanna Hundred*. Charlestown, Md.: Cecil County Genealogical Society, 1988.

Ragan, Nathan M. and M. Frances Taylor. *Patent List: 8th District of Cecil County, Maryland, or Octoraro Hundred*. Charlestown, Md.: Cecil County Genealogical Society, 1986.

Wood, Jane E. *Index to Simon J. Martenet's 1850 Map of Cecil County, Maryland, Containing 2,500 Names and Residences*. North East, Md.: By the author, 1982.

Wright, F. Edward. *Maryland Militia, War of 1812*. Vol. 3, *Cecil & Harford Counties*. Silver Spring, Md.: Family Line Publications, 1980.

———. *Newspaper Abstracts of Cecil and Harford Counties, 1822–1830*. Silver Spring, Md.: Family Line Publications, 1984.

Charles County

(also see Southern Maryland)

Bates, Marlene Strawser and F. Edward Wright. *Early Charles County, Maryland Settlers, 1658–1745*. Westminster, Md.: Family Line Publications, 1995.

Bell, Annie W. Burns. *Index to Court Records, Charles County, Maryland*, 2 volumes. Annapolis, Md.: By the compiler, c1939.

———. *Index, Rent Rolls [of] Charles County, Maryland, 1642–1725*. Baltimore: By the compiler, 1942.

———. *Maryland Wills, Charles County Will Book Nos. 7–16, 1777–1850*. Annapolis, Md.: By the compiler, 1939.

Brown, Jack D., et al. *Charles County, Maryland: A History*. South Hackensack, N.J.: Custombook, 1976.

Clark, Raymond B. Jr. *Index to Charles County, Maryland Wills, 1658–1777*. Arlington, Va.: By the compiler, 1981.

A Guide to Maryland State Archives Holdings of Charles County Records on Microform. Annapolis: Maryland State Archives, 1989.

Jourdan, Elise Greenup. *Charles County Court and Land Records, 1658–1722*. 3 volumes. Westminster, Md.: Family Line Publications, 1993, 1994.

Keen, Gladys, et al. *Charles County, Maryland 1800 Census*. 1967. Reprint, Westminster, Md.: Family Line Publications, 1992.

Klapthor, Margaret Brown, and Paul Dennis Brown. *The History of Charles County, Maryland*. LaPlata, Md.: Charles County Tercentenary, Inc., 1958. [This volume contains the 1790 census of the county and a map.]

Newman, Harry Wright. *Charles County Gentry*. 1940. Reprint, Baltimore: Genealogical Publishing Company, 1971, 1997.

Peden, Henry C. Jr. *Revolutionary Patriots of Charles County, Maryland, 1775–1783*. Westminster, Md.: Family Line Publications, 1997.

Schaepman, Rona R., ed. *Charles County, Maryland: A History*. Leonardtown, Md.: Charles County Bicentennial Comm, 1976.

Stewart, Rose Marie, comp. *Charles County 1850 Census*. Oxon Hill, Md.: By the compiler, n.d.

Volkel, Charlotte A., Lowell M. Volkel, and Timothy Q. Wilson. "An Index to the 1800 Federal Census of Caroline, Cecil, Charles, Frederick, and Kent Counties, Maryland." Maryland Historical Society Library, 1968. [Typescript.]

Wearmouth, Roberta J. *Abstracts from the Port Tobacco Times and Charles County Advertiser, 1844–1875.* 3 volumes. Bowie, Md.: Heritage Books, Inc., 1990, 1991, 1993.

Wright, F. Edward. *Maryland Militia, War of 1812.* Vol. 5, *St. Mary's and Charles Counties.* Silver Spring, Md.: Family Line Publications, 1983.

Dorchester County

(also see Eastern Shore)

Arps, Walter E. Jr. *Before the Fire: Genealogical Gleanings from the Cambridge Chronicle, 1830–55.* Lutherville, Md.: Bettie S. Carothers, 1978.

Bell, Annie W. B. *Dorchester County Marriage Licenses, 1780–1843.* 2 volumes. Annapolis, Md.: By the compiler, 1939.

Clark, Raymond B. Jr. *Index to Dorchester County, Maryland, Wills, 1669–1777.* Arlington, Va.: By the compiler, 1982.

A Guide to Maryland State Archives Holdings of Dorchester County Records on Microform. Annapolis: Maryland State Archives, 1989.

Jones, Elias. *New Revised History of Dorchester County, Maryland.* Cambridge, Md.: Tidewater Publishing, 1966.

Marshall, Nellie M. *Tombstone Records of Dorchester County, Maryland, 1678–1964.* Cambridge, Md.: Dorchester County Historical Society, Inc., 1965.

———. *Additional Tombstone Records of Dorchester County, Maryland.* St. Michaels, Md.: Raymond B. Clark, 1982.

———. *Bible Records of Dorchester County, Maryland, 1612–1969 and Baptismal and Marriage Records, 1855–1866, Zion United Methodist Church, Cambridge, Maryland.* Cambridge, Md.: Dorchester County Historical Society, 1971.

McAllister, James A. Jr. *Abstracts from Land Records of Dorchester County, Maryland.* 17 volumes. Cambridge, Md.: By the compiler, 1960–64. *Supplementary Index.* volumes 1–10. n.d.

———. *Indian Lands in Dorchester County, Maryland.* Cambridge, Md.: By the compiler, 1962.

———. *Records of Choptank Parish, Dorchester County.* 3 volumes. Cambridge, Md.: By the compiler, 1968.

Mowbray, Calvin W. *First Dorchester Families.* 1984. Reprint, Westminster, Md.: Family Line Publications, 1991.

———. *The Dorchester County Fact Book: An Historical Survey of Churches,*

Mills, Post Offices, Transportation, and Revolutionary War Participants. Silver Spring, Md.: Family Line Publications, 1981.

Mowbray, Calvin W. and Mary I. Mowbray. *The Early Settlers of Dorchester County and Their Lands.* 2 volumes. Woolford, Md.: By the authors, 1981.

Mowbray, Calvin W. and Maurice D. Rimpo. *Close-ups of Early Dorchester County History.* Silver Spring, Md.: Family Line Publications, 1987.

Molisani, Jackie. *1860 Census of Dorchester County, Maryland.* Silver Spring, Md.: Family Line Publications, 1984.

Moxey, Debra Smith. *Dorchester Genealogical Magazine.* Madison, Md.: Dorchester County Historical Society, 1981–.

———. *1830 Census of Dorchester County, Maryland.* Silver Spring, Md.: Family Line Publications, 1984.

———. *1850 Census of Dorchester County, Maryland.* Westminster, Md.: Family Line Publications, 1984.

———. *Abstracts of Dorchester County Distributions, 1852–1885.* Madison, Md.: By the compiler, 1987.

Palmer, Katherine W. *Dorchester County, Maryland Marriage License Records, 1780–1855.* Cambridge, Md.: By the compiler, 1960.

Peden, Henry C. Jr. *Revolutionary Patriots of Dorchester County, Maryland, 1775–1783.* Westminster, Md.: Family Line Publications, 1998.

Price, Mrs. Hargis. "Dorchester County, Maryland 1800 Census," *Maryland Genealogical Society Bulletin.* Vols. 16 & 17 in 1976, 1977. Reprint, Westminster, Md.: Family Line Publications, ?????.

Skinner, V. L. *Other Wills in the Prerogative Court for Somerset and Dorchester Counties, 1664–1776.* Silver Spring, Md.: Family Line Publications, 1988.

Turner, Henry B. "Marriage Licenses Issued in Dorchester County, Maryland, 1790–1802." *The Publications of the Pennsylvania Genealogical Society,* 8: 252–60.

Volkel, Lowell M. and Timothy Q. Wilson. *Index to the 1800 Federal Census of Dorchester, Harford, Montgomery, Prince George's, and Queen Anne's Counties, State of Maryland.* Maryland Historical Society Library, 1968. [Typescript.]

Webster, Roger G. *Dorchester Memorial Park Cemetery.* Cambridge, Md.: By the compiler, 1982.

Eastern Shore

Barnes, Robert W, and F. Edward Wright. *Colonial Families of the Eastern Shore of Maryland.* Vols. 1–3. Westminster, Md.: Family Line Publications, 1996–97.

Carroll, Kenneth. *Joseph Nichols and the Nicholites*. Easton, Md.: Easton Publishing Company, 1962.

————. *Quakerism on the Eastern Shore*. Baltimore: Maryland Historical Society, 1970.

Chesapeake Cousins. Easton, Md.: Published by the Upper Shore Genealogical Society.

Christou, Christos, and F. Edward Wright. *Colonial Families of the Eastern Shore of Maryland*. Vol. 4. Westminster, Md.: Family Line Publications, 1998.

Clark, Charles B. *The Eastern Shore of Maryland and Virginia*. 3 volumes. New York, 1950.

Earle, Swepson. *Maryland's Colonial Eastern Shore: Historical Sketches of Counties and Some Notable Structures*. Baltimore, 1916.

More from the Shore. Salisbury, Md.: Lower Delmarva Genealogical Society, 1982– .

Peden, Henry C. Jr. *Revolutionary Patriots of Worcester & Somerset Counties, Maryland, 1775–1783*. Westminster, Md.: Family Line Publications, 1999.

Peden, Henry C. Jr. and F. Edward Wright. *Colonial Families of the Eastern Shore*. Vol. 5. Westminster, Md.: Family Line Publications, 1999.

————. *Colonial Families of the Eastern Shore*. Vol. 6. Westminster, Md.: Willow Bend Books & Family Line Publications, 1999.

————. *Colonial Families of the Eastern Shore*. Vol. 7. Westminster, Md.: Willow Bend Books, 2000.

————. *Colonial Families of the Eastern Shore*. Vol. 8. Westminster, Md.: Willow Bend Books, 2000.

————. *Colonial Families of the Eastern Shore*. Vol. 9. Lewes Del.: Delmarva Roots, 2000.

Peterman, Thomas Joseph. *Catholics in Colonial Delmarva*. Devon, Pa.: Cooke Publishing Company, 1996.

Portrait & Biographical Record of the Eastern Shore of Maryland. New York: n.p., 1898.

Preston, Dixon J. *Newspapers of the Eastern Shore*. Queenstown, Md.: Queen Anne Press and Centreville, Md.: Tidewater Publishers, 1968.

Priesler, Julian H. *Jewish Cemeteries of the Delmarva Peninsula*. Westminster, Md.: Family Line Publications, 1995.

Pritchett, Morgan and Susan R. Woodcock. *The Eastern Shore of Maryland: An Annotated Bibliography*. Queenstown, Md.: Queen Anne Press, 1980.

Riley, Janet. *Eastern Shore Mortality Schedules*. 2 volumes. 1870, 1880.

Skinner, Vernon L. and F. Edward Wright. *Colonial Families of the Eastern Shore*. Vol. 10. Lewes Del.: Delmarva Roots, 2000.

Upper Shore Genealogical Society of Maryland. See *"Chesapeake Cousins."*

Wicomico Bicentennial Commission. *The 1877 Atlases and Other Early Maps of the Eastern Shore of Maryland*. Salisbury, Md.: By the Commission, 1976.

Wright, F. Edward. *Marriages & Deaths of the Lower Delmarva, 1835–1840.* Silver Spring, Md.: Family Line Publications, 1987. [These notices were collected from the newspapers of Dorchester, Somerset, and Worcester Counties, Md.]

———. *Citizens of the Eastern Shore of Maryland, 1659–1750.* Silver Spring, Md.: Family Line Publications, 1986.

———. *Maryland Militia, War of 1812.* Vol. 1, *Eastern Shore.* Silver Spring, Md.: Family Line Publications, 1979.

———. *Maryland Eastern Shore Newspaper Abstracts, 1790–1834.* 8 volumes. Silver Spring, Md.: Family Line Publications, 1981–85.

———. *Vital Records of the Jesuit Missions of the Eastern Shore, 1760–1800.* Silver Spring, Md.: Family Line Publications, 1986.

———. *Maryland Eastern Shore Vital Records, 1648–1825.* 5 volumes. Silver Spring, Md.: Family Line Publications, 1982–86. [All extant church records for counties of Kent, Queen Anne's, Caroline, Talbot, Dorchester, Somerset, and Worcester to date. Volumes 3 and 4 do not include Catholic records contained in *Vital Records of the Jesuit Missions.*]

———. *Sketches of Maryland Eastern Shoremen.* Silver Spring, Md.: Family Line Publications, 1985, 1988.

Frederick County

(also see Western Maryland)

Andersen, Patricia Abelard. *Frederick County, Maryland Land Records, 1748–1768.* [Libers B through K] 6 volumes. Gaithersburg, Md.: GenLaw Resources, 1995–97.

Barnes, Robert W. "Marriages and Deaths, 1802–1815, from the *Fredericktown Herald.*" Maryland Historical Society, 1970. [Typescript.]

Bodner, Nancy Willmann. *Buckey's Town, A Village Remembered.* Buckeystown, Md.: By the author, 1984.

Bolin, Coral Gordon. *Records of the Lutheran Congregation of the Saint Peter's Church, Woodsboro, Frederick County, Maryland, 1767–1857.* Baltimore, 1962.

Bond, Isaac. *Map of Frederick County, Maryland.* Baltimore: E. Sachse, 1853.

Cavey, Kathleen Tull-Burton. *Tombstones and Beyond: Prospect United Methodist Church and Cemetery and Marvin Chapel Church and Cemetery.* Westminster, Md.: Family Line Publications, 1995. [This volume includes Jacob M. Holdcraft's field records and caretakers' records.]

Clark, Raymond B. Jr. "Frederick County, Maryland, Naturalizations, 1787–1799." *The Maryland & Delaware Genealogist,* 6: 16–18, 37–39, 58–59, 80–81.

———. *Frederick County, Maryland, Naturalizations, 1799–1850*. St. Michaels, Md.: By the author, 1974.

———. *Index to Frederick County, Maryland, Wills, 1748–1777*. Arlington, Va.: By the author, 1982.

Eader, Edith Olivia, and Trudie Davis-Long. *The Jacob Engelbrecht Marriage Ledger of Frederick County, Maryland, 1820–1890*. Monrovia, Md.: Paw Prints, Inc., 1994.

———. *The Jacob Engelbrecht Death Ledger of Frederick County, Maryland, 1820–1890*. Monrovia, Md.: Paw Prints, Inc., 1995.

———. *The Jacob Engelbrecht Property and Almshouse Ledgers of Frederick, Maryland*. Monrovia, Md.: Paw Prints, 1996.

Flowers, Susanne Files. *Frederick County, Maryland, Will Index, 1744–1946*. Monrovia, Md.: Paw Prints, Inc., 1998.

Fogle, Patricia A. *Baptisms, Marriages, and Burials: A Compilation of the Records Kept by the Pastors of Christ Reformed Church, Middletown, Maryland, 1830–1966*. Middletown, Md.: By the author, 1996.

———. *Lutheran Congregation of Zion Church, Middletown, Maryland: Pastoral Records of Baptisms, Marriages, and Burials, 1780–1996*. Middletown, Md.: By the author, 1997.

———. *A Time to Live and a Time to Die: A Census of the Graves and Stones in the Christ Reformed, United Church of Christ, Cemetery, Middletown, Maryland*. Middletown, Md.: By the author, 1997.

———. *Names from the Past: A Compilation of the Reading of Tombstones in the Old Union Cemetery, the Jefferson United Church of Christ, Old Reformed Cemetery, and the St. Paul's Lutheran Cemetery, Jefferson, Frederick County, Maryland*. Middletown, Md.: By the author, 1998.

———. *Pastoral Records of the Jefferson and Feagaville Lutheran Parishes, Frederick County, Maryland, 1850–1998*. Middletown, Md.: By the author, 1998.

Frederick Directory: City Guide and Business Mirror, 1859–. Reprint, Silver Spring Md.: Family Line Publications, 1985 [Without advertisements.]

Gilland, Steve. *Early Families of Frederick County, Maryland and Adams County, Pennsylvania*. Westminster, Md.: Family Line Publications, 1997.

———. *Frederick County Backgrounds*. Westminster, Md.: Family Line Publications, 1995. [This volume contains articles about early residents published in Emmitsburg's *Chronicle* in the 1930s and 1940s.]

Gordon, Paul P. *The Jews Beneath the Clustered Spires*. Hagerstown, Md.: Hagerstown Bookbinding & Printing Company, 1971.

Grove, William J. *History of Carrollton Manor, Frederick County, Maryland*. Lime Kiln, Md., 1928.

A Guide to Maryland State Archives Holdings of Frederick County Records on Microform. Annapolis: Maryland State Archives, 1989.

Hinke, William J. and E. W. Reinecke. *Records of the Evangelical Church in Frederick, Maryland, 1746–1800.* Silver Spring, Md.: Family Line Publications, 1986.

Helfenstein, Ernest. *History of All Saints Parish in Frederick County, Maryland, 1742–1932.* Frederick, Md., 1932.

Helman, James A. *A History of Emmitsburg, Maryland.* 1906. Reprint, by Frederick, Md.: Chronicle Press, 1975.

Hiatt, Marty. *Early Church Records of Loudoun County, Virginia, 1745–1800.* Westminster, Md.: Family Line Publications, 1995. [This volume contains many references to people from Frederick County, Maryland.]

Hitselberger, Mary F. and John P. Dern. *A Bridge in Time: The Complete 1850 Census of Frederick County, Maryland.* Redwood City, Calif.: Monocacy Books, 1978.

Holdcraft, Jacob Mehrling. *Names in Stone: 75,000 Cemetery Inscriptions from Frederick County, MD.* 2 volumes. 1966 Reprint, Redwood City, Calif.: Monocacy Books, 1972.

———. *More Names in Stone.* Redwood City, Calif.: Monocacy Books, 1972.

Jefferson United Church of Christ Historical Committee. *A Listing of the Members of the Jefferson United Church of Christ, 1823– September, 1997.* Jefferson, Md.: By the Church's Historical Committee, 1998.

Keiffer, Elizabeth C. *Baptismal Records of Apple's Church. Lutheran and Reformed Near Thurmont, Maryland, 1773–1848.* Hudson, Wis.: Star Observer Print, 1963.

Lake, D. J. *Atlas of Frederick County, Maryland.* 1873. Reprint, Evansville, Ind.: Unigraphic, 1976.

Mallick, Sallie A. and F. Edward Wright. *Frederick County Militia in the War of 1812.* Westminster, Md.: Family Line Publications, 1992.

Miller, Edith. "Maryland Marriage Licenses, 1778–1800, Recorded in Frederick County, Maryland." *Daughters of the American Revolution Magazine,* 85: 61. Washington, D.C.: By the DAR, 1951.

Moore, L. Tilden. *Index to the Administration Account Records of Frederick County, Maryland, 1750–1816.* Westminster, Md.: Family Line Publications, 1996.

———. *Abstracts of Marriages and Deaths and Other Articles of Interest in the Newspapers of Frederick and Montgomery Counties, Maryland, 1831–1840.* Westminster, Md.: Family Line Publications, 1991.

Myers, Margaret E. *Marriage Licenses of Frederick County, Maryland, 1778–1865.* 3 volumes. Westminster, Md.: Family Line Publications, 1986–88, 1997.

———. *Myersville, Maryland, Lutheran Baptisms 1832–1849, 1861–1897: St. John's. Church Hill; St. Mark's. Wolfs-ville; St. Paul's, Myersville.* Middletown, Md.: Catoctin Press, 1986.

———. *Births and Baptisms from Evangelical Lutheran Church, Frederick,*

Maryland, October 21, 1848 to December 26, 1855. Frederick, Md.: By the author, 1998.

Oerter, Rev. A. L. "The History of Graceham, Frederick County, Maryland." Printed as part of Vol. 9 of *Transactions of the Moravian Historical Society*. Bethlehem, Pa., 1913.

Peden, Henry C. Jr. *Revolutionary Patriots of Frederick County, Maryland, 1775–1783*. Westminster, Md.: Family Line Publications, 1995.

Phillips, Hugh J. *The Catholic Settlement in the Monocacy Valley*. Emmitsburg, Md.: Mount St. Mary's College, 1976.

Polk's Frederick, Maryland, City Directory: Rural Routes. Baltimore: R. L. Polk & Company, various years.

Ranck, James B., et al. *A History of the Evangelical Reformed Church, Frederick, Maryland*. Frederick, Md.: n.p., 1964.

Reed, Amy Lee Huffman, and Marie LaForge Burns. *In and Out of Frederick County: Colonial Occupations*. Frederick, Md.: By the authors, 1985.

Rice, Millard Milburn. *New Facts and Old Families from the Records of Frederick County, Maryland*. Redwood City, Calif.: Monocacy Books, 1976.

————. *This was the Life: Excerpts from the Judgment Records of Frederick County, Maryland, 1748–1765*. Redwood City, Calif.: Monocacy Book Company, 1979.

Russell, Donna Valley. *Frederick County, Maryland, Genealogical Research Guide*. Middletown, Md.: Catoctin Press, 1987, revised 1991.

Scharf, J. Thomas. *History of Western Maryland, Being a History of Frederick, Montgomery, Carroll, Washington, Allegany and Garrett Counties*. 2 volumes. 1882. Reprint, Baltimore: Regional Publishing Company, 1968. [For indices to each county, see "Western Maryland."]

Schildknecht, C. E., ed. *Monocacy and Catoctin: Some Early Settlers of Frederick and Carroll County, Maryland and Adams County, Pennsylvania*. 3 volumes. Gettysburg, Pa.: By the author, 1985, 1989, 1994.

Schultz, Edward T. *First Settlements of Germans in Maryland*. 1896. Reprint, Miami, Fla.: Ethra, Inc., 1976.

Seubold, Helen W. and Frank H. "Frederick County, Maryland 1800 Census." *Maryland Genealogical Society Bulletin*, 18: 60–166. Baltimore: Maryland Genealogical Society, 1977. Reprint, Westminster, Md.: Family Line Publications, 1992. [This is the only complete 1800 census available to the public. Two pages of the original are missing from the microfilm copy by the National Archives.]

Shaffer, Stefanie R. *Inhabitants of Frederick, Maryland*. Vol. 1, *1750–1790*. Westminster, Md.: Family Line Publications, 1998.

Tracey, Grace L. and John P. Dern. *Pioneers of Old Monocacy: The Early Settlements of Frederick County, Maryland, 1721–1743*. Baltimore: Genealogical Publishing Company, 1987, 1998.

Varle Map of Frederick & Washington Counties. Reprint, of Charles Varle's 1808 map by Frederick County Landmarks Foundation, 1990.

Volkel, Charlotte A., Lowell M., Volkel, and Timothy Q. Wilson. "An Index to the 1800 Federal Census of Caroline, Cecil, Charles, Frederick, and Kent Counties, Maryland." Maryland Historical Society Library, 1968. [Typescript.]

Weiser, Frederick S. *Records of Marriages and Burials in the Monocacy Church in Frederick County, Maryland in the Evangelical Congregation in the City of Frederick, Maryland, 1743–1811.* Washington, D.C.: National Genealogical Society, 1972.

Weiser, Frederick S., editor and translator. *Maryland German Church Records.* Vol. 1, *Christ Reformed Church of Middletown, Maryland, 1770–1840.* Manchester, Md.: Noodle-Doosey Press, 1986.

Weiser, Frederick S. editor and Charles T. Zahn, translator. *Maryland German Church Records.* Vol. 2, *Zion Lutheran Church, Middletown, Maryland, 1781–1826.* Manchester, Md.: Noodle-Doosey Press, 1987.

Weiser, Frederick S., editor and translator. *Maryland German Church Records.* Vol. 3, *Monocacy Lutheran Congregation and Evangelical Lutheran Church Baptisms 1742–1779, Frederick, Maryland.* Manchester, Md.: Noodle-Doosey Press, 1987.

———. *Maryland German Church Records.* Vol. 4, *Evangelical Lutheran Church, Frederick, Frederick County, Maryland, Baptisms, 1780–1811.* Westminster, Md.: Historical Society of Carroll County, 1989.

Weiser, Frederick S., editor and William J. Hinke, translator. *Maryland German Church Records.* Vol. 5, *Evangelical Reformed Church, Frederick, Frederick County, Maryland, 1746–1789.* Westminster, Md.: Historical Society of Carroll County, 1991.

———. *Maryland German Church Records.* Vol. 6, *Evangelical Reformed Church, Frederick, Frederick County, Maryland, 1790–1828.* Westminster, Md.: Historical Society of Carroll County, 1992.

Weiser, Frederick Sheely and W. E. Hutchinson. *Frederick Evangelical Lutheran Church, Frederick, Maryland, Parish Records, Books I and II, 1743–1811.* 2 volumes. Gettysburg, Pa.: A. R. Wentz Library, Lutheran Theological Seminary, 1969.

Weiser, Frederick S. *Maryland German Church Records. Volume 11: Apple's Church near Thurmont, Frederick County, Maryland, Lutheran and Reformed Records, 1773–1849, Union Church, Creagerstown, Frederick County, Maryland, Lutheran and Reformed Records, 1789–1863.* Westminster, Md.: Historical Society of Carroll County, 1996.

———. *Maryland German Church Records. Vol. 16, St. Peter's Lutheran Church, now Grace Lutheran Church, near Woodsboro, 1767–1854; Glade Ref. Church, now the Glade United Church of Christ, Walkersville, 1769–1836; Mount Zion Lutheran and Reformed Church formerly St. Paul and St.*

Matthias Church, 1798–1834. Westminster, Md.: Family Line Publications, 1998.

————. *Marriages & Burials from the Frederick, Maryland, Evangelical Lutheran Church, 1743–1811*. n. p. 1972.

Wentz, Abdel Ross. *History of the Evangelical Lutheran Church of Frederick, Maryland, 1738–1938*. Harrisburg, Pa., 1938.

Williams, C. S. *Williams' Frederick Directory, City Guide and Business Mirror.* Vol. 1, *1859–1860*. Reprint, Westminster, Md.: Family Line Publications, 1985.

Williams, T. J. C. and Folger McKinsey. *History of Frederick County, Maryland*. 2 volumes. 1910. Reprint, Baltimore: Regional Publishing Company, 1967, 1997. [Surname index to book by Jacob Mehrling Holdcraft. Baltimore, 1936.]

Wireman, George W. *Gateway to the Mountains*. Hagerstown, Md., 1969.

Wright, F. Edward. *Early Lists of Frederick Countians, 1765–1775*. Silver Spring, Md.: Family Line Publications, 1986.

————. *Marriages and Deaths in Newspapers of Frederick and Montgomery Counties, Maryland, 1820–1830*. Silver Spring, Md.: Family Line Publications, 1987.

————. *Newspaper Abstracts of Frederick County, 1811–1819*, 2 volumes. Westminster, Md.: Family Line Publications, 1992, 1993.

Young, Henry James. *The Moravian Families of Graceham, Maryland, 1759–1871*. 1942. Reprint, Westminster, Md.: Family Line Publications, 1988, 1998.

Garrett County

(also see Western Maryland)

The Bloomington Story. Keyser, W. Va.: Keyprint, Bloomington Bicentennial Commission, 1976.

Daughters of the American Revolution, Youghiogheny Glades Chapter. *Maryland's Garrett County Graves*. Oakland, Md., and Parsons, W. Va.: McClain Printing Company, 1987.

Garrett County Historical Society. *Hoye's Pioneer Families of Garrett County*. Oakland, Md.: By the Society, 1988.

The Glades Star. Oakland, Md.: Garrett County Historical Society, 1941.

Gude, Gilbert. *Where the Potomac Begins: A History of the North Branch Valley*. Cabin John, Md.: Seven Locks Press, 1984.

A Guide to Maryland State Archives Holdings of Garrett County Records on Microform. Annapolis: Maryland State Archives, 1989.

Historical Records Survey, WPA. *Inventory of the County and Town Archives of Maryland, No. 11, Garrett County*. Baltimore, 1938.

Hume, Joan, editor. *Index to Wills of Garrett County, 1872–1960, and Harford County, 1774–1960*. Baltimore: Magna Carta Book Co., 1970.

Michael, D. O., compiler and ed. *Western Maryland Materials in Allegany and Garrett County Libraries.* Cumberland, Md.: Allegany County Local History Program, 1977.

Olson, Evelyn Guard. *Indian Blood.* Parsons, W. Va.: McClain Printing Company, 1967. [This includes a history of Pennsylvania counties and Garrett County, Maryland, with brief history of Indian dealings.]

Scharf, J. Thomas. *History of Western Maryland, Being a History of Frederick, Montgomery, Carroll, Washington, Allegany and Garrett Counties.* 2 volumes. 1882. Reprint, Baltimore: Regional Publishing Company, 1968. [For indices see Western Maryland section.]

Schlosnagle, Stephen. *Garrett County, A History of Maryland's Tableland.* Oakland, Md.: Garrett County Bicentennial Commission, 1978.

Weeks, Thekla Fundenberg. *Oakland, Garrett County, Maryland, Centennial History, 1849–1949.* Oakland, Md.: Oakland Centennial Commission, 1949.

Harford County

Biographical Records of Harford and Cecil Counties, Maryland. 1897. Reprint of the biographies with a new index by the Harford County Genealogical Society. Westminster, Md.: Family Line Publications, 1989.

Bishop, Margaret S. *Index to Naturalization Records of Harford County, Maryland.* 2 volumes. Aberdeen, Md.: Harford County Genealogical Society, 1991.

Carothers, Bettie S. *Index to the 1810 Federal Census of Harford County, Maryland.* Chesterfield, Mo.: By the author, 1972.

Davis, Helene M. *Abstracts of Death Certificates from Files of Herbert S. Bailey, Funeral Director, Darlington, Maryland, 1921–1961.* 2 volumes. Aberdeen, Md.: Harford County Genealogical Society, 1990.

A Guide to Maryland State Archives Holdings of Harford County Records on Microform. Annapolis: Maryland State Archives, 1989.

Harford County Directory. Baltimore: State Directories Publishing Company, 1953.

Harford County Genealogical Society Newsletter. Aberdeen, Md.: Published by the Society, 1979– .

Harford County 1783 Maryland Tax List from the Collections of the Maryland Historical Society. Philadelphia, 1970.

Hume, Joan, ed. *Index to Wills of Garrett County, 1872–1960, and Harford County, 1774–1960.* Baltimore, 1970.

Joerndt, Clarence V. *St. Ignatius, Hickory, and Its Missions.* Baltimore: Publication Press, 1972.

Livezey, Jon Harlan. *United States Census of 1900 for Town and Precinct of Aberdeen, Harford County, Maryland.* Aberdeen, Md.: Harford County Genealogical Society, 1993.

———. *1831 Tax List for Harford County, Maryland.* Aberdeen, Md.: Harford County Genealogical Society, 1995.

———. *United States Census of 1880 for Churchville Precinct, Third Election District, Harford County, Maryland.* Aberdeen, Md.: Harford County Genealogical Society, 1999.

Livezey, Jon Harlan and Helene Maynard Davis. *Harford County Marriage Licenses, 1777–1865.* Westminster, Md.: Family Line Publications, 1993.

Mason, Samuel Jr. *Historical Sketches of Harford County, Maryland.* Darlington, Md.: Little Pines Farm, 1955.

Meyer, Mary K. *Free Blacks in Harford, Somerset and Talbot Counties, Maryland, 1832.* Finksburg, Md.: Pipe Creek Publications, 1991.

Morgan, Ralph H. Jr. *Harford County Wills, 1774–1800.* Westminster, Md.: Family Line Publications, 1990.

Peden, Henry C. Jr. *Abstracts of the Orphans Court Proceedings of Harford County, Maryland, 1778–1800.* Westminster, Md.: Family Line Publications, 1990.

———. *Revolutionary Patriots of Harford County, Maryland, 1775–1783.* Bel Air, Md.: By the author, 1985; repr. 1986; rev. 1987. Reprint, Westminster, Md.: Family Line Publications, 1991.

———. *St. John's & St. George's Parish Registers, 1696–1851, Baltimore and Harford Counties, Maryland.* Silver Spring, Md.: Family Line Publications, 1987.

———. *Heirs and Legatees of Harford County, Maryland, 1774–1802.* Westminster, Md.: Family Line Publications, 1989.

———. *Heirs and Legatees of Harford County, Maryland, 1802–1846.* Westminster, Md.: Family Line Publications, 1988.

———. *Early Harford Countians.* Westminster, Md.: Family Line Publications, 1993. Reprint, Westminster, Md.: Willow Bend Books, 1999. [In three parts: Vol. 1, A–K, Vol. 2, L–Z, Vol. 3, Supplement.]

———. *Harford County Children: Indentures and Guardianships, 1801–1830.* Westminster, Md.: Family Line Publications, 1994.

———. *Harford County Taxpayers in 1870, 1872, and 1883.* Aberdeen, Md.: Harford County Genealogical Society, 1992.

———. *A Medical Ledger of Dr. John Archer of Harford County, Maryland, 1786–1796.* Aberdeen, Md.: Harford County Genealogical Society, 1992.

———. *Dr. John Archer's First Medical Ledger, 1767–1769.* Aberdeen, Md.: Harford County Genealogical Society, 1997.

———. *A Survey Field Book of David and William Clark in Harford County, Maryland, 1770–1812.* Aberdeen, Md.: Harford County Genealogical Society, 1998.

————. *Abstracts of the Ledgers and Accounts of the Bush Store and Rock Run Store, 1759–1771.* Aberdeen, Md.: Harford County Genealogical Society, 1999.

————. *Harford County, Maryland, Divorce Cases, 1827–1912: An Annotated Index.* Bel Air, Md.: By the author, 1999.

————. *Union Chapel United Methodist Church Cemetery Tombstone Inscriptions, Wilna, Harford County, Maryland.* Bel Air, Md.: By the author, 1999.

————. *Inhabitants of Harford County, Maryland, 1791–1800.* Westminster, Md.: Willow Bend Books, 1999.

————. *Bible and Family Records of Harford County, Maryland.* 2 volumes. Aberdeen Md.: Harford County Genealogical Society, 1996, 2000.

Polk's Aberdeen – Havre de Grace. Harford County City Directory. Richmond, Va.: R. L. Polk & Company, various years.

Portrait and Biographical Record of Harford and Cecil Counties, Maryland. New York, 1897.

Preston, Walter W. *History of Harford County, Maryland, from 1608 to the close of the War of 1812.* 1901. Reprint, Baltimore: Regional Publishing Company, 1972. Reprint, Westminster, Md.: Family Line Publications, 1988. [With an added index of names by the Harford County Genealogical Society.]

Randers–Pehrson, Glenn. *Index to Herrick's 1858 Map of Harford County, Maryland.* Aberdeen, Md.: Harford County Genealogical Society, 1991.

————. *Harford Circuit of the Methodist Church: Birth and Marriage Register, 1809–1815, and Minutes of the Quarterly Conferences, 1831–1842.* Aberdeen, Md.: Harford County Genealogical Society, 1994.

————. *Deaths and Marriages in Harford County, Maryland and Vicinity, 1873–1904.* Aberdeen, Md.: Harford County Genealogical Society, 1995.

Reamy, Bill and Martha Reamy. *St. George's Parish Registers, 1689–1793.* Silver Spring, Md.: Family Line Publications, 1988.

Reightler, Shirley L. *Death Notices from The Bel Air Times, 1882–1899.* Aberdeen, Md: Harford County Genealogical Society, 1987.

————. *Bible and Family Records of Harford County, Maryland.* 2 volumes. Aberdeen, Md.: Harford County Genealogical Society, 1988–89.

————. *Illegitimate Children of Harford County, Maryland, 1800–1900: From the Minutes Books of the Harford County Circuit Court.* Aberdeen, Md.: Harford County Genealogical Society, 1993.

Rowe, Ella. *1800 Census of Harford County, Maryland.* Baltimore: Maryland Genealogical Society, 1972. Reprint, Westminster, Md.: Family Line Publications, 1992.

Turner, Joseph Brown. "Marriage Licenses Issued in Harford County, Maryland, 1779–1838." *The Publications of the Pennsylvania Genealogical Society,* 8 (March 1922): 151–63. Philadelphia: Pennsylvania Genealogical Society, 1922.

Volkel, Lowell M. and Timothy Q. Wilson. "An Index to the 1800 Federal Census of Dorchester, Harford, Montgomery, Prince George's and Queen Anne's Counties, State of Maryland." Maryland Historical Society Library, 1968. [Typescript.]

Wright, C. Milton. *Our Harford Heritage: A History of Harford County, Maryland.* Glen Burnie, Md.: French-Bray Printing Company, 1967.

Wright, F. Edward. *Maryland Militia, War of 1812.* Vol. 3, *Cecil and Harford Counties.* Silver Spring, Md.: Family Line Publications, 1980.

————. *Newspaper Abstracts of Cecil and Harford Counties, 1822–1830.* Silver Spring, Md.: Family Line Publications, 1984, 1995.

Howard County

Daughters of the American Revolution, Colonel Thomas Dorsey Chapter. "Marriage Licenses in Howard District of Anne Arundel County, 1840–1851." Maryland Historical Society Library, 1966. [Typescript.]

Daughters of the American Revolution, Colonel Thomas Dorsey Chapter. "Tombstone Inscriptions of a few Cemeteries in Howard County, Maryland." Maryland Historical Society Library, 1960. [Typescript.]

The Family Tree. Columbia, Md.: Howard County Genealogical Society, 1977–.

Filby, Vera Ruth. *Savage, Maryland.* Savage, Md., 1964.

A Guide to Maryland State Archives Holdings of Howard County Records on Microform. Annapolis: Maryland State Archives, 1989.

Historical Records Survey, WPA. *Inventory of the County and Town Archives of Maryland. No. 13, Howard County.* Baltimore, 1939.

Holland, Celia. *Ellicott City, Maryland, Mill-town, U.S.A.* University Park, Md.: By the author, 1970.

Hopkins, G. M. *Atlas of Fifteen Miles Around Baltimore, Including Howard County, Maryland.* 1878. Reprint, Ellicott City, Md.: Howard County Bicentennial Commission, 1975. [This volume has an index by Anita Cushing.]

Howard County Genealogical Society. *Howard County, Maryland Records.* Vol. 1, *Cemeteries.* Columbia, Md.: By the Society, 1979.

————. *Howard County, Maryland Records.* Vol. 2, *More Cemeteries.* Columbia, Md.: By the Society, 1981.

————. *Howard County, Maryland Records.* Vol. 3, *Even More Cemeteries.* Columbia, Md.: By the Society, 1982.

————. *Howard County, Maryland Records.* Vol. 4, *Additional Cemeteries Plus Manumission Records.* Columbia, Md.: By the Society, 1985.

————. *Howard County, Maryland Records.* Vol. 5, *More Cemetery Inscriptions*

Plus Family Bible Data. Columbia, Md.: By the Society, 1985.

———. *Howard County, Maryland Records*. Vol. 6, *A Continuation of Howard County Cemetery Inscriptions*. Columbia, Md.: By the Society, 1988.

———. *Howard County, Maryland Records*. Vol. 7, *St. John's Cemetery Inscriptions from St. John's Episcopal Church, Columbarian*. Columbia, Md.: By the Society, 1991.

Hume, Joan, ed. *Maryland: Index to the Wills of Howard County, 1840–1950: Kent County 1642–1960*. Baltimore: Magna Carta Book Co., 1970.

Stein, Charles F. Jr. *Origin and History of Howard County, Maryland*. Baltimore: By the author, 1972.

Tyson, Martha Ellicott. *A Brief Account of the Settlement of Ellicott's Mills*. Baltimore: J. Murphy, 1871.

Warfield, J. D. *The Founders of Anne Arundel and Howard Counties, Maryland*. 1905. Reprint, Baltimore: Regional Publishing Company, 1967; Westminster, Md.: Family Line Publications, 1990.

Zimmerman, Kenneth Edwin. *Guide to Research in Howard County, Maryland*. Woodstock, Md.: By the author, 1997.

Kent County

(also see Eastern Shore)

Bell, Annie W. B. *Shrewsbury Parish Register, Kent County, Maryland*. Annapolis, Md.: By the author, 1939.

Buckey, Ethel Close. *Kent County, Maryland and Vicinity, List of Militia and Oaths of Allegiance, June, 1775*. 1948. Reprint, Westminster, Md.: Family Line Publications, 1985.

Christou, Christos, and John A. Barnhouser. *Abstracts of Kent County, Maryland Wills, 1777–1816*. 2 volumes. Westminster, Md.: Family Line Publications, 1997.

Clark, Raymond B. Jr. *Index to Kent County, Maryland Wills, 1642–1777*. Arlington, Va.: By the author, 1982.

Clark, Sara Seth and Raymond B. Clark Jr. *Kent County, Maryland, Marriage Licenses, 1799–1850*. St. Michaels, Md.: By the authors, 1972.

Cooper, Carolyn E. *Worton Gleanings: A History of Union M. E. Church and Development of the Area, [at] Worton, Maryland*. Silver Spring, Md.: Family Line Publications, 1983.

Denroche, Chris T. *A Souvenir History of the Parish of St. Paul's, Kent County, Maryland*. Chestertown, Md.: Chestertown Transcript Steam Book Print, 1893.

Hanson, George A. *Old Kent: The Eastern Shore of Maryland*. 1876. Reprint, Baltimore: Regional Publishing Company, 1967, 1996.

Historic Graves, Private Burial Grounds, and Cemeteries of Kent County,

Maryland: Gone But Not Forgotten. Silver Spring, Md.: Family Line Publications, 1985, 1997. [Compiled by Historical Society of Kent County members, 1969–72.]

Hume, Joan, ed. *Maryland: Index to the Wills of Howard County, 1840–1950: Kent County 1642–1960.* Baltimore: Magna Carta Book Co., 1970.

Hynson, Jerry M. *The African-American Collection.* Vol. 1, *Kent County, Maryland.* Westminster, Md.: Family Line Publications, 1998.

————. *Maryland Freedom Papers,* Vol. 2, *Kent County.* Westminster, Md.: Family Line Publications, 1997.

Keeney, Floretta J. *1800 Census of Kent County, Maryland.* Baltimore: Maryland Genealogical Society. Reprint, Westminster, Md.: Family Line Publications, 1992.

Lake, Griffing, & Stevenson. *An Illustrated Atlas of Kent and Queen Anne Counties, Maryland.* Philadelphia: Lake, Griffing, & Stevenson, 1877.

Peden, Henry C. Jr. *Revolutionary Patriots of Kent and Queen Anne's Counties, Maryland, 1775–1783.* Westminster, Md.: Family Line Publications, 1995.

————. *Inhabitants of Kent County, Maryland, 1637–1787.* Westminster, Md.: Family Line Publications, 1994.

Volkel, Charlotte A., Lowell M. Volkel, and Timothy Q. Wilson. "An Index to the 1800 Federal Census of Caroline, Cecil, Charles, Frederick and Kent Counties, State of Maryland." Maryland Historical Society Library, 1967. [Typescript.]

Montgomery County

Annals of Sandy Spring: History or History of a Rural Community in Maryland. 4 volumes. Baltimore: Cushings & Bailey, 1884–1929. [Volume 2 was published by Thomas & Evans, Baltimore. Volume 3 was published by King Brothers, Baltimore. Volume 4 was published by Times Printing Company, Westminster, Md.]

Ball, Walter V. *The History of Mount Pleasant.* Rockville, Md.: Montgomery County Historical Society, 1977.

Barrow, Healan, and Kristine Stevens. *Olney: Echoes of the Past.* Westminster, Md.: Family Line Publications, 1994.

Bell, Annie W. B. *Saint Peter's Parish, Montgomery County, Maryland, Register of Births and Baptisms, 1797–1854.* Baltimore: By the author, 1940.

————. *Index to the Register of Births, Marriages, and Deaths in Prince George's Parish, Montgomery County, Maryland.* By the author, n.p., n.d.

Bowman, Tressie Nash. *Montgomery County, Maryland, Marriage Licenses Issued, 1796–1850.* Rockville, Md., 1966.

Boyd, Thomas H. S. *History of Montgomery County, Maryland from Its Earliest Settlement in 1650 to 1879*. 1879. Reprint, Baltimore: Regional Publishing Company, 1968, 1972.

Carothers, Bettie Sterling. *Index to the 1810 Federal Census of Montgomery County, Maryland*. Chesterfield, Mo., 1972.

Cook, Eleanor M. V. *Guide to the Records of Montgomery County: Genealogical and Historical*. Westminster, Md.: Family Line Publications, 1989, revised, 1997.

Cuttler, Dona Lou. *The History of Hyattstown, Maryland*. Bowie, Md.: Heritage Books, Inc., 1998.

———. *The Cemeteries of Hyattstown*. Bowie, Md.: Heritage Books, Inc., 1999.

———. *The History of Comus*. Bowie, Md.: Heritage Books, Inc., 1999.

Cuttler, Dona Lou and Ida Lu Brown. *The History of Barnesville and Sellman, Maryland*. Bowie, Md.: Heritage Books, Inc., 1999.

Duffy, C. E. Mrs. *Montgomery County 1800 Census*. 1972. Reprint, Westminster, Md.: Family Line Publications, 1992.

Farquhar, Roger Brooke. *Old Homes and History of Montgomery County, Maryland*. 1952 Rev. Silver Spring, Md., 1962.

———. *Annals of Sandy Spring or 20 Years History of a Rural Community in Maryland*. Volume 1. Baltimore: Cushing & Bailey, 1884.

Frain, Elizabeth. *Monocacy Cemetery, Bealls-ville, Maryland*. Westminster, Md.: Family Line Publications, 1997.

A Guide to Maryland State Archives Holdings of Montgomery County Records on Microform. Annapolis: Maryland State Archives, 1989.

Heibert, Ray Eldon and Richard K. MacMaster. *A Grateful Remembrance: The Story of Montgomery County, Maryland*. Rockville, Md.: Montgomery County Government and Montgomery County Historical Society, 1976.

Historical Records Survey, WPA. *Inventory of County and Town Archives of Maryland. No. 15, Montgomery County*. Baltimore, 1939.

Hopkins, G. M. *Atlas of Fifteen Miles Around Washington, D.C., Including the County of Montgomery*. 1879. Reprint, Rockville, Md.: Montgomery County Historical Society, 1975.

Hurley, William N. Jr. *Montgomery County, Maryland, 1860 Census*. Bowie, Md.: Heritage Books, Inc., 1998.

Lord, Elizabeth M. *Burtonsville Heritage, Genealogically Speaking: A Brief Historical Sketch of Burtonsville, Maryland, Plus Genealogical Data of Over 100 Area Families*. Baltimore: Gateway Press, Inc., 1978.

Malloy, Mary G., et al. *Abstracts of Wills of Montgomery County, Maryland*. Vol. 1, *1776–1825,* and Vol. 2, *1826–1875*. Westminster, Md.: Family Line Publications, 1977, 1989.

———. "Montgomery County, Maryland Land Records, Liber A, 1777–1781." *Maryland & Delaware Genealogist*. Vol. 19. St. Michaels, Md., 1978.

Malloy, Mary G. and Jane C. Sween. *A Selective Guide to the Historic Records of Montgomery County, Maryland.* Rockville, Md.: Montgomery County Department of Public Library, 1974.

Malloy, Mary Gordon, and Marian W. Jacobs. *Genealogical Abstracts, Montgomery County, 1855–1899.* Rockville, Md.: Montgomery County Historical Society, 1986.

Manuel, Janet D. *Montgomery County, Maryland, Marriage Licenses, 1798–1898.* Westminster, Md.: Family Line Publications, 1987.

Martenet, Simon J. *Martenet and Bond's Map of Montgomery County, Maryland.* Baltimore: Simon J. Martenet, 1865.

Moore, L. Tilden. *Abstracts of Marriages and Deaths and Other Articles of Interest in the Newspapers of Frederick and Montgomery Counties, Maryland, 1831–1840.* Westminster, Md.: Family Line Publications, 1991.

Nelson's Suburban Directory of Maryland and Virginia Towns Adjacent to the District of Columbia. Washington, D.C.: J. C. Nelson Company, 1912.

Omans, Donald James, and Nancy West Omans. *Montgomery County Marriages, 1798–1875.* Athens, Ga.: Iberian Publishing, Potomack River Chapter, National Society, Colonial Dames of the XVII Century, 1987.

Peden, Henry C. Jr. *Revolutionary Patriots of Montgomery County, Maryland, 1776–1783.* Westminster, Md.: Family Line Publications, 1996.

Polk's Maryland – Washington Suburban Montgomery and Prince George's Counties, Maryland Directory. Washington, D.C.: R. L. Polk & Company, various years

Riggs, Donald Paul, compiler. *The Montgomery Sentinel: Newspaper Abstracts, 1855–1856.* Washington, D.C.: By compiler, 1978.

Scharf, J. Thomas. *History of Western Maryland, Being a History of Frederick, Montgomery, Carroll, Washington, Allegany and Garrett Counties.* 2 volumes. 1882. Reprint, Baltimore: Regional Publishing Company, 1968. [For the index see Western Maryland.]

Volkel, Lowell M. and Timothy Q. Wilson. "An Index to the 1800 Federal Census of Dorchester, Harford, Montgomery, Prince George's and Queen Anne's Counties, State of Maryland." Maryland Historical Society Library, 1967. [Typescript.]

Wright, F. Edward. *Maryland Militia, War of 1812.* Vol. 7, *Montgomery County.* Silver Spring, Md.: Family Line Publications, 1986.

———. *Marriages and Deaths in the Newspapers of Frederick and Montgomery Counties, Maryland, 1820–1830.* Silver Spring, Md.: Family Line Publications, 1987.

Prince George's County

Ackerson, Constance Pelzer. *Holy Trinity– Collington, Her People and Their Church: 275 Years*. Bowie, Md.: By the author, 1978.

Baltz, Shirley V. and George E. Baltz. *Prince George's County, Maryland, Marriages and Deaths in Nineteenth Century Newspapers*. 2 volumes. Bowie, Md.: Heritage Books, Inc., 1995.

A Bibliography of Published Genealogical Source Records; Prince George's County, Maryland. Bowie, Md.: Prince George's County Genealogical Society, 1975.

Bell, Annie W. B. *General Index to Wills of Prince George's County, 1698– 1899*. Annapolis, Md.: By the author, 1939.

———. *Prince George's County Index to Executors and Administrators Accounts*. Annapolis, Md.: By the author, 1939.

Boogher, William F. *Prince George's County, Maryland, Marriage License Record, 1777–1825*. n.p., 1968.

Bowie, Effie Gwynn. *Across the Years in Prince George's County*. 1947. Reprint, Baltimore: Genealogical Publishing Company, 1975, 1996.

Brown, Helen W. *Index to Register of Queen Anne Parish, 1686–1777*. Annapolis, Md.: Daughters of the American Revolution, 1960.

———. *Index to Register of Prince George's Parish, Prince George's and Montgomery Counties, Maryland*. Baltimore: Daughters of the American Revolution, 1961.

———. *Index of Marriage Licenses, Prince George's County, Maryland, 1777–1886*. 1971. Reprint, Baltimore: Genealogical Publishing Company, 1973, 1995.

———. *Prince George's County, Maryland, Indexes of Church Registers, 1685–1885*. 2 volumes. 1979. Reprint, Westminster, Md.: Family Line Publications, 1988, 1994.

Clark, Raymond B. Jr. *Index to Prince George's County, Maryland Wills, 1695–1777*. St. Michaels, Md.: By the author, 1987.

Daughters of the American Revolution, Toaping Castle Chapter. "Index to Registers of St. Matthew's Parish, Hyattsville, Prince George's County, Maryland, 1834–1926." Maryland Historical Society Library, 1981. [Typescript.]

A Guide to Maryland State Archives Holdings of Prince George's County Records on Microform. Annapolis: Maryland State Archives, 1989

Hienton, Louise Joyner. *Prince George's County Heritage*. Baltimore: Maryland Historical Society, 1972.

Hopkins, G. M. *Atlas of Fifteen Miles Around Washington, D.C, Including the County of Prince George's*. 1878. Reprint, Riverdale, Md.: Prince George's County Historical Society, 1975.

Index to Probate Records of Prince George's County, Maryland, 1696–1900. Bowie, Md.: Prince George's County Genealogical Society, 1988.

Jourdan, Elise Greenup. *The Land Records of Prince George's County, Maryland, 1702–1743*. 5 volumes. Westminster, Md.: Family Line Publications 1990, 1995, 1996, 1997.

————. *Colonial Settlers of Prince George's County*. Westminster, Md.: Family Line Publications, 1998.

Lucas, Olive. *Prince George's County, Maryland 1800 Census*. 1969. Reprint, Westminster, Md.: Family Line Publications, 1992.

"Marriage Licenses in Prince George's County, Maryland, 1777–1824." *New England Historical & Genealogical Register*, 73 (April, July, and October, 1919). Boston.

Martinet, Simon J. *Martenet's Map of Prince George's County, Maryland*. 1861. Reprint, Riverdale, Md.: Prince George's County Historical Society, 1976.

Peden, Henry C. Jr. *Revolutionary Patriots of Prince George's County, Maryland, 1775–1783*. Westminster, Md.: Family Line Publications, 1997.

Polk's Maryland – Washington Surburban. Montgomery and Prince George's Counties, MD Directory. Washington, D.C.: R. L. Polk & Company, various years.

Polk's Laurel. Prince George's County, MD City Directory. Richmond, Va.: R. L. Polk & Company, various years.

Prince George's County Deed Book B. Bowie, Md.: Prince George's County Genealogical Society, 1982.

Prince George's County Land Records. Vol. A, *1698–1702*. Bowie, Md.: Prince George's County Genealogical Society, 1976.

Prince George's County, Maryland 1800 Census. 1969. Reprint, Westminster, Md.: Family Line Publications, 1992.

Prince George's County Genealogical Society Bulletin. Vol. 1, No. 1. Bowie, Md., 1961

Sargent, Jean A, ed. *Stones and Bones: Cemetery Records of Prince George's County, Maryland*. Bowie, Md.: Prince George's County Genealogical Society, 1984.

Skarda, D. D. *Berwyn Heights: History of a Small Maryland Town*. n.p., c1976.

Smith, Dorothy H. *Orphans & Infants of Prince George's County, Maryland, 1696–1750*. Annapolis, Md., 1976.

Smith, Joseph H. and Philip A. Crowe, eds. *Court Records of Prince George's County, Maryland, 1696–1699* [American Legal Records. Vol. 9]. Washington, D.C.: American Historical Association, 1964.

Tombstones of Queen Anne's County, Maryland. 2 volumes. Easton, Md.: Upper Shore Genealogical Society, 1994.

Van Horn, R. Lee. *Out of the Past: Prince Georgians and Their Land*. Riverdale, Md.: Prince George's County Historical Society, 1976.

Volkel, Lowell M. and Timothy Q. Wilson. "An Index to the 1800 Federal

Census of Dorchester, Harford, Montgomery, Prince George's and Queen
Anne's Counties, State of Maryland. Maryland Historical Society Library,
1968. [Typescript.]

Wilcox, Shirley Langdon, ed. *1850 Census, Prince George's County,
Maryland.* Bowie, Md.: Prince George's County Genealogical Society,
1978.

———. *1828 Tax List, Prince George's County, Maryland.* Bowie, Md.: Prince
George's County Genealogical Society, 1985.

Wright, F. Edward. *Maryland Militia, War of 1812.* Vol. 6, *Prince George's
County.* Silver Spring, Md.: Family Line Publications, 1985.

Queen Anne's County

(also see Eastern Shore)

Bell, Annie W. B. *Queen Anne's County: Orphan Court Record, Guardian
Accounts, Book No. W. H. N, #1, 1798–1803.* Annapolis, Md.: By the
author, 1939.

———. *Index to Rent Roll of Queen Anne's County, Maryland, 1640–1724.*
Annapolis, Md.: By the author, 1939.

Carley, Rev. E. B. *The Origins and History of St. Peter's Church and
Congregation, Queenstown, Maryland.* Centreville, Md.: n.p., By the
author. 1976. [This volume contains few vital records.]

Clark, Raymond B. Jr. *Index to Queen Anne's County, Maryland, Wills.*
Arlington, Va.: By the author, 1981.

Clark, Sara S. and Raymond B. Jr. *Queen Anne's County, Maryland Marriage
Licenses, 1817–1858.* Washington, D.C.: By the authors, 1963.

Emory, Frederic. *Queen Anne's County, Maryland: Its Early History and
Development.* Baltimore: Maryland Historical Society, 1950.

*A Guide to Maryland State Archives Holdings of Queen Anne's County on
Microform.* Annapolis: Maryland State Archives, 1989.

Lake, Griffing, & Stevenson. *An Illustrated Atlas of Kent and Queen Anne
Counties, Maryland.* Philadelphia: Lake, Griffing, & Stevenson, 1877.

Leonard, R. Bernice. *Queen Anne's County, Maryland, Land Records, 1701–
1755.* 4 volumes. Westminster, Md.: Family Line Publications, 1992–94.

Volkel, Lowell M. and Timothy Q. Wilson. "An Index to the 1800 Federal
Census of Dorchester, Harford, Montgomery, Prince George's and Queen
Anne's Counties, State of Maryland." Maryland Historical Society Library,
1967. [Typescript.]

Wilson, George B. *1800 Census of Queen Anne's County, Maryland.* 1972.
Reprint, Westminster, Md.: Family Line Publications, 1992.

St. Mary's County

(also see Southern Maryland)

Beitzel, Edwin W. *A History of St. Francis Xavier Roman Catholic. Old Newton Manor of Little Bretton, St. Mary's County, Maryland*. Newton, Md.: St. Francis Xavier Parish, 1962.

———. *The Jesuit Missions of St. Mary's County*. Abell, Md.: By the author, 1959.

———. *St. Mary's County, Maryland, in the American Revolution: Calendar of Events*. Leonardtown, Md.: St. Mary's County Bicentennial Commission, 1975.

———. *Point Lookout Prison Camp for Confederates*. Abell, Md.: By the author, 1972.

Bell, Annie Walker Burns. *Index, Rent Roll, St. Mary's County, Maryland, 1639–1724*. By the author, n.d.

———. *Index to Persons and Places, St. Mary's County, Maryland* [1639–1724]. By the author, n.d.

———. *Maryland Wills, Charles and St. Mary's Counties, 1644–1722*. By the author, n.d.

Callum, Agnes Kane. *Black Marriages in St. Mary's County, Maryland, 1800–1900*. Baltimore: Mullac Publications, 1991.

Chronicles of St. Mary's. Monthly News Bulletin of the St. Mary's County Historical Society. Leonardtown, Md.: St. Mary's County Historical Society, 1953–.

Clark, Raymond B. Jr. *Index to St. Mary's County, Maryland, Wills, 1634–1777*. St. Michaels, Md.: By author, 1987.

Colleary, Shirley. *1860 Census of St. Mary's County, Maryland*. Valley Lee, Md.: By the compiler, 1982.

Cryer, Leona. *Deaths and Burials in St. Mary's County, Maryland*. Westminster, Md.: Family Line Publications, 1995.

1850 Census of St. Mary's County, Maryland. Leonardtown, Md.: Genealogical Committee of St. Mary's County Historical Society, 1980.

Fresco, Margaret K., compiler. *Marriages and Deaths in St. Mary's County, Maryland, 1634–1900*. Ridge, Md.: By the compiler, 1982.

The Generator. 1978– . St. Mary's County Genealogical Society. Calloway, Md.: By the Society. [Quarterly.]

A Guide to Maryland State Archives Holdings of St. Mary's County Records on Microform. Annapolis: Maryland State Archives, 1989.

Hammett, Regina Combs. *History of St. Mary's County, Maryland*. Ridge, Md.: n.p., 1977. Reprint, Washington, D.C.: Kirby Lithographic, 1980. [Sponsored by the St. Mary's County Bicentennial Commission.]

Historical Map of St. Mary's County, Maryland. Leonardtown, Md.: St. Mary's County Historical Society, 1980.

Hume, Joan, ed. *Maryland: Index to the Wills of St. Mary's County, 1662–1960, and Somerset County, 1664–1955.* Baltimore: Magna Carta Book Co., 1970.

Knight, George Morgan Jr. *Intimate Glimpses of Old Saint Mary's.* Baltimore: Meyer and Thalheimer, 1938.

Loffler, Grace. *A History of the Methodist Churches in St. Mary's County, Maryland.* Leonardtown, Md.: Printing Press, 1984.

Norris, Joseph E. Jr. *Chaptico: A History of St. Mary's Fourth District.* Leonardtown, Md.: n.p., n.d.

O'Rourke, Timothy J. *Catholic Families of Southern Maryland: Records of Catholic Residents of St. Mary's County in the Eighteenth Century.* Baltimore: Genealogical Publishing Company, 1985.

Peden, Henry C. Jr. *Revolutionary Patriots of Calvert & St. Mary's Counties, Maryland, 1775–1783.* Westminster, Md.: Family Line Publications, 1996.

Polk's Lexington Park and Leonardtown. St. Mary's County, Maryland Directory, Including California, Callaway and Great Mills. Richmond, Va.: R. L. Polk & Company, various years.

Pogue, Robert E. T. *Yesterday in Old St. Mary's.* New York: Carlton Press, 1968.

Reno, Linda Davis. *Abstracts of the Levy Court Records for St. Mary's County, Maryland, 1829–1877.* By the compiler, 1993.

Roberts, David, ed. *Index to St. Mary's County Graves.* Morganza, Md.: Chaptico High School, 1976.

St. Mary's County, Maryland, 1800 Census. Baltimore: Maryland Genealogical Society, 1972. Reprint, Westminster Md.: Family Line Publications, 1992.

Tice, Janet, et al. *Burials from Tombstones, Grave Markers, and Church Registers of St. Mary's County, Maryland, 1634–1994.* Leonardtown, Md.: St. Mary's County Historical Society, 1996.

Volkel, Lowell M. and Timothy Q. Wilson. "An Index to the 1800 Federal Census of St. Mary's, Somerset, Talbot, Washington and Worcester Counties, State of Maryland." Maryland Historical Society Library, 1968. [Typescript.]

Walton, James, S.J. *The Diary of Father James Walton, S.J.: A List of Baptisms in St. Mary's County, Maryland from 1766 through August, 1794.* Compiled by Thomas Wilbur Jennings. Baltimore: n. p., 1975.

Wright, F. Edward. *Maryland Militia, War of 1812.* Vol. 5, *St. Mary's and Charles Counties.* Silver Spring, Md.: Family Line Publications, 1983.

Somerset County

(also see Eastern Shore)

Barnes, John C. *Maryland, Somerset County, 1860 Census*. San Diego: Ruth T. Dryden, 1988.

———. *Maryland, Somerset County, 1870 Census*. San Diego: Ruth T. Dryden, 1988.

Batchelder, Pauline Manning, ed. *A Somerset Sampler: Families of Old Somerset County, Maryland, 1700–1776*. Baltimore: Gateway Press, Inc., 1994. [Published for the Lower Delmarva Genealogical Society in Salisbury, Md.]

Bischof, Hermann. *Rehoboth by the River: A Sketch of the Ancient Presbyterian Church at Rehoboth, Maryland*. n.p., 1933.

Clark, Raymond B. Jr. *Index to Somerset County Maryland Wills, 1666–1777*. Arlington, Va.: By the author, 1982.

Clary, Helen Bowie. *Coventry Parish Records, 1736 to 1828, Somerset County, Maryland*. Washington, D.C.: Mary Turpin Layton, 1936.

Crockett-Tabb, Nancy. *1860 Census of Somerset County, Maryland*. Silver Spring, Md.: Family Line Publications, 1985.

Dryden, Ruth T. *Land Records of Somerset County, Maryland*. San Diego: By the author, 1985, 1992.

———. *Somerset County, Maryland, 1850 Census*. El Cajon, Calif.: By the author, 1974.

———. *Somerset County, Maryland Rent Rolls, 1663–1723*. San Diego: By the author, 1982.

———. *Somerset County, Maryland Will Books, 1777–1859*, 7 volumes. San Diego: By the compiler, n.d.

———. *Somerset County, Maryland Will Book, 1748–1749, including Accounts and Inventories, 1678–1749*. San Diego: By the compiler, n.d.

———. *Somerset County, Maryland Wills, 1750–1772*. San Diego: By the compiler, n.d.

———. *1783 Tax Lists, Somerset and Worcester Counties, Maryland*. San Diego: By the compiler, n.d.

———. *Somerset Parish Records*. San Diego: By the compiler, 1987.

———. *Cemetery Records of Somerset County, Maryland*. San Diego: By the compiler, 1988.

———. *Stepney Parish Records of Somerset County, Maryland: St. Bartholomew's at Green Hill and St. Mary's at Tyaskin*. San Diego: By the compiler, 1988.

A Guide to Maryland State Archives Holdings of Somerset County Records on Microform. Annapolis: Maryland State Archives, 1989.

Heise, David V. *Somerset County, Maryland, Orphans Court Proceedings, 3* volumes: 1777–1792 and 1811–1823, 1823–1838, 1838–1852. Westminster, Md.: Family Line Publications, 1996–97.

Helton, Dorothy. *Somerset County, Maryland 1800 Census*. 1974, 1975. Reprint, Westminster, Md.: Family Line Publications, 1992.

Hume, Joan, ed. *Maryland: Index to the Wills of St. Mary's County, 1662–1960, and Somerset County, 1664–1955*. Baltimore: Magna Carta Book Co., 1970.

Lankford, Wilmer O. *Genealogical Data from Somerset County, Maryland Court Records, 1675–1677*. Westminster, Md.: Family Line Publications, 1988.

Meyer, Mary K. *Free Blacks in Harford, Somerset, and Talbot Counties, Maryland*. Mt. Airy, Md.: Pipe Creek Publications, 1991.

Peden, Henry C. Jr. *Revolutionary Patriots of Worcester & Somerset Counties, Maryland, 1775–1783*. Westminster, Md.: Willow Bend Books & Family Line Publications, 1999.

Pollitt, Roy C. *Somerset County, Maryland, Marriage Records, 1796–1871*. Prince George, Va.: Old Somersett House, 1986.

Powell, Jody. *Somerset County, Maryland, 1739 Tax List*. Roanoke, Tex.: 1990.

Reedy, Tom. *The 1798 Federal Direct Tax of Somerset County, Maryland*. Westminster, Md.: Family Line Publications, 1999.

Rent Rolls of Somerset County, Maryland, 1663–1723. Westminster, Md.: Family Line Publications, 1987.

Russo, Jean. *Tax Lists of Somerset County, 1730–1740*. Westminster, Md.: Family Line Publications, 1992, 1995.

Skinner, Vernon L. Jr. *Somerset County Wills, Liber EB #9, 1667–1748*. Westminster, Md.: Family Line Publications, 1987.

———. *Somerset County Will Books, Liber EB #5, 1770–1777, 1675–1710*. Westminster, Md.: Family Line Publications, 1987.

———. *Other Wills in the Prerogative Court for Somerset and Worcester Counties, 1664–1775*. Westminster, Md.: Family Line Publications, 1988.

Torrence, Clayton. *Old Somerset on the Eastern Shore of Maryland: A Study in Foundations and Founders*. 1935. Reprint, Baltimore: Regional Publishing Company, 1966, 1992.

Volkel, Lowell M. and Timothy Q. Wilson. "An Index to the 1800 Federal Census of St. Mary's, Somerset, Talbot, Washington and Worcester Counties, State of Maryland." Maryland Historical Society Library, 1967. [Typescript.]

Wilson, Woodrow T. *Thirty-four Families of Old Somerset County, Maryland*. Baltimore: Gateway Press, Inc., 1974.

———. *Crisfield, Maryland, 1676–1976*. Baltimore: Gateway Press, Inc., 1977.

————. *Quindocqua, Maryland, Indian Country*. Baltimore: Gateway Press, Inc., 1980.

Wright, F. Edward. *Marriages and Deaths of the Lower Delmarva, 1835–1840, from Newspapers of Dorchester, Somerset and Worcester Counties*. Silver Spring, Md.: Family Line Publications, 1987.

Southern Maryland

Jourdan, Elise Greenup. *Colonial Records of Southern Maryland*. Westminster, Md.: Family Line Publications, 1997.

————. *Early Families of Southern Maryland*, 8 volumes. Westminster, Md.: Family Line Publications, 1992–99.

Maryland Genealogies. 2 volumes. Baltimore: Genealogical Publishing Company, 1980, 1997. [This book is a consolidation of articles from the *Maryland Historical Magazine*.]

Peden, Henry C. Jr. *Quaker Records of Southern Maryland, 1658–1800*. Westminster, Md.: Family Line Publications, 1992.

Talbot County

(also see Eastern Shore)

Callahan, Loleta, et al. *The History of St. Joseph's Mission, Cordova, Maryland, 1765–1965*. Cordova, Md.: Cordova Church, 1965. [Also includes baptisms and marriages, 1760–1802.]

Clark, Raymond B. Jr. *Index to Talbot County, Maryland Wills, 1662–1777*. Arlington, Va.: By the author, 1982.

————. *Talbot County Wills, 1744–1753*. St. Michaels, Md.: By the author, 1989.

Clark, Sara Seth and Raymond B. Clark Jr. *Talbot County, Maryland, Marriage Licenses, 1657–1691, 1738–1751, 1781*. 3 volumes. St. Michaels, Md.: By authors, 1972.

————. *Talbot County, Maryland, Marriage Licenses, 1794–1824*. Washington, D.C.: By the authors, 1965.

Daughters of the American Revolution. *Talbot County, Maryland, Marriage Licenses, 1825–1850, with Biographical Sketches of the Ministers*. St. Michaels, Md.: By the authors, 1967.

A Guide to Maryland State Archives Holdings of Talbot County Records on Microform. Annapolis: Maryland State Archives, 1989.

Leonard, R. Bernice. *Bound to Serve: The Indentured Children in Talbot*

County, Maryland, 1794–1920. St. Michaels, Md.: By the author and The Anundsen Publishing Company, Decorah, Iowa, 1983.

———. *Talbot County, Maryland, Marriage Licenses, 1850–1875.* Decorah, Iowa: The Anundsen Publishing Company, 1986.

———. *Talbot County, Maryland, Land Records, 1662–1790.* 15 volumes. Decorah, Iowa: The Anundsen Publishing Company, 1987–1990.

McGhee, Lucy Kate. *Maryland Quaker Records of Third Haven, Tred Avon, Talbot County.* 6 volumes. Washington, D.C.: By the author, 1950.

Meyer, Mary K. *Census of the Free Blacks in Harford, Somerset and Talbot Counties, Maryland.* Mt. Airy, Md.: Pipe Creek Publications, 1991.

Peden, Henry C. Jr. *Revolutionary Patriots of Talbot County, Maryland, 1775–1783.* Westminster, Md.: Family Line Publications, 1998.

Preston, Dickson J. *Talbot County: A History.* Centreville, Md.: Tidewater Publications, 1983.

Riley, Janet Wilson. *1860 Census of Talbot County, Maryland.* Silver Spring, Md.: Family Line Publications, 1985.

Tilghman, Oswald. *History of Talbot County, Maryland, 1661–1861.* 2 volumes. 1915. Reprint, Baltimore: Regional Publishing Company, 1967.

Upper Shore Genealogical Society. *Tombstones of Talbot County, Maryland.* 4 volumes. Easton, Md.: By the society, 1989–94.

Volkel, Lowell M. and Timothy Q. Wilson. "An Index to the 1800 Federal Census of St. Mary's, Somerset, Talbot, Washington and Worcester Counties, State of Maryland." Maryland Historical Society Library, 1968. [Typescript.]

Wilson, George B. *Talbot County, Maryland 1800 Census.* 1974. Reprint, Westminster, Md.: Family Line Publications, 1992.

Upper Shore Genealogical Society. *Tombstones of Talbot County, Maryland.* 4 volumes. Easton, Md.: By the Society, 1989–1994.

Washington County

(also see Western Maryland)

Antietam Ancestors. Waynesboro, Pa.: Mount Airy Press, 1983. [Quarterly.]

Barron, Barbara and Lee D., *Abstracts of Estate Distributions of Washington County, Maryland, 1778–1835.* 4 volumes. Center, Mo.: Traces, 1982.

———. *The History of Sharpsburg, Maryland.* Center, Mo.: Traces, 1972.

———. *Index to Wills of Washington County, Maryland, 1776–1890.* Center, Mo.: Traces, 1982.

———. *Marriages, Washington County, Maryland, 1799–1860.* 4 volumes. Center, Mo.: Traces, 1982.

————. *References and Sources for All Data Presented in the History of Sharpsburg, Maryland.* Center, Mo.: Traces, 1973.

Bell, Herbert C. *History of the Leitersburg District, Washington County, Maryland,* 3d edition. 1898. Reprint, Waynesboro, Pa.: Caston Press, 1985. [With new index.]

Bible Records of Washington County, Maryland. Westminster, Md.: Family Line Publications in cooperation with Washington County Historical Society, Hagerstown, Md., 1992.

Brake, Donald C. *For Five Shillings Current: The Story of the Lutheran Church at Jerusalem. Funkstown, Washington County, Maryland, 1771–1983.* Shippensburg, Pa.: Beidel Printing House, 1984.

Clark, Linda B, ed. *An Index to Hagerstown Newspapers: The Washington Spy, August, 1790–February, 1797.* Hagerstown, Md.: Washington County Free Library, 1982.

————. *An Index to Hagerstown Newspapers: The Maryland Herald, and the Maryland Herald and Elizabethtown Weekly Advertiser, March, 1797–December, 1804.* Hagerstown, Md.: Washington County Free Library, 1982.

————. *An Index to Hagerstown Newspapers: The Hagerstown Gazette, and the Maryland Herald & Hagerstown Weekly Advertiser.* Hagerstown, Md.: Washington County Free Library, 1983.

————. *An Index to Hagerstown Newspapers: The Maryland Herald and Hagerstown Weekly Advertiser, and the Torch Light and Public Advertiser.* 2 volumes: January, 1815–December, 1824 and January, 1820–December, 1824. Hagerstown, Md.: Washington County Free Library, 1985.

Clark, Raymond B. Jr. *Washington County, Maryland 1800 Census.* Washington, D.C.: By the author, 1964.

Fuller, Marsha L. *Naturalizations of Washington County, Maryland, Prior to 1880.* Hagerstown, Md.: Desert Sheik Press, 1998.

————. *African American Manumissions of Washington County, Maryland.* Hagerstown, Md.: Desert Sheik Press, 1998.

A Guide to Maryland State Archives Holdings of Washington County Records on Microform. Annapolis: Maryland State Archives, 1989.

Hartman, J. Stewart. *The History of Christ Reformed Church, Cavetown, Maryland, 1827–1927: A Century.* Hagerstown, Md.: Maryland Printery, 1927.

Historical Records Survey, WPA. *Inventory of County and Town Archives of Maryland, No. 21, Washington County.* Baltimore, 1937.

Keller, Roger. *Roster of Civil War Soldiers from Washington County, Maryland.* Westminster, Md.: Family Line Publications, 1993.

Lake, Griffing & Stevenson. *An Illustrated Atlas of Washington County, Maryland.* 1877. Reprint, Evansville, Ind.: Unigraphic, Inc., 1975.

McGinley, Charles R. *A History of Saint Mark's Episcopal Church, Lappans,*

Washington County, Maryland. Boonsboro, Md.: Saint Mark's Episcopal Church, 1986.

Morrow, Dale Walton, editor, and Samuel Webster Piper, compiler. *Washington County Cemetery Records.* 7 volumes. 1935. Reprint, Westminster, Md.: Family Line Publications, 1992–94.

Morrow, Dale Walton and Deborah Sue Jensen. *Wills of Washington County, Maryland: An Index, 1776–1890.* Center, Mo.: Traces, 1977.

Morrow, Dale Walton and Deborah Jensen Morrow. *Marriages of Washington County, Maryland Marriages: An Index, 1799–1860.* 4 volumes. Center, Mo.: Traces, 1982.

———. *Distribution of Estate Accounts: Washington County, Maryland, 1778–1835.* 4 volumes [1778–1805, 1806–1816, 1817–1827, 1828–1835]. Center, Mo.: Traces, 1982. Reprint, Westminster Md.: Family Line Publications, 1992. [In 1 volume with index.]

———. *Washington County, Maryland: Surname List of Deeds, 1776–1932.* Center, Mo.: Traces, 1982.

———. *Washington County, Maryland, Bibliography.* Center, Mo.: Traces, 1984.

Peden, Henry C. Jr. *Revolutionary Patriots of Washington County, Maryland, 1776–1783.* Westminster, Md.: Family Line Publications, 1998.

Polk's Hagerstown. Washington County, Maryland City Directory. Richmond, Va.: R. L. Polk & Company, various years.

Russell, George Ely, C.G. *Washington County, Maryland, Genealogical Research Guide.* Middletown, Md.: Catoctin Press, 1993.

Scharf, J. Thomas. *History of Western Maryland: Being a History of Frederick, Montgomery, Carroll, Washington, Allegany and Garrett Counties,* 2 volumes. 1882. Reprint, Baltimore: Regional Publishing Company, 1968.

Schwartz, Frank and Rachel. *Old Zion: History of the First German Reformed Church in Hagerstown, 1770–1970.* Chambersburg, Pa.: The Craft Press, 1970.

Sword, Gerald J. *The Minutes and Proceedings of the Washington County Court Held in Elizabeth Town, 1776–1810.* Hagerstown, Md.: By the compiler, 1983.

Varle, Charles. *A Map of Frederick and Washington Counties, State of Maryland, 1868.* Reprint, Frederick, Md.: Frederick County Landmarks Foundation, 1990.

Volkel, Lowell M. and Timothy Q. Wilson. "An Index to the 1800 Federal Census of St. Mary's, Somerset, Talbot, Washington and Worcester Counties, State of Maryland." Maryland Historical Society Library, 1968. [Typescript.]

Weiser, Frederick S. *Maryland German Church Records.* Vol. 12, *Zion Evangelical and Reformed Church, Hagerstown, Washington County, Maryland, 1771–1849.* Westminster, Md.: Historical Society of Carroll County, 1998.

Williams, Thomas J. C. *A History of Washington County, Maryland.* 2 volumes. 1906. Reprint, Baltimore: Regional Publishing Company, 1968. [Surname index to biographical section only prepared by Bryan T. Winter, San Rafael, Calif., 1986.]

Wright, F. Edward. *Newspaper Abstracts of Allegany and Washington Counties, Maryland, 1811–1815.* Westminster, Md.: Family Line Publications, 1989.

—————. *Newspaper Abstracts of Allegany and Washington Counties, Maryland, 1820–1830.* Westminster, Md.: Family Line Publications, 1987.

—————. *Washington County Church Records of the 18th Century, 1768–1800.* Westminster, Md.: Family Line Publications, 1987.

Western Maryland

Long, R. Helen. *Index to Scharf's History of Western Maryland.* 7 volumes. Manhattan and Topeka, Kan.: Claflin Books. [Each county section is indexed separately, as is the general history section: Frederick County, 1986; Washington County, 1988; Montgomery County, 1988; Garrett County, 1988; Carroll County, 1989; Allegany County, 1990; general history, 1991.]

Portrait and Biographical Record of the Sixth Congressional District, Biographies of Many Well Known Citizens. New York and Chicago: Chapman Publishing Company, 1898. [This volume includes Allegany, Frederick, Garrett, Montgomery, and Washington Counties.]

Scharf, J. Thomas. *History of Western Maryland Being a History of Frederick, Montgomery, Carroll, Washington, Allegany, and Garrett Counties.* 2 volumes. 1882. Reprint, Baltimore: Genealogical Publishing Company, 1968.

Stanton, Thomas J. *A Century of Growth, Or the History of the Catholic Church in Western Maryland.* 2 volumes. Baltimore: John Murphy Company, 1900.

Western Maryland Genealogy. Quarterly. January, 1985–October, 1998, by editor and publisher Donna Valley Russell. Middletown, Md.: Catoctin Press; Vol. 15, No. 1, January, 1999, by editor and publisher Patricia Abelard Andersen. Gaithersburg, Md.: GenLaw Resources.

Wright, F. Edward. *Western Maryland Newspaper Abstracts, 1786–1810.* 3 volumes. Silver Spring, Md.: Family Line Publications, 1985–87.

Wicomico County

(also see Eastern Shore)

Barnes, John C. *Maryland, Wicomico County, 1870 Census*. San Diego: By the author and Ruth T. Dryden, 1988.

Cooper, Richard W. *Profile of a Colonial Community: Salisbury Town & Wicomico County on Maryland's Eastern Shore*. Baltimore: Gateway Press, Inc., 1986.

Dryden, Ruth T. *Stepney Parish Records*. San Diego: By the author, 1988.

———. *Land Records of Wicomico County, Maryland, 1666–1810*. San Diego: By the author, 1986.

A Guide to Maryland State Archives Holdings of Wicomico County Records on Microform. Annapolis: Maryland State Archives, 1989.

Historical Records Survey, WPA. *Inventory of County and Town Archives of Maryland, No. 22, Wicomico County*. Baltimore, 1940.

Jacob, John E. Jr. *Graveyards and Gravestones of Wicomico*. Salisbury, Md.: The Salisbury Advertiser, 1971, 1996.

———. *Store Account of John Nelms of Salisbury, 1758–1787*. Westminster, Md.: Family Line Publications, 1990.

Torrence, Clayton. *Old Somerset on the Eastern Shore of Maryland: A Study in Foundations and Founders*. 1935. Reprint, Baltimore: Regional Publishing Company, 1966, 1992.

Worcester County

(also see Eastern Shore)

Barnes, John C. *1860 Census, Worcester County*. San Diego: By the author and Ruth T. Dryden, 1988.

———. *1870 Census, Worcester County*. San Diego: By the author and Ruth T. Dryden, [1990].

Clark, Raymond B. Jr. *Index to Worcester County, Maryland, Wills, 1742–1777*. Arlington, Va.: By the author, 1982.

Dryden, Ruth T. *Worcester County, Maryland, Administrators Bonds and Inventories, 1783–1790*. San Diego: By the author, n.d.

———. *1850 Census, Worcester County*. San Diego: By the author, n.d..

———. *Worcester County, Maryland Will Books, 1742–1851*. 9 volumes. San Diego: By the author, n.d. [Note: LDS has 1769–1851.]

———. *1783 Tax Lists, Somerset and Worcester Counties*. San Diego: By the author, n.d.

———. *Land Records of Worcester County, Maryland* [1666–1810]. San Diego: By the author, 1987.

————. *Cemetery Records of Worcester County, Maryland.* San Diego: By the author, 1988.

A Guide to Maryland State Archives Holdings of Worcester County Records on Microform. Annapolis: Maryland State Archives, 1989.

Heise, David V. *A Closer Look at Worcester County Wills, 1666–1851.* Westminster, Md.: Family Line Publications, 1991.

————. *Worcester County Wills, Book JW No. 13, 1783–1790.* Westminster, Md.: Family Line Publications, 1991.

————. *Worcester County Orphans Court Proceedings.* Vol. 1, *1777–1780.* Westminster, Md.: Family Line Publications, 1998.

Jones, Sharon A. *Worcester County Wills, Book JW No. 2, 1742–1758.* Silver Spring, Md.: Family Line Publications, 1986.

————. *Worcester County Wills, Book JW No. 3, 1759–1759.* Silver Spring, Md.: Family Line Publications, 1987.

Long, Mary Beth and Vanessa. *Worcester County, Maryland, Marriage Licenses, 1795–1865.* Westminster, Md.: Family Line Publications, 1990.

Murray, Rev. James. *History of Pocomoke City, Formerly Newtown.* 1883. Reprint, Westminster Md.: Family Line Publications, 1986. [With new index.]

Page, Isaac Marshall. *Old Buckingham by the Sea on the Eastern Shore of Maryland.* Philadelphia: Westminster Press, 1936.

Peden, Henry C. Jr. *Revolutionary Patriots of Worcester & Somerset Counties, Maryland, 1775–1783.* Westminster, Md.: Willow Bend Books & Family Line Publications, 1999.

Scott, Mrs. F. Paul. *1800 Census of Worcester County, Maryland.* 1977. Reprint, Westminster, Md.: Family Line Publications, 1990.

Skinner, Vernon L. Jr. *Other Wills in the Prerogative Court for Somerset and Worcester Counties, 1664–1775.* Westminster, Md.: Family Line Publications, 1988.

————. *Abstracts of Worcester County Estate Docket No. ET, 1742–1820.* Westminster, Md.: Family Line Publications, 1988.

Truitt, Reginald Van Trump, and Millard G. Les Callette. *Worcester County, Maryland's Arcadia.* Snow Hill, Md.: Worcester County Historical Society, 1977.

Volkel, Lowell M. and Timothy Q. Wilson. "An Index to the 1800 Federal Census of St. Mary's, Somerset, Talbot, Washington and Worcester Counties, State of Maryland." Maryland Historical Society Library, 1968.

Wright, F. Edward. *Marriages & Deaths of the Lower Delmarva, 1835–1840.* Westminster, Md.: Family Line Publications, 1987. [These entries were abstracted from area newspapers.]

General References

Allan, Christopher N. and Les White. *Newspapers of Maryland: A Guide to the Microfilm Collection of Newspapers at the Maryland State Archives.* Annapolis: Maryland State Archives, 1990.

Ancestral Records and Portraits. Colonial Dames of America, Chapter 1 [Baltimore]. 2 volumes. 1910. Reprint, Baltimore: Genealogical Publishing Company, 1969.

Andrews, Mathew Page. *History of Maryland: Province and State.* Hatboro, Pa.: Tradition Press, 1965.

Andrews, Mathew Page. *Tercentenary History of Maryland.* 4 volumes. Deluxe supplement. Chicago: n.p., 1925.

Annual Report of the Society for the History of Germans in Maryland. Baltimore, 1887–1966. 32 volumes. Baltimore: Society for the Preservation of the History of Germans in Maryland, 1968. [Continued from volume 33 as *The Report: A Journal of German-American History.*]

Baldwin, Jane. See "Cotton, Jane Baldwin."

Barnes, Robert W. *British Roots of Maryland Families.* Baltimore: Genealogical Publishing Company, 1999.

———. *Gleanings from Maryland Newspapers, 1727–1795.* 4 volumes. Lutherville, Md.: Bettie S. Carothers, 1975–76.

———. *Marriages and Deaths from the Maryland Gazette, 1727–1839.* Baltimore: Genealogical Publishing Company, 1973, 1979.

———. *Marriages and Deaths from Baltimore Newspapers, 1796–1816.* Baltimore: Genealogical Publishing Company, 1978.

———. *Maryland Marriages, 1634–1777.* Baltimore: Genealogical Publishing Company, 1976, 1995.

———. *Maryland Marriages, 1778–1800.* Baltimore: Genealogical Publishing Company, 1978, 1993.

———. *Maryland Marriages, 1801–1820.* Baltimore: Genealogical Publishing Company, 1993.

———, ed. *Inventory of Maryland Bible Records.* Vol. 1. [See "Genealogical Council of Maryland" below.]

The Biographical Cyclopedia of Representative Men of Maryland and the District of Columbia. Baltimore, 1879.

Blizzard, Dennis F. and Thomas L. Hollowak. *A Chronicle of War of 1812 Soldiers, Seamen and Marines.* Westminster, Md.: Published by Family Line Publications for The Society of the War of 1812 in the State of Maryland, Inc., 1993.

Brewer, John M. and Lewis Mayer. *The Laws and Rules of the Land Office of Maryland.* Baltimore: Kelley, Piet & Co., 1871. [This volume includes a list of officers and soldiers entitled to lots west of Fort Cumberland,

Allegany Co, for Revolutionary service. It also includes a list of patented military lots.]

Brown, Mary Ross. *An Illustrated Genealogy of the Counties of Maryland and the District of Columbia as a Guide to Locating Land Records.* Baltimore: French-Bray Printing Co., 1967.

Browne, William Hand, et al., editors. *Archives of Maryland.* 72 volumes. (Baltimore: Maryland Historical Society, 1883–1972). [The *Archives of Maryland,* vols. 1–72 are available electronically at the Maryland State Archives web site (see Maryland State Archives entry in Part I). The series has been expanded and includes volume I, New Series, *Historical Lists* (Annapolis: Maryland State Archives, 1990), and multiple volumes of the *Maryland Manual.*]

Brumbaugh, Gaius M. *Maryland Records: Colonial, Revolutionary, County and Church, from Original Sources.* 2 volumes. 1915, 1928. Reprint, Baltimore: Genealogical Publishing Company, 1967, 1975, 1993.

Brumbaugh, Gaius M. and Margaret R. Hodges. *Revolutionary Records of Maryland.* Part I. Rufus H. Darby Printing Co., 1924. Reprint, Baltimore: Genealogical Publishing Company, 1978.

Bulletin No. 17: A Guide to the Index Holdings at the Hall of Records. Annapolis: State of Maryland, Department of General Services, 1972, 1988.

Bureau of the Census. *Heads of Families at the First Census of the United States Taken in the Year 1790, Maryland.* 1907. Reprint, Baltimore: Genealogical Publishing Company, 1952, 1966, 1972, and Spartansburg, S.C.: Reprint Company, 1965.

Burns, Annie Walker. *Abstracts of [Maryland] Will Book No. 38, 1770–1772,* 2 volumes. n.d. Reprint, Lutherville, Md.: n.p., 1975.

———. *Maryland Early Settlers.* 6 volumes. Annapolis, Md.: By the author, 1936.

———. *1752 Maryland Account Book No. 33.* n.d. Reprint, Lutherville, Md.: By the author, 1974.

———. *Maryland Balances of Final Distribution Books, Prerogative Court, Province of Maryland, 1751–1775.* Annapolis, Md.: By the author, 1936.

———. *Maryland Inventories and Accounts.* 5 volumes. Annapolis, Md., 1938. [Titles of each volume differ slightly.]

———. *Maryland Record of Deaths 1718–1777.* Annapolis, Md., 1936. [2 parts.]

———. *Maryland Death Records as Taken from Maryland Account Book No. 15, 1736–1737.* Annapolis, Md., [1936].

———. *Maryland Marriage Records.* 25 volumes. Washington, D.C.: By the author, 1938. [This series contains marriage inferences, 1659–1807.]

———. *Maryland Will Books Nos. 24–38, 1744–1773.* 15 volumes. Annapolis, Md.: By the author, 1938–45.

Calendar of Maryland State Papers. The Hall of Records Commission Publications No. 1, 5, 6, 7, 8, 10, 11. Annapolis, Md.: Hall of Records Commission, 1943–58.

Calendar of Maryland State Papers, Publication No. 1, The Black Books. Annapolis, Md.: Hall of Records Commission, 1943. Reprint, Baltimore: Regional Publishing Company, 1967, 1993.

Calendar of Maryland State Papers, Publication No. 3, The Brown Books. By Roger Thomas. Annapolis, Md.: Hall of Records Commission, 1948.

Calendar of Maryland State Papers, Publication No. 7, The Red Books. Annapolis, Md.: Hall of Records Commission, 1950, 1973.

Callum, Agnes Kane. *Colored Volunteers of Maryland, Civil War, 7th Regiment, U.S. Colored Troops, 1863–1866.* Baltimore: Mullac Publications, 1990.

Carothers, Bettie S. *Maryland Slave Owners and Superintendents, 1798.* 2 volumes. Lutherville, Md.: By the compiler, 1974.

———. *Maryland Soldiers Entitled to Lands Westward of Fort Cumberland.* Lutherville, Md.: By the compiler, 1973.

———. *Maryland Source Records.* 2 volumes. Lutherville, Md.: By author, 1975, 1979. Reprint, Silver Spring, Md.: Family Line Publications, 1987.

———. *Signers of the Oaths of Fidelity to Maryland,* 2 volumes. Lutherville, Md.: By the author, 1974. Reprint in one volume, *Maryland Oaths of Fidelity,* Silver Spring, Md.: Family Line Publications, 1995.

———. *1776 Census of Maryland.* Chesterfield, Mo.: By the compiler, 1972.

———. *1778 Census of Maryland.* Chesterfield, Mo.: By the compiler, 1973.

Clark, Raymond B. Jr. *The Maryland & Delaware Genealogist.* 11 volumes. St. Michaels, Md.: By the author, 1959–90.

Clements, S. Eugene and Wright, F. Edward. *Maryland Militia in the Revolutionary War.* Silver Spring, Md.: Family Line Publications, 1987.

Coldham, Peter Wilson. *Lord Mayor's Court of London Depositions Relating to Americans, 1641–1736.* Washington, D.C.: National Genealogical Society, 1980.

———. *English Convicts in Colonial America.* 2 volumes. New Orleans: Polyanthos, Inc., 1974.

———. *English Convicts in Colonial Maryland.* 5 volumes. Baltimore: Genealogical Publishing Company, 1982.

———. *The King's Passengers to Maryland and Virginia.* Westminster, Md.: Family Line Publications, 1997.

———. *Settlers of Maryland, 1679–1700.* Baltimore: Genealogical Publishing Company, 1995.

———. *Settlers of Maryland, 1701–1730.* Baltimore: Genealogical Publishing Company, 1996.

———. *Settlers of Maryland, 1731–1750.* Baltimore: Genealogical Publishing Company, 1996.

————. *Settlers of Maryland, 1751–1765.* Baltimore: Genealogical Publishing Company, 1996.

————. *Settlers of Maryland, 1766–1783.* Baltimore: Genealogical Publishing Company, 1996.

Collins, Linda M. *Resource Directory of Historical Organizations.* Prince Frederick, Md.: By the author, 1998.

Cordell, Eugene Fauntleroy. *The Medical Annals of Maryland, 1799–1899.* Baltimore: n.p., 1903. [This volume contains short biographical sketches of early physicians of Maryland.]

Cotton, Jane Baldwin and Roberta B. Henry. *The Maryland Calendar of Wills, 1635–1743.* 8 volumes. 1904–28. Reprint, Baltimore: Genealogical Publishing Company, 1968. Reprint, Family Line Publications, 1988. [Also see *Maryland Calendar of Wills, 1744–1749,* etc., which continues this important series to 1777.]

Cunz, Dieter. *The Maryland Germans, A History.* 1948. Reprint, Port Washington, N.Y.: Kennikat Press, 1972.

Daughters of the American Revolution, Maryland Society. *Directory of the Maryland State Society, Daughters of the American Revolution and Their Revolutionary Ancestors, 1892–1965.* 2 volumes. Bel Air, Md.: n.p., 1966.

Dobson, David. *Scots on the Chesapeake, 1607–1830.* Baltimore: Genealogical Publishing Company, 1992.

Dryden, Ruth T. *State of Maryland Mortality Schedules, 1850 and 1860.* San Diego: By the author, 1982.

Echternamp, Jorg. "Emerging Ethnicity: The German Experience in Antebellum Baltimore." *Maryland Historical Magazine,* 86 (1991): 1–16.

Ellis, Donna M. and Karen A. Stuart. *Calvert Papers: Calendar and Guide to the Microfilm Edition.* Baltimore: Maryland Historical Society, 1989.

Filby, P. William. *Passenger and Immigration Lists Bibliography, 1538–1900.* Detroit: Gale Research Company, 1981.

Filby, P. William and Dorothy Lower. *Passenger and Immigration Lists Index.* Detroit: Gale Research Company, 1986, supplements.

Filby, P. William and Mary K. Meyer. *Passenger and Immigration Lists Index.* 7 volumes. Detroit: Gale Research Company, 1981–85.

Ford, Paul Leicester, ed. *Orderly Book of the Maryland Loyalist Regiment, June 18th, 1778 to October 12th, 1778, kept by Capt. Caleb Jones.* Brooklyn, 1891.

Gahn, Bessie W. *Original Patentees of Land at Washington Prior to 1700.* 1936. Reprint, Baltimore: Regional Publishing Company, 1969.

Gannett, Henry. *A Gazetteer of Maryland and Delaware.* 1904. Reprint, Baltimore: Genealogical Publishing Company, 1979.

Genealogical Council of Maryland. *Inventory of Maryland Bible Records.* Vol. 1. Robert W. Barnes, ed. Westminster, Md.: Family Line Publications, 1990.

————. *Directory of Maryland Burial Grounds.* Vol. 1. Westminster, Md.: Family Line Publications, 1996.

Genealogies Catalogued by the Library of Congress Since 1986: With a List of Established Forms of Family Names and a List of Genealogies Converted to Microform Since 1983. Washington, D.C.: Library of Congress, 1991.

Gibb, Carson. *A Supplement to the Early Settlers of Maryland.* Annapolis: The Maryland State Archives, 1997.

Goettner, Harold C. and Wayne K. Goettner. *Confederate Cemeteries in Maryland: Loudon Park, Baltimore; Mt. Olivet, Frederick; Rosehill, Hagerstown; Point Lookout, Prison Camp, St. Mary's County.* Baltimore, n.p., n.d.

Ghirelli, Michael. *A List of Emigrants from England to America, 1662–1692.* Baltimore: n.p., 1968.

Goldsborough, William W. *The Maryland Line in the Confederate Army, 1861–1865.* 1900. Reprint, Port Washington, N.Y.: Kennikat Press, 1972.

Green, Karen Mauer. *The Maryland Gazette, 1727–1761: Genealogical and Historical Abstracts.* Galveston, Tex.: Frontier Press, 1989.

A Guide to Government Records at the Maryland State Archives: A Comprehensive List by Agency and Records Series. Annapolis: Maryland State Archives, 1991.

A Guide to Newspapers and Newspaper Holdings in Maryland: The Newspaper Project. Baltimore: Maryland Department of Education, Division of Library Development and Services, 1991.

Hargreaves-Mawdsley, R. transcriber. *Bristol and America: A Record of the First Settlers in the Colonies of North America, 1654–1685.* Reprint, Baltimore: Genealogical Publishing Company, 1967, 1970.

Harper, Irma Sweitzer. *Maryland Marriage Clues.* 3 volumes. St. Michaels, Md.: By the compiler, 1980, 1981, 1982.

Hartzler, Daniel D. *Marylanders in the Confederacy.* Westminster, Md.: Family Line Publications, 1986, 1990.

————. *Band of Brothers.* Westminster, Md.: Family Line Publications, 1995. [This volume includes a photographic epilogue to *Marylanders in the Confederacy.*]

Hartsook, Elizabeth and Gust Skordas. *Land Office and Prerogative Court Records of Colonial Maryland.* Annapolis, Md.: Hall of Records, 1946. Publication No. 4. Reprint, Baltimore: Genealogical Publishing Company, 1968.

Hayes, Robert Jr, ed. *The Maryland Historical and Genealogical Bulletin.* 21 volumes. Originally *The Maryland Genealogical Bulletin.* Baltimore: By the author, 1930–50.

Henninghausen, Louis P. *History of the German Society of Maryland.* Baltimore, 1909.

Henry, J. Maurice. *History of the Church of the Brethren in Maryland*. Elgin, Ill., 1936.

Hickman, Nathaniel, ed. *The Citizen Soldiers at North Point and Fort McHenry*. n.d. Reprint, Baltimore, 1889.

Historical Records Survey, WPA. *Inventory of the Church Archives in the District of Columbia: Protestant Episcopal Church, Diocese of Maryland*. 2 volumes. Washington, D.C., 1940.

Historical Records Survey, WPA. *Inventory of the Church Archives of Maryland: Protestant Episcopal Church, Diocese of Maryland*. Baltimore, 1940.

Hofstetter, Eleanore O. and M. S. Eustes. *Newspapers in Maryland Libraries: A Union List*. Baltimore: Maryland State Dept. of Education, 1977.

Hollowak, Thomas L. *Index to Marriages and Deaths in the. Baltimore Sun, 1837–1850*. Baltimore: Genealogical Publishing Company, 1978.

————. *Index to Marriages in the. Baltimore Sun, 1851–1860*. Baltimore: Genealogical Publishing Company, 1978.

————. *Polish Heads of Households in Maryland: An Index to the 1910 Census for Maryland*. Westminster, Md.: Family Line Publications, 1990.

Hooper, Debbie. *Abstracts of Chancery Court Records of Maryland, 1669–1782*. Westminster, Md.: Family Line Publications, 1996.

Hotten, John Camden. *The Original Lists of Persons of Quality, Emigrants, Religious Exiles, Political Rebels, Serving Men and Others Who Went from Great Britain to the American Plantations*. 2d edition. 1880. Reprint, Baltimore: Genealogical Publishing Company, 1962, 1968.

Hynson, Jerry M. *Free African–Americans of Maryland, 1832*. Westminster, Md.: Family Line Publications, 1998.

Index to the Maryland Line in the Confederate Army, 1861–1865. Publication No. 5. Annapolis, Md.: Hall of Records, 1945.

Jackson, Ronald Vern. *Heads of Families at the First Census of the United States Taken in 1790: Maryland*. Bountiful, Utah: Accelerated Indexing Systems, 1978.

Jackson, Ronald Vern, ed. *Maryland 1800 Census Index*. Bountiful, Utah: Accelerated Indexing Systems International, 1973.

————. *Maryland 1810 Census Index*. Bountiful, Utah: Accelerated Indexing Systems International, 1976.

Jackson, Ronald Vern, et al., eds. *Maryland 1820 Census Index*. Bountiful, Utah: Accelerated Indexing Systems International, 1977.

Jackson, Ronald Vern and Gary Ronald Teeples. *Early Maryland,* Vol. 1, *1700–1709; 1740–1749*. Bountiful, Utah: Accelerated Indexing Systems International, 1980.

————. *Maryland 1830 Census Index*. Bountiful, Utah: Accelerated Indexing Systems International, 1978.

————. *Maryland 1850 Census Index*. Bountiful, Utah: Accelerated Indexing Systems International, 1976.

————. *Maryland 1860 Census Index*. Salt Lake City: Accelerated Indexing Systems International, 1988.

————. *Maryland 1850 Slave Schedule Census Index*. Salt Lake City: Accelerated Indexing Systems International, 1988.

————. *Maryland 1840 Census Index*. Bountiful, Utah: Accelerated Indexing Systems International, 1977.

Jacobsen, Phebe R. *Quaker Records in Maryland*. Annapolis, Md.: Hall of Records Commission, 1966.

————. *Researching Black Families at the Maryland Hall of Records*. Annapolis: Maryland State Archives, 1984.

Johnson, Richard S. *How to Locate Anyone Who Is or Has Been in the Military*. 4th edition. Ft. Sam Houston, Tex.: Military Information Enterprises, 1991. [Armed Forces Locator Directory.]

Kaminkow, Jack and Marion J., *A List of Emigrants from England to America, 1718–1759*. Baltimore: n.p., 1964.

————. *Original Lists of Emigrants in Bondage from London to the American Colonies, 1713–1744*. Baltimore: n.p., 1967.

Kaminkow, Marion J. *Maryland A to Z: A Topographical Dictionary*. Baltimore: Magna Carta Book Company, 1985.

Kanely, Edna A. *An Alphabetical List of Baltimore and Ohio R.R. Employees Who Worked During the Months of April, 1852, September, 1852, February, 1855, November, 1857*. Baltimore: By the compiler, 1982.

————. *Directory of Ministers and the Maryland Churches They Served, 1634–1990*. 2 volumes. Annapolis: Maryland State Archives, 1992.

————, ed. *Directory of Maryland Church Records*. Westminster, Md.: Family Line Publications, 1982. Published for the Genealogical Council of Maryland.

Kenny, Hamill. *Origin and Meaning of Indian Placenames of Maryland*. Baltimore: Waverly Press, 1961.

————. *Placenames of Maryland: Their Origin and Meaning*. Baltimore: Maryland Historical Society, 1984, 1999.

Laws of Maryland, 1634 to Date. [Titles and publishers will vary. Much genealogical information in laws passed for relief of private parties. Includes early naturalizations, revolutionary pension records, divorces, name changes, insolvent debtor listings, paupers, business and church incorporations, roads laid out, escheated land, permission for aliens to own land, etc. Nineteenth–century volumes indexed.]

Ljungstedt, Milnor, ed. *The County Court Notebook: A Little Bulletin of Heraldry and Genealogy and Ancestral Proofs and Probabilities*, 10 volumes. 1921–31. Reprint, Baltimore: Genealogical Publishing Company, 1972. [One-volume edition.]

Magruder, James M. Jr. *Index of Maryland Colonial Wills, 1634–1777, in the Hall of Records*. 1933. Reprint, Baltimore: Genealogical Publishing Company,

1967, 1975, 1986. [Includes additions and new introduction.] Reprint, Westminster, Md.: Family Line Publications, 1991. [Single-volume edition.]

————. *Magruder's Maryland Colonial Abstracts, Wills, Accounts, and Inventories, 1772–1777.* 5 volumes. 1934–39. Reprint, Baltimore: Genealogical Publishing Company, 1968. [One volume.]

Maguire, Joseph C. Jr. *Index to Obituaries and Marriages in the Baltimore Sun, 1861–1865.* Westminster, Md.: Family Line Publications, 1992.

Marine, William M. *The British Invasion of Maryland, 1812–1815.* Reprint, Baltimore: Genealogical Publishing Company, 1977. [With an appendix containing 11,000 names of soldiers in War of 1812 by Louis H. Dielman, 1913.]

Martenet, Simon J. *New Topographical Atlas of the State of Maryland and the District of Columbia, with Descriptions Historical, Scientific and Statistical.* Baltimore, 1872.

Maryland Calendar of Wills. [F. Edward Wright continued the will series started by Jane Baldwin Cotton.] Vols. 9–16, 1744–1777. Westminster, Md.: Family Line Publications, 1991–95. [Volume 16 contains wills probated through May 1777.]

Maryland Department of State Planning. *Maryland Manual of Coordinates.* Baltimore: n.p., 1969. [Lists cities and villages, etc., with their locations.]

Maryland Genealogical Society Bulletin. Baltimore: By the society, 1960–.

Maryland Genealogical Society. *Index for the Maryland Genealogical Society Bulletin.* Vols. 1–5, 6, 7, 8, 9, 10, 12, and 13. Baltimore: By the Society, various dates.

Maryland Genealogies: A Consolidation of Articles from the Maryland Historical Magazine. 2 volumes. Baltimore: Genealogical Publishing Company, 1980.

Maryland Historical Society. *Maryland Magazine of Genealogy.* 5 volumes. Baltimore: By the Society, 1978–83.

Maryland in World War II: Register of Service Personnel. 5 volumes. Baltimore: Maryland Historical Society, War Records Division, 1965.

Maryland in the World War, 1917–1919. 5 volumes. Baltimore: Maryland War Records Commission, 1933.

Maryland Original Research Society of Baltimore. Bulletin, Vols. 1–3. 1906–13. Reprinted in 1 volume. Baltimore: Genealogical Publishing Company, 1973.

Maryland State Planning Commission and Department of Geology, Mines & Water Resources. *Gazeteer of Maryland.* Baltimore, 1941.

Mathews, Edward B. "The Counties of Maryland, Their Origins, Boundaries, and Election Districts." *Maryland Geological Survey.* Vol. 6. Baltimore, Johns Hopkins Press, 1907.

Men of Mark in Maryland: Biographies of the Leading Men of the State. 4 volumes. Washington, D.C., 1907–12.

Metcalf, Frank J. and George H. Martin. *Marriages and Deaths, 1800–1820, from the Intelligencer, Washington, D.C.* Washington, D.C.: National Genealogical Society, Special Publication No. 34, 1968. [This volume contains the names of many Marylanders.]

Meyer, Mary Keysor. *Divorces and Names Changed in Maryland by Act of Legislature, 1634–1854.* 1970, updated to 1867. Reprint, Finksburg, Md.: Pipe Creek Publications, 1991.

———. *Directory of Genealogical Societies in the U.S.A. and Canada.* 9th edition. Mt. Airy, Md.: Libra Publications, 1992.

———. *Westward of Fort Cumberland: Military Lots Set Off for Maryland's Revolutionary Soldiers.* Finksburg, Md.: Pipe Creek Publications, 1994.

Middleton, Canon Arthur Pierce. *Tercentenary Essays Commemorating Anglican Maryland, 1692–1792.* Virginia Beach, Va.: The Donning Company, 1992.

Morrison, Charles. *An Outline of the Maryland Boundary Disputes and Related Events.* Parsons, W. Va.: McLain Printing Company, 1974.

Muster Rolls and Other Records of Service of Maryland Troops in the American Revolution, 1775–1783. 1900. Reprint, Baltimore: Genealogical Publishing Company, 1972. *Archives of Maryland,* Vol. 18.

Nead, Daniel Wunderlich. *The Pennsylvania-German in the Settlement of Maryland.* Lancaster, Pa.: The Pennsylvania-German Society, 1914. Reprint, Baltimore: Genealogical Publishing Company, 1975, 1980, 1991.

New, M. Christopher. *Maryland Loyalists in the American Revolution.* Westminster, Md.: Family Line Publications, 1997.

Newman, Harry Wright. *The Flowering of the Maryland Palatinate.* Washington, D.C.: By the author, 1961. Reprint, Baltimore: Genealogical Publishing Company, 1985.

———. *Heraldic Marylandia.* Washington, D.C.: n.p., 1968.

———. *Maryland Revolutionary Records.* 1938. Reprint, Baltimore: Genealogical Publishing Company, 1967, 1993.

———. *Seigniory in Early Maryland, with a List of Manors and Manor Lords.* Baltimore: n.p., 1949.

———. *To Maryland from Overseas.* Baltimore: Genealogical Publishing Company, 1982, 1991.

O'Rourke, Timothy J. *Maryland Catholics on the Frontier: The Missouri and Texas Settlements.* Parsons, Kan.: Brefney Press, 1973, 1980.

Oszakiewski, Robert A. *Maryland Naturalization Abstracts.* Vol. 2, *The County Court of Maryland, 1779–1851, The United States Circuit Court for Maryland, 1790–1851.* Westminster, Md.: Family Line Publications, 1996. [For volume 1, see "Baltimore City and County."]

Owings, Donnell M. *His Lordships' Patronage: Offices of Profit in Colonial Maryland.* Baltimore: Maryland Historical Society, 1953.

Papenfuse, Edward C. *An Historical List of Public Officials of Maryland.* Annapolis: Maryland State Archives, 1991.

Papenfuse, Edward C., Alan F. Day, David W. Jordan, and Gregory A. Stiverson. *A Biographical Dictionary of the Maryland Legislature, 1635–1789.* 2 volumes. Baltimore: The Johns Hopkins University Press, 1979, 1985.

Papenfuse, Edward C., Christopher N. Allan, Patricia V. Melville, Kevin Swanson, and Constance R. Neale. *A Guide to Government Records at the Maryland State Archives: A Comprehensive List by Agency and Record Series.* Annapolis: Maryland State Archives, 1991.

Papenfuse, Edward C., Christopher N. Allan, Patricia V. Melville, Kris T. Lucas, Timothy D. Pyatt, and Dean K. Yates. *A Guide to State Agency Records at the Maryland State Archives: State Agency Histories and Series Descriptions.* Annapolis: Maryland State Archives, 1994.

Parran, Alice Norris. *Register of Maryland's Heraldic Families: Period from March 25, 1634 to March 25, 1935.* 2 volumes. Baltimore: H. G. Roebuck & Son, 1935–38.

Parsons, Richard, ed. "A Bibliography of In-Print Maryland Material." *Maryland Libraries,* 3 (Fall, 1969), 4 (Winter, 1970), 4 (Spring, 1970). Towson, Md.: Baltimore County Public Library, 1969, 1970.

———, editor and compiler. *Guide to Specialized Collections in Maryland Libraries.* Towson, Md.: Baltimore County Public Library, 1974.

Passano, Eleanor P. *An Index of the Source Records of Maryland: Genealogical, Biographical, Historical.* 1940. Reprint, Baltimore: Genealogical Publishing Company, 1967, 1984, 1994.

Peden, Henry C. Jr. *Maryland Deponents, 1634–1799.* Westminster, Md.: Family Line Publications, 1991.

———. *More Maryland Deponents, 1716–1799.* Westminster, Md.: Family Line Publications, 1992.

———. *Marylanders to Kentucky, 1775–1825.* Westminster, Md.: Family Line Publications, 1991.

———. *More Marylanders to Kentucky, 1778–1828.* Westminster, Md.: Family Line Publications, 1997.

———. *Marylanders to Carolina: Migration of Marylanders to North and South Carolina Prior to 1800.* Westminster, Md.: Family Line Publications, 1994.

———. *More Marylanders to Carolina: Migration of More Marylanders to North and South Carolina Prior to 1800.* Westminster, Md.: Family Line Publications, 1999.

———. *Quaker Records of Northern Maryland, 1716–1800.* Westminster, Md.: Family Line Publications, 1993.

———. *Quaker Records of Southern Maryland, 1658–1800.* Westminster, Md.: Family Line Publications, 1992.

———. *A Collection of Maryland Church Records.* Westminster, Md.: Family Line Publications, 1997. [This volume spans the years 1689 to 1845 and consists mainly of Baltimore City and Baltimore, Harford, and Frederick County records.]

————. *Maryland Society, Sons of the American Revolution, Centennial History, 1889–1989.* Baltimore: Maryland Historical Society in cooperation with Family Line Publications, 1989.

————. *Revolutionary Patriots of Maryland 1775–1783: A Supplement.* Westminster, Md.: Willow Bend Books, 2000.

Pedley, Avril J. M. *Manuscript Collections of the Maryland Historical Society.* Baltimore: Maryland Historical Society, 1968.

Pierce, Alycon Trubey. *Selected Final Pension Payment Vouchers, 1818–1864, Maryland: Baltimore.* Westminster, Md.: Family Line Publications, 1997.

Portrait and Biographical Record of the Sixth Congressional District, Maryland. 2 volumes. New York, 1898.

Radoff, Morris L., Gust Skordas, and Phoebe R. Jacobsen. *The County Courthouses and Records of Maryland. Part I: The Courthouses. Part II: The Records.* Annapolis, Md.: Hall of Records Commission, 1963.

Radoff, Morris L, et al. *The Old Line State, A History of Maryland: A Source Edition Recounting the Early and Contemporary History of Maryland Through the Medium of Extensive Research and the Life Histories of Its Most Constructive Members, Chronicling Backgrounds and Achievements of Its Prominent Families and Personages.* 3 volumes. Hopkinsville, Ky.: n.p., 1956.

Reamy, Martha and Bill Reamy. *Immigrant Ancestors of Marylanders, as Found in Local Histories.* Finksburg, Md.: Pipe Creek Publications, 1993.

Retzer, Henry J. *German Regiments of Maryland and Pennsylvania in the Continental Army, 1776–1781.* Westminster, Md.: Family Publications, 1991, 1996.

Richardson, Hester D. *Side-Lights on Maryland History, with Sketches of Early Maryland Families.* 2 volumes. 1913. Reprint, Baltimore: Genealogical Publishing Company, 1995.

Ridgely, Helen W. *Historic Graves of Maryland and the District of Columbia.* 1908. Reprint, Baltimore: Genealogical Publishing Company, 1967.

Rifman, Judge Avrum K. "Centennial of Eastern European Jewish Immigration." Maryland Historical Society Library. [Typescript.]

Riley, Hugh Ridgely and Charles S. Carrington. *Roster of the Soldiers and Sailors who Served in Organizations from Maryland During the Spanish–American War: Compiled Under the Authority of the House of Delegates of Maryland.* 1901. Reprint, with new index Westminster, Md.: Family Line Publications, 1991.

Sams, Conway W. and Elihu S. Riley. *The Bench and Bar of Maryland: A History, 1634–1801.* 2 volumes. Chicago, 1901.

Scarpaci, Jean. *The Ethnic Experience in Maryland: A Bibliography of Resources.* Baltimore: Towson State University, 1977.

Scharf, J. Thomas. *History of Maryland from the Earliest Period to the Present*

Day. 1879. Reprinted in 3 volumes with a new index. Hatboro, Pa.: Tradition Press, 1967.

Scharf, J. Thomas. *Separate Printing of New Index bound into Scharf's History of Maryland.* Compiled by Ray Lincoln. Hatboro, Pa.: Tradition Press, 1967.

Schultz, Edward T. *First Settlements of Germans in Maryland to Which Items of Historical Interest Referring to Frederick City and County Added.* 1896. Reprint, Miami, Fla.: n.p., 1976.

Schweitzer, George K. *Maryland Genealogical Research.* Knoxville, Tenn.: By the author, 1991.

———. *Revolutionary War Genealogy.* Knoxville, Tenn.: By the author, 1987.

Scott, Kenneth. *British Aliens in the United States During the War of 1812.* Baltimore: Genealogical Publishing Company, 1979.

Semmes, Raphael. *Crime and Punishment in Early Maryland.* 1938. Reprint, Montclair, N.J.: Patterson-Smith Company, 1970.

Skinner, Vernon L. Jr. *Abstracts of the Inventories of the Prerogative Court of Maryland, 1718–1777.* 17 volumes. Westminster, Md.: Family Line Publications, 1988–91.

———. *Abstracts of the Administration Accounts of the Prerogative Court of Maryland, 1718–1777.* 10 volumes. Westminster, Md.: Family Line Publications, 1995–99.

———. *Abstracts of the Inventories and Accounts of the Prerogative Court of Maryland, 1674–1718.* 11 volumes and 1 supplement. Westminster, Md.: Family Line Publications, 1992–94.

———. *Provincial Families of Maryland.* Vol. 1. Westminster, Md.: Family Line Publications, 1998.

Skirven, Percy G. *The First Parishes of the Province of Maryland, Wherein are Given Historical Sketches of the Ten Counties and of the Thirty Parishes in the Province at the Time of the Establishment of the Church of England in Maryland in 1692.* 1923. Reprint, n.p., 1994.

Skordas, Gust. *The Early Settlers of Maryland: An Index to Names of Immigrants Compiled from Records of Land Patents, 1633–1680.* Baltimore: Genealogical Publishing Company, 1968, 1974, 1979.

Society of Colonial Wars of Maryland, Vol. 1. [By Christopher Johnston.] Baltimore, 1905.

Society of Colonial Wars of Maryland, Vol. 2. [By Francis B. Culver.] Baltimore, 1940.

Society for History of Germans in Maryland. [See *"Annual Report of . . ."* above.]

Sowell, Thomas. *Ethnic America: A History.* New York: Basic Books, Inc., 1981.

Spalding, Thomas W. *The Premiere See: A History of the Archdiocese of Baltimore, 1789–1989.* Baltimore: Johns Hopkins University Press, 1989.

Spencer, Richard H., ed. *Genealogical and Memorial Cyclopedia of the State of Maryland,* 2 volumes. New York, 1919.

Steuart, Rieman. *The Maryland Line: A History of the Maryland Line in the Revolutionary War, 1775–1783.* Baltimore: Society of the Cincinnati, 1969.

Sullivan, Larry, and Richard Cox. *A Guide to the Research Collections of the Maryland Historical Society.* Baltimore: Maryland Historical Society, 1980.

Tepper, Michael H., editor, and Elizabeth P. Bentley, transcriber. *Passenger Arrivals at the Port of Baltimore, 1820–1834: From Customs Passenger Lists.* Baltimore: Genealogical Publishing Company, 1982.

Thomas, James Walter. *Chronicles of Colonial Maryland.* 1900. Reprint, Westminster, Md.: Family Line Publications, 1995.

Toomey, Daniel C. *The Civil War in Maryland.* Linthicum, Md.: Toomey Press, 1983.

———. *Marylanders at Gettysburg.* Linthicum, Md.: Toomey Press, 1995.

Towle, Laird C. *Genealogical Periodical Annual Index.* Bowie, Md.: Heritage Books, Inc., 1962–.

Webb, Benjamin A. *The Centenary of Catholicity in Kentucky.* Louisville Ky: Charles A. Rogers, Co., 1884. [This volume contains considerable information on early Maryland families who established Catholicism in the State of Kentucky.]

Wells, Charles J. *Maryland and District of Columbia Volunteers in the Mexican War.* Westminster, Md.: Family Line Publications, 1991.

White, Frank F. Jr. *The Governors of Maryland, 1777–1970.* Annapolis, Md.: The Hall of Records Commission, Publication No. 15, 1970.

White, Les. *Guide to the Newspaper Collection on Microfilm at Maryland State Archives.* Annapolis: Maryland State Archives, 1991.

Whittaker, Mary-Jean. *Genealogy and Local History: A UMBC Bibliography.* Baltimore: University of Maryland, Baltimore County, 1979.

Williams, Harold A. *A History of the Hibernian Society of Baltimore, 1803–1957.* Baltimore: The Hibernian Society of Baltimore, 1957.

Wilmer, L. Allison, et al. *The History and Roster of Maryland Volunteers, War of 1861–1865.* 2 volumes. 1898–99. Reprint, Westminster, Md.: Family Line Publications, 1990. [Indexed by Bill and Martha Reamy.]

Winchester, Paul and Frank D. Webb, eds. *Newspapers and Newspapermen of Maryland, Past and Present.* Baltimore, 1905.

Wood, Gregory A. *The French Presence in Maryland.* Baltimore: Gateway Press, Inc., 1978.

———. *A Guide to the Acadians in Maryland in the Eighteenth and Nineteenth Centuries.* Baltimore: Gateway Press, Inc., 1995.

Wyand, Jeffrey A. and Florence L. *Colonial Maryland Naturalizations.* Baltimore: Genealogical Publishing Company, 1975.

Wright, Lauren. *1997 Pocket Guide to Genealogical Resource Centers of the Mid-Atlantic.* Westminster, Md.: Family Line Publications, 1997.

Yeager, Gerry, Thomas L. Hollowak, Elizabeth Schaaf, and Kristen Stevens, eds. *Baltimore's Past: A Directory of Historical Sources*. Baltimore: The Baltimore History Network, University of Baltimore, 1989.

Compact Disks

Census Index: Baltimore, Chicago, & St. Louis, 1870. Published by Broderbund Software, Inc., Banner Blue Division, 1997.

Church Records: Maryland and Delaware, 1600s–1800s. Images of 27 books on early Maryland and Delaware church records published by Family Line Publications through 1997. Published by Broderbund Software, Inc., Banner Blue Division, for Family Line Publications, 1998.

Family History: Colonial Families of Maryland, 1600s–1900s. Images of the pages of 17 volumes of Maryland genealogies and family histories. Published by Broderbund Software, Inc., Banner Blue Division for Family Line Publications, 1998.

Family History: Maryland Marriages and Genealogies, 1634–1820. Images from *Maryland Genealogies*. 2 volumes taken from *Maryland Historical Magazine*; and Robert Barnes' *Baltimore County Families, 1659–1759*; and *Maryland Marriages, 1634–1820*. 3 volumes. Published by Broderbund Software, Inc., Banner Blue Division, for Genealogical Publishing Co, Inc., 1998.

Genealogical Records: Maryland Probate Records, 1674–1778. Images from the following collections of Maryland probate records: *Maryland Calendar of Wills*. Vols. 1–16; *Abstracts of Inventories and Accounts of the Prerogative Court of Maryland*, *Abstracts of the Balance Books of the Prerogative Court of Maryland*, and *Abstracts of the Inventories of the Prerogative Court of Maryland*. Published by Broderbund Software, Inc., Banner Blue Division, for Family Line Publications, 1997.

Genealogical Records: Maryland Genealogical Society Bulletin, Vols. 1–38. Images of the pages from volumes 1–38 of the *Maryland Genealogical Society Bulletin*, 1960–97. Published by Broderbund Software, Inc., Banner Blue Division for Maryland Genealogical Society, 1998.

Marriage Index: Selected Counties of MD, NC, VA, 1624–1915. Published by Broderbund Software, Inc., Banner Blue Division.

Marriage Index: Maryland, 1665–1850. Published by Broderbund Software, Inc., Banner Blue Division.

Revolutionary Patriots, Maryland and Delaware, 1775–1783. Images of 11 volumes of Family Line Publications' *Revolutionary Patriots* series by Henry C. Peden, Jr. which cover the state of Delaware and eleven Maryland counties: Anne Arundel, Baltimore, Calvert, Charles, Frederick, Harford, Kent,

Montgomery, Prince George's, Queen Anne's, St. Mary's. Published by Broderbund Software, Inc., Banner Blue Division, for Family Line Publications, 1998.

PUBLISHERS AND PURVEYORS
OF MARYLAND GENEALOGY

Ancestry, Inc.
P. O. Dept. SRV, Box 538
Salt Lake City, Utah 84410
Web Site: www.ancestry.com

Anne Arundel Genealogical Society
P. O. Box 221
Pasadena, Maryland 21122
[see "Genealogical Societies"]

Anundsen Publishing Company
108 Washington Street
Decorah, Iowa 52101

Baltimore County Genealogical Society
P. O. Box 10085
Towson, Maryland 21285-0085
[see "Genealogical Societies"]

Catoctin Press
P. O. Box 505
New Market, Maryland 21774-0505

Cecil County Genealogical Society
P. O. Box 11
Charlestown, Maryland 21914
[see "Genealogical Societies"]

Clearfield Press
200 East Eager Street
Baltimore, Maryland 21202
Telephone: 410-625-9004

Closson Press
1935 Sampson Drive
Apollo, PA 15613-9208
Telephone: 724-337-4482
Fax number: 724-337-9484
Web Site: www.clossonpress.com

155

Delmarva Roots
   120 Schley Avenue
   Lewes, Delaware 19958
   Telephone: 302-644-2798; 800-576-8608
   Email – fedwright@excite.com

Desert Shiek Press
   c/o Marsha L. Fuller
   P. O. Box 3623
   Hagerstown, MD 21742

Ruth T. Dryden
   2414 Front Street, #425
   San Diego, CA 92101

Family Line Publications
   [see "Willow Bend Books"]

Patricia A. Fogle
   120 Locust Blvd.
   Middletown, MD 21769

Gateway Press, Inc.
   1001 North Calvert Street
   Baltimore, Maryland 21202
   Telephone: 410-837-8271

Genealogical Publishing Company
   1001 North Calvert Street
   Baltimore, Maryland 21202
   Telephone: 410-837-8271

GenLaw Resources
   9346 Bremerton Way
   Gaithersburg, Maryland 20886-1427
   Web Site: www.genlawresources.com
   E-mail: genlaw@mindspring.com

Harford County Genealogical Society
   P. O. Box 15
   Aberdeen, Maryland 21001
   [see "Genealogical Societies"]

Hearthstone Bookshop
Potomac Square
8405-H Richmond Highway
Alexandria, Virginia 22309

Heritage Books, Inc.
1540-E Pointer Ridge Place
Bowie, Maryland 20716
Telephone: 800-398-7709 or 301-390-7709
Fax number: 800-276-1760 or 301-390-7153
E-mail: heritagebooks@usa.pipeline.com
Web Site: www.heritagebooks.com

Maryland Historical Society
201 West Monument Street
Baltimore, Maryland 21201
Telephone: 410-685-3750
Web Site: www.mdhs.org

Monacacy Book Company
P. O. Box 765
Redwood City, California 94063

Mountain Press
P. O. Box 400
Signal Mountain, TN 37377-0400
Telephone: 615-886-6369
Fax number: 615-886-5312

Margaret E. Myers
409 Culler Avenue
Frederick, MD 21701-4111

Noodle-Doosey Press
P. O. Box 716
Manchester, Maryland 21102

Prince George's County Genealogical Society
P. O. Box 819
Bowie, Maryland 20716
[see "Genealogical Societies"]

Scholarly Resources, Inc.
  104 Greenhill Avenue
  Wilmington, Delaware 19805

Tidewater Publishers
  Bay Country Publishing Co.
  Cambridge, Maryland 21613

Traces
  P. O. Box 68
  Center, Missouri 63436

Charles E. Tuttle Company
  P. O. Box 541
  Rutland, Vermont 05701

Western Maryland Genealogy
  P. O. Box 9187
  Gaithersburg, Maryland 20898-0187
  E-mail: genlaw@mindspring.com

Willow Bend Books and Family Line Publications
  65 East Main Street
  Westminster, Maryland 21157-5036
  Telephone: 410-876-6101
  Phone or fax: 800-876-6103
  E-mail: willowbend@mediasoft.net
  Web Site: www.willowbend.net

Who's Who in Genealogy
  8944 Madison Street
  Savage, Maryland 20763

Ye Olde Map Shoppe
  5818 Mineral Hill Road
  Eldersburg, Maryland 21784

GLOSSARY

Abstract: essential items selected from an original document — names, dates, places, and relationships.

Abstract of Title: a condensed history of the title of a piece of real estate; includes every conveyance, restrictions, and a statement of all liens or charges against it. Abstracts often include maps, plats, and surveys.

Account of sales: a record of the personal property listed in the inventory of the deceased.

Ad litem: for this case only; A guardian ad litem represents a minor in this specific case.

Administration: settling an estate usually when there is no will. The term administration is almost always associated with intestate cases.

Administration bond: a written obligation by the administrator of an estate requiring that he/she, under penalty of stated monetary amount, faithfully perform their duties in the settlement of an estate.

Administrative account: a detailed statement of receipts and payments filed by the administrator of an estate.

Administrator/administratix: a person appointed by the court to administer the assets and liabilities of the deceased. If named in a will, the person is an executor/executrix.

Administrator de bonis non: a person appointed by the court to administer the effects of a decedent that have not been included in a former administration.

Administer with will annexed: one appointed as administrator of an estate after the executor named in the will either refused or was unable to act.

Affidavit: a statement made under oath, usually in writing.

Agreement: implies that the parties have given mutual assent to a particular matter that might change some of their rights or obligations.

Alienation: the transfer of land from one person to another.

Alienation fee/fine: the tax or fee levied when land is transferred.

159

Antenuptial Contract: a contract in which a man and woman delineate the property rights of one or the other. These agreements are usually made prior to a second marriage for the purpose of securing property for the children of a former marriage.

Apprenticeship: when a person or a guardian acting for a minor child, agreed to work and live with another family to learn a trade, craft, or possession. These arrangements were sometimes made by court order.

Assignment: the legal grant of certain types of property rights, such as leases, life estates, trusts, and mortgages.

Assigns: anyone acting in place of or on the behalf of the nominal owner.

Banns: public announcements that a marriage is about to take place. Persons knowing any reason why the marriage should not take place are encouraged to stand up and speak out or forever hold their peace. Banns were usually read in church three consecutive weeks prior to the marriage.

Bastardy: the record of illegitimacy or an attempt to identify the father of an illegitimate child.

Bishop's transcripts: official copies of local church birth, marriage, and death registers submitted to the bishop.

Bounty Land: land awarded as a bonus to attract soldiers to enlist or as payment in addition to or in lieu of wages for military service.

Caveat: literally "beware," it is a warning to investigate before action is taken.

Certificate of survey: the official description of a plot of land.

Codicil: a section added to a will after it has been witnessed and signed that alters the provisions of the original will; may also apply to other legal documents.

Collateral: descended from a common ancestor through a different line such as a cousin, aunt, or uncle.

Conveyance: see Deed

Covert: a married woman.

Debt books: the proprietary records listing the landowners and those who owed an annual rent to Lord Baltimore.

Decedent: a deceased person.

Decennial: every ten years.

Deed: the document by which title of property is transferred from one person to another.

Deed of Release: a document executed by a lien holder once the lien or mortgage has been paid; gives complete title to the owner.

Deed of Trust: a transfer of property to someone who will hold the property for another.

Delinquent lands: lands on which payment of taxes, fees, or specific requirements for title are past due.

Deposition: written testimony of a witness to a certain matter, certified by the court official in charge of taking it. These statements were often taken to verify land titles and boundary disputes.

Distributions: the divisions and apportionment of an estate to the legal heirs after the debts and charges have been paid.

Dower: a life estate, usually the widow's one-third interest in her former husband's property, to be used to support herself and her children.

Ejectments: the suits in the Provincial Courts usually regarding title to land in which one party sues to "eject" the other.

Entail: entailed lands automatically descend to a specific person and his/her lineal descendents. The key phrase is "to x and the heirs of his/her body legally begotten." The phrase "to his heirs and assigns forever" is not an entail; it is a freehold.

Enumerator: the person who records the census or tax information.

Escheat: the reversion of property title to the state, country, or lord of the manor when there are no legal heirs to inherit.

Estate: the total property, of whatever kind, owned by a decedent.

Fee simple: ownership of land that can be inherited by any heirs; generally direct descendents.

Free man of color: a black free born or given freedom papers many years earlier.

Freedman: an emancipated slave.

Freehold: a landholding that could be bought, sold, inherited, or bequeathed by will.

Freeholder: the owner of enough property to vote, serve on a jury, or hold public office.

Freeman: in legal terms, is most always a white man; a man not bound in servitude.

Gift Deed: a deed whereby real estate is transferred without normal costs and fees as in a parent to a child.

Grantee: the person buying the property.

Grantor: the person selling the property.

Griff: a person of mixed Native American and African American ancestry.

Guardian: any person lawfully invested with the authority to take care of an orphan and to manage that child's property.

Guardian account: an annual record filed by the guardian listing receipts, payments, and balances due the orphan.

Headright: a term applied to the land distribution system in Maryland and Virginia by which immigrants (including minor children) were entitled to a specific number of acres for transporting oneself and/or others into the province. Headrights could be sold or assigned to others.

Heir-at law: during the colonial period was the eldest son; if deceased, his heir-at-law; in the absence of a son, daughters inherited jointly as heirs-at-law. After 1790, all children inherited equal shares and other family members inherited as stipulated by the law.

Indenture: a contract in two or more copies binding one person to labor for another and learn a specific trade during a specific period of time. Also is used to describe any written contract between two persons, such as in land transactions.

Intestate: the term used when a person dies without leaving a will.

Inventory: an itemized list of the possessions and property of the deceased with their estimated or actual values.

Kindred: persons related by blood; not necessarily children.

Letter of Attorney: see Power of Attorney

Letters Testamentary: the formal instrument of administration given to the executor by the court when a will is brought to probate; it empowers the executor to discharge his/her duties and act on behalf of the estate.

Lien: a claim by one party upon the property of another for security in the payment of a debt.

Lis pendens: court action pending; usually applies to land title claims.

Lis: a lawsuit.

Litigation: a lawsuit before the courts.

Manifest: a detailed list of cargo, crew, and passengers on board a ship, signed and authenticated by a ship's officer.

Manumission: a formal, often written, act that frees a slave.

Marshaling lists: may be part of a distribution account. It is a distribution of assets "marshaled" on the personal estate of the deceased.

Measurements of Land: common units of measure found in old land records

      acre — 43,560 square feet, 160 square rods

      chain — 66 feet or 22 yards (100 links)

      furlong — 660 feet or 220 yards (10 chains)

      link — 7.92 inches (there are 25 links in a rod and 100 links in a chain)

      mile — 5,280 feet (80 chains, 32 rods, or 8 furlongs)

      perch — 51/2 yards or 161/2 feet; also called rod or pole

      pole — see perch

      rod — see perch

Meridian: a line or circle of longitude from which map lines are projected.

Metes and Bounds: property described by natural boundary markers such as "to the large white oak on the south corner of Richard Brown's land," or along the banks of the Gunpowder River from . . . " instead of lineal measures.

Mortgage: a conditional transfer of legal title to real property as security for payment of a debt. It is much like a deed in form, but if the conditions are met (the debt is paid) then the mortgage becomes void. Actual legal title is transferred to the mortgagee and he/she then has the right to own the land.

Nee: literally "born" and is used to identify women's maiden names.

Palatinate: a region west of the Rhine River in Germany.

Partition: when two or more parties are co-tenants of one piece of real estate and wish to divide it among themselves (usually when children inherit property from a parent). A deed of partition, or partition, is made and recorded showing the parts taken by each person.

Patent: a document granting ownership to a previously unpatented tract of land.

Patronymics: the custom of using the father's given name or some form of it as a surname for the children.

Perambulation: literally "to walk around." The practice of walking the boundaries of local property in a group so every male over age eighteen knows the boundaries of his neighbor's property. Boundary markers that had been obliterated or moved were repositioned. This practice prevented litigation and boundary disputes.

Personality: a collective term for all of a person's personal and moveable property.

Petition: a request made to the court for action in a matter not the subject of a suit.

Power of Attorney: a document drawn by one person stating that another person may act for him/her. The person thus appointed becomes the attorney in fact in the performance of the specified duties.

Probate: the court procedure by which a person makes a disposition of his/her property after death.

Proprietary leases: leases granted by the proprietor or his agent for lands on the proprietary manors.

Quadroon: a person one-fourth black and three-fourths white.

Quaker dating system: month, day, year; as in 11th mo. 10th day 1845.

Quitclaim Deed: an instrument by which the person releases all title, interest, or claim that he/she may possess in certain real properties.

Quitrent: an annual rent paid to the proprietor in lieu of required feudal service; the amount of the quitrent (actually a real estate tax) is recorded in the patent.

Redemptioner: an immigrant who redeems passage money by becoming a bond servant for a specific number of years. This is different from indentured servants in that the immigrant is sold to the highest bidder after arrival, rather than contracting his/her labor before emigrating.

Release: a document by which a person gives up his/her right to something in which he/she has a just claim.

Release of Dower: the document signed by a widow in which she gives up all claim to her former husband's property. Without this signature, the widow may return at any time to claim ownership of the property.

Rent rolls: proprietary records of land tract owners.

Renunciation: the act of giving up title or claim to property; also applies to estate executors who renounce their duties to the court.

Sexton: the person at the church responsible for burying the dead and keeping a record of the burial.

Statute: a law enacted by a legislative body.

Surrender: like a deed in its form and involves giving up a lease before its term is expired. It is made with the agreement of both parties.

Tenure: a specific holding in land.

Testate: the term used when a person dies leaving a will.

Tripartite conveyance: a deed involving three parties in which title to the land is cleared and re-granted in one document; most commonly executed by multiple heirs of a single tract.

Warrant: directs the surveyor to map the land and issue a certificate of survey.

Ward: a political subdivision of a city or someone under the care of a guardian.

Watch and Ward: an old custom of patrolling towns and cities watching for lawbreakers, fire, or other dangers to persons or property; the forerunner of the modern police department.

Whole blood: a person biologically descended from both sides of the family; as opposed to a "half" blood sibling.

Will: the instrument by which a person makes a disposition of his/her property to take effect after death. A holographic will is one that is written, signed, and dated by the testator. A nuncupative will is one made by the verbal declaration of the testator and, by law, is required to be put in writing by at least three witnesses within six days.

Writ: an official order of the court delivered under seal.

ABBREVIATIONS

A,a – acre or acres
acct. – account
admr. – administrator
ae., aet – age or aged
A.G. – Accredited Genealogist
a.k.a. – also known as
alias – an assumed name, or the married or maiden name of a woman
anon. – anonymous
ante – before, or prior
app. – appendix
assn. – association
b. – born
bap., bapt., bp. – baptized
bef. – before
bet. – between
BK, Bks – books
BLWT – bounty land warrant
bpl – birthplace
bro – brother
bro/o – brother of
b.s. – bill of sale
ca. – circa (about)
cert. – certified
cf – compare
comp. – compiler
d. – died, deceased
dau. – daughter
d/o, da/o, dau/o – daughter of
DB – deed book
do. – ditto
D.o.G. – deed of gift
D.o.T. – deed of trust
doc. – document
d.s.p. – decessit sine prole (died without issue)
d.s.p.m. – decessit sine prole mascula (died without male issue)
d.s.p. s. – decessit sine prole supersite (died without surviving issue)

d.v.m. – decessit vita matris (died in the mother's lifetime)
d.v.p. – decessit vita patris (died in the father's lifetime)
e.g. – for example
ed. cit. – edition cited
ed. – editor
esp. – especially
Esq. – esquire
est. – estate
et al. – et alli (and others)
et ux. – et uxor (and wife)
exec., extx. – executor, executrix
f. – female
f., fa. – father
f., ff. – following page or pages
facs. – facsimile
fig. – figure
fn – footnote
fol. - folio (page)
gdn. – guardian
Gent. – gentleman
gr. – grant, granted, grantor, grantee
h. – heir, husband
hic jacet – here lies
hic sit – here is buried
h/o – husband of
H.S. – hic sepultus (here is buried)
Hun. – hundred
i.e. – that is
ibid – in the same place
imp. – in the first place
in esse. - in being (an unborn child)
inf., inft. – infant
infra – below
int. – intestate, interest, interred
inst. – (instant) in the same month
ills. – illustrated
issue – child or children
jour. – journal
J.P. – Justice of the Peace
Jur. – jury, juror or jurat
l. – line, lived
L. – libra (pound)
L.G.O. – Land Grant Office

Lib. – liber (book)
Lic. – license
loc. cit. – in the place cited
L.S. – locus sigilii – the place of the seal
£.s.d. – pounds, shillings, pence
m. – married, male, mother
mar. – married
mo., mos. – month, months
MS – manuscript
M.G. – Minister of God
M.M. – monthly meeting (Quakers)
Mr. – Master or Mister
Mrs. – a married woman or an unmarried woman of high social standing
N. – note or notes
N.B. – nota bene – take note
n.d. – no date
n.n. – no name
n.p. – no place
next friend – one acting legally for another
no. – number
nr. – near
ob. – obit (died)
op. – opus (work)
op.cit. – opere citato (in the work cited)
O.S. – old style (calendar)
p., pp. – page, pages
P.A. – Power of Attorney
par. – paragraph
passim. – here and there
pat. – paternal
per. – by means of
pltf. – plaintiff
P.R., p.r. – probate record
pref. – preface
pt. – part
pvd. – proved
q.v. – quod vide (which see)
R. – range (legal land description)
R.G. – record group
Rev. – revised
R.I.P. – rest in peace
rpt. – reprint
s. – son, shilling

s.p. – sine prole (without issue)
s.p.s. – sine prole supersite (without surviving issue)
sec. – section
ser. – series
sic – thus
sine die – without date
s/o – son of
soc. – society
supra – above
T. – township
t. – temp, tempore (in the time of)
trans. – translator
twp. – township
ult. – ultimo (in the month immediately preceding)
ux. – wife
V. – verso (the back page)
v. – versus (against), vidi (see)
v.d. – various dates
viz. – videlicet (namely)
vol. – volume
vs. – versus
w. – wife or widow
w/o – wife of, widow of, without
Y.M. – yearly Meeting (Quakers)
yr., yrs. – year, years

INDEX

tax records, 81
World War II list, 75
Maryland Genealogical Society
    donations to, 34
as publisher, 157
web site, 3, 157
*Maryland in World War II: Register of
    Service Personnel,* 75
*Maryland Loyalists Regiment, Orderly Book
    of* (Jones), 73
Maryland Magazine of Genealogy
    article on Maryland ethnic associations,
    85
Maryland Militia, War of 1812 (Wright,
    comp.), 73
"Maryland Muster Rolls, 1757–1758"
    (article), 71
*Maryland Records: Colonial, Revolution-
    ary, County and Church* (Brumbaugh),
    5, 64
*Maryland Soldiers Entitled to Lands West of
    Fort Cumberland* (Carothers), 73
Maryland State Archives
    African American resources (guide),
        89
    American Revolution muster rolls, 72
    birth records, 55–56
    Blue Books (colonial soldier lists), 71
    Catholic records, 68
    Civil War records, 75
    cost policy for copies, 8
    debt books, 82
    Genealogical Council of Maryland
        files, 11
    guides published by, 62–63, 81
    holdings of, 1, 7–9
    land records, by county, 78–81
    marriage records in, 57
    Methodist circuit records, 15
    military records, 71–72
    naturalization records, 89
    pension records, 73
    probate records, 58–63
    rent rolls, 82
    Society of Friends records, 68
    tax records, 81
    web site, 9
Maryland State Law Library
    Baltimore Sun file, 9
    census records, 65
    guide to research in, 10

Maryland Gazette file, 9
    tax lists in, 82
    web site, 9
Maryland War Records Commission
    World Wars I and II records, 75
"Maryland's Ethnic Organizations" (article),
    83
Mayer, Lewis, 72
McKeldin Library, 24
Melville, Patricia V.
    article by, on Maryland State Archives
    web site, 9
Methodist Episcopal Southern Conference.
    See United Methodist Historical Society
Methodist records, 15, 19, 21, 69
Mexican War
    records of, 76
Meyer, Gary E.
    German immigration collection of, 10
Meyer, Mary Keysor, 27, 57
    article on muster rolls, 71
    as original author, *Genealogical
        Research in Maryland*
    purposes of, ix
    quoted on "turmoil" in genealogy, vii
microfiche, 3, 35
microfilmed records, 1–3, 7, 9, 13, 15–
    19, 21–23, 25, 31, 35, 38–39, 41, 43,
    58, 66, 68, 74–75, 81–82, 88
    census records on, 65
    Civil War records, 75
    debt books, 82
    probate records on, 58
    religious records on, 66, 68
    rent rolls, 82
    ship passenger lists, 88
    and Soundex system, 88
    tax lists, 81–82
Mid-Atlantic Germanic Society (MAGS),
    34
military records, ix, xiv–xv, 25, 40, 70–
    76
militias, xv, 70, 72
Milton S. Eisenhower Library, 10, 20
    holdings of, 20
ministers, 15, 44, 66, 69
Monrovia, Maryland, 31
Montgomery County, Maryland
    bibliography, 123–26
    census records, 65
    land records, 80

probate records, 61
Montgomery County Historical Society, Inc., 21
  Genealogy Club of, 31
  holdings of, 46
Montgomery County Public Libraries, 21
Montgomery County Sentinel
  file of, 31
Monumental City (Howard), 4
Mormon Church. *See* Church of Jesus Christ of Latter Day Saints, The
Museum of Rural Life. *See* Caroline County Historical Society, Inc.
museums, historical, 3–5, 14, 37, 39, 41–45, 47–49
muster rolls, 11, 71–73

Nabb Research Center. *See* Edward H. Nabb Research Center for Delmarva History and Culture
National Archives and Records Administration, 2, 65
  Civil War records
    Confederate deaths at Point Lookout, 74
    Marylanders in Confederate Army, 74–75
  index, "City Passenger Lists," 11, 88
  military records, 70, 74–76
  pension records, 72–74, 76
  web site, genealogy, 50
National Park Service, U.S., 50
National Register of Historic Places, 44
naturalization, 11–12, 35, 83, 89
Naval Academy. *See* United States Naval Academy
naval records, 25
Newberger, Adele M., 86
Newman Collection. *See* Harry Wright Newman Collection
newsletters, genealogical, 28, 30–32, 34–36, 43
newspapers, 4, 9, 13, 17–21, 23, 25, 31, 38, 40–41, 43, 46–47, 49
Nimitz Library. *See* United State Naval Academy: Admiral Chester A. Nimitz Library
Nimmo, Nannie Ball, 4
Nimmo Genealogical Collection. *See* Maryland Historical Society
Norris Harris Church Index. *See* Maryland

Historical Society
  Notebook, The (journal), 29

Oakland, Maryland, 19, 42
Old Jail Museum. *See* St. Mary's County Historical Society, Inc.
Old Somerset on the Eastern Shore of Maryland (Torrence), 56
oral history, 19, 23
Orphan's Court, 8–9, 58

Papenfuse, Edward C., 81
Parker, Mrs. Sumner A.
  as founder, genealogical contest, 5–6
Pasadena, Maryland, 28
Passenger and Immigration Lists Index (Filby and Meyer, comps.), 10, 74
passenger lists, ship, 4, 10, 24, 74, 83–84, 87–88
Peabody, George, 10
Peabody Library. See George Peabody Library of the Johns Hopkins University
Peden, Henry C., Jr., 70, 73
Pedley, Avril J. M., 5, 81
pension records, 46, 70–73
Peskin, Larry A.
  article on bounty land warrants, 71
Phillips, Christopher, 90
photographic records, xiv, 3, 14, 19, 23, 29, 37–38, 40, 42–44, 46, 49
Pikesville, Maryland, 74
Poffenberger, Moses, 74
Point Lookout, Maryland, 74
Pratt Library. *See* Enoch Pratt Free Library
preachers. *See* ministers
Preliminary Voter Registration Books, 1882–1889, 12
Prerogative Court, 8, 39, 57–59
priests, 68
Prince Frederick, Maryland, 38
Prince George's County, Maryland
  bibliography, 126–28
  census records, 64–65
  land records, 80
  probate records, 59, 61
  as publisher, 157
Prince George's County Genealogical Society, 35, 46
Prince George's County Memorial Library, 22

Princess Anne, Maryland, 47
probate records, ix, 7–8, 31, 47, 51, 57–63
Protestant Episcopal Church. *See* Episcopal Diocese of Maryland
Provincial Families of Maryland (Genealogical Council of Maryland), 11
public libraries, ix
  Allen County Library (Indiana)
    as major genealogy collection, 50, 65
  Baltimore County Public Library System, 16
  C. Burr Artz Central Library, 18–19
  Caroline County Public Library, 17
  Carroll County Public Library, 17, 29
  Cecil County Public Library, 17–18
  Charles County Community Center, 18
  Dorchester County Public Library, 18
  Easton Public Library, 68
  Frederick County Public Libraries, 18
  Greenbelt Library, 35
  Harford County Public Library, 19–20
  Leonardtown Library, 35
  Montgomery County Public Libraries, 21
  Prince George's County Memorial Library, 22
  Ruth Enlow Library of Garrett County, 19
  St. Mary's County Public Library, 22
  Talbot County Public Library
    See Historical Society of Talbot County
  Washington County Free Library, 25
  Worcester County Library, 25–26
  See also research libraries
publishers, genealogical materials, viii, 155–58

Quaker Records in Maryland (Jacobsen), 68
Quakers. *See* Society of Friends
Queen Anne's County, Maryland, 36
  bibliography, 128–29
  census records, 64–65
  land records, 80
  probate records, 59, 61–62
Queen Anne's County Historical Society, 47

Record, The (newspaper)

file, Harford County Public Library, 20
Records of Baltimore's Private Organizations, The (Guertler and Newberger), 86
Register of Wills, 7, 9, 58–59
Reisterstown, Maryland, 16
religious records, ix, xiv–xvi, 4–5, 7, 10–11, 13–15. 19, 21, 28–29. 31–32, 35, 37–38, 40–41, 44–47, 49, 51, 54, 66–69, 86
rent rolls, viii, 47, 82, 165
research, genealogical, xv
  complex nature of, xiii
  and customs of the past, 51
  efficient time use, xiii
  familiarization with institutions, 1–2, 14–18, 23, 25–26
  making charts for, xiii
  strategy for working backward, xiii
research centers, ix, 1–2
  Anne Arundel Genealogical Society, 28–29, 37
  The Baltimore City Archives, 11–12
  The Church of Jesus Christ of Latter Day Saints, 68
  locations, 14
  fees, 15
  The George Peabody Library of the Johns Hopkins University, 10–11
  The Jewish Museum of Maryland, 14–15
  Kuethe Library Historical and Genealogical Research Center, 28
  Maryland Historical Society, 3–5
  Maryland State Archives, 7–9
  Maryland State Law Library, 9–10
  Prince George's County Genealogical Society
    Rainwater-Miles Research Center, 35
  research assistance available from, 5, 8, 12
  Tudor Hall Research Center. *See* St. Mary's County Historical Society, Inc.
  United Methodist Historical Society, 15, 69
research libraries, ix, 3–6, 9–10, 14
  Baltimore County Public Library System, 16
  C. Burr Artz Central Library, 18–19

slavery, 44, 46–47, 65
    manumission, 89
Snow Hill, Maryland, 25, 49
Social Security Administration, 50
Society of Colonial Wars in the State of
    Maryland
    records of, 23, 73
        See also under University of
        Baltimore: Langsdale Library
Society of Friends (Quakers)
    records of, 21, 68–69
Society of the War of 1812 in the State of
    Maryland
    records of, 23–24, 73
        See also under University of
        Baltimore: Langsdale Library
Solomons, Maryland, 39
Somerset County, Maryland, 47
    bibliography, 131–33
    census records, 65
    land records, 80
    probate records, 59, 62
Somerset County Historical Society, 47–48
Sons of the American Revolution,
    Maryland Society of
    records of, 5, 24, 73
    See also under University of Baltimore:
    Langsdale Library
Sons of Union Veterans of the Civil War
    records of, 24
Soundex system
    instruction for, 88
*Sources of Basic Genealogical Research in
    the Maryland State Law Library, A
    Sampler* (pamphlet), 10
Southern Maryland Studies Center, 22–23
    Harry Wright Newman Collection of,
    23
Spanish-American War
    service and pension records, 76
Steamship Historical Society of America.
    See University of Baltimore
store ledgers, 39
Sullivan, Larry E., 5, 85
surnames, 34, 38
    file maps for, 35
surveyors' records, 40

Talbot County, Maryland, 36, 48
    bibliography, 133–34
    census records, 64

land records, 80–81
probate records, 59, 62
Talbot County Public Library. *See*
    Historical Society of Talbot County
tax records, 11, 22, 31, 40, 43, 46–47, 81
Torrence, Clayton, 56
Town Commissioners Survey Book, 1729
    See also under the Baltimore City
    Archives
Towson, Maryland, 16, 29

United Daughters of the Confederacy,
    74–75
    manuscripts of, 44
United States Naval Academy
    Admiral Chester A. Nimitz Library of,
    25
University of Baltimore
    Langsdale Library, 23–24, 73–74
        Sons of the American Revolution
        records in, 5, 73–74
        Steamship Historical Society of
        America records in, 24, 48
University of Maryland
    McKeldin Library of, 24
University of Maryland Baltimore County,
    24
"Unpublished Revolutionary Records of
    Maryland" (typescript), 72
Upper Shore Genealogical Society of
    Maryland, 36

vertical files, xiv, 17–18, 29, 40, 43, 46,
    49
Vietnam War
    service and pension records of, 76
voting records, 12, 44

Waldorf, Maryland, 68
War Memorial Commission
    discharge records in, 76
War of 1812, 23–24, 73–74
War of the Rebellion, 40, 44
Washington County, Maryland, 48, 72
    bibliography, 136–39
    land patents, 40
    land records, 81
    probate records, 62
Washington County Free Library, 25
Washington County Genealogical Society,
    36